The Use of Performance Indicators in Higher Education

The Challenge of the Quality Movement

Third Edition

also in the Higher Education Policy Series

Standards and Quality in Higher Education
Edited by John Brennan, Peter de Vries
and Ruth Williams
ISBN 1 85302 423 6

Dimensions of Evaluation in Higher Education
Report of the IHME Study Group on Evaluation
in Higher Education
Urban Dahllöf, John Harris, Michael Shattock,
André Staropoli and Roeland in't Veld
ISBN 1 85302 526 7

Self-Regulation in Higher Education
A Multi-National Perpective on Collaborative
Systems of Quality Assurance and Control
H.R. Kells
ISBN 1 85302 528 3

Assessing Quality in Further and Higher Education
Allan Ashworth and Roger Harvey
ISBN 1 85302 539 9

Staffing Higher Education
Meeting New Challenges
Maurice Kogan, Elaine El-Khawas and Ingrid Moses
ISBN 1 85302 541 0

Evaluating Higher Education
Edited by Maurice Kogan
ISBN 1 85302 510 0

Goals and Purposes of Higher Education
in the 21st Century
Edited by Arnold Burgen
ISBN 1 85302 547 X

Higher Education Policy Series 34

The Use of Performance Indicators in Higher Education
The Challenge of the Quality Movement
Third Edition

**Martin Cave, Stephen Hanney,
Mary Henkel and Maurice Kogan**

Jessica Kingsley Publishers
London and Bristol, Pennsylvania

First published in 1988
by Jessica Kingsley Publishers
116 Pentonville Road
London N1 9JB, UK
and
400 Market Street, Suite 400
Philadelphia, PA 19106, USA

www.jkp com

Second impression 1991
Third impression 1997
Printed digitally since 2006

Library of Congress Cataloging in Publication Data
A CIP catalog record for this book is available from the Library of Congress

British Library Cataloguing in Publication Data
Cave, Martin
The use of performance indicators in higher education· the challenge of the
quality movement −3rd ed − (Higher education policy; 34)
1 Educational evaluation 2. Education, Higher − Evaluation 3. Performance
Standards
I. Title II Hanney, Stephen III. Henkel, Mary IV. Kogan, Maurice 379.1'54

ISBN-13. 978 1 85302 345 3
ISBN-10· 1 85302 3450

Contents

List of Figures

List of Tables

Preface to the Third Edition

This book is an updated account of the present use and status of performance indicators (PIs) in British higher education. As in the previous editions, our descriptions and conclusions are set against the developing literature and experience of PIs in the USA and other countries. In particular, we have been able to draw upon current research being undertaken in Norway by Dr Ivar Bleiklie of the University of Bergen and in Sweden by Professor Marianne Bauer of the University of Gothenburg. They, together with Mary Henkel who has joined us in writing this edition, and other colleagues, are undertaking a major international study of the nature of higher education reforms which includes analyses of the developments and impacts of the quality movement.

Writing about PIs must be set against the background of major shifts in higher education policy in the UK and other countries. In the UK over the last decade, a series of governments and central agency reports and policy announcements have altered the landscape of higher education policy. We attempt to give a dispassionate account of the changes so that higher education teachers and researchers, those who administer institutions and systems, and those who are interested in their performance can make informed choices about the uses to which they would put performance indicators. The book thus provides a critical survey of the range of devices now being proposed but also, in its concluding chapter, points to possible patterns or strategies of use.

This is a particularly opportune time to update this work because 1995 saw the final edition of the *University Management Statistics and Performance Indicators in the UK*. This will have been replaced in 1996 by a series of publications embodying a new emphasis on management statistics rather than on performance indicators. Furthermore, it has been possible to review the changing role of PIs in relation to the various exercises to assess research and teaching.

We are grateful to colleagues who contributed to previous editions: Juliet Poole, Richard Bell and Gillian Trevett. Several people have been kind enough to read the manuscripts of different editions and comment on them – notably Philip Chatwin, Duncan Harris, Richard Miller, John Sizer and Paul Clark. We emphasise that the performance of this task in no way implies that they share our views.

The bibliography in this edition contains all previous as well as current references in the hope that it will prove a useful source of information to readers.

We also express gratitude to Sally Harris who expertly collated and reproduced contributions from our team and saw all three editions to the press, and to Tom Kogan who has been a valued source of support in preparing the text for publication.

M. Cave, S. Hanney, M. Henkel and M. Kogan
Faculty of Social Sciences
Brunel University, 1996

Chapter 1

Key Issues in the Development of Performance Indicators

1.1 Introduction

A decade on from the controversial introduction of performance indicators (PIs) into higher education policy in the UK, their history is at a critical juncture. From being a largely externally imposed government initiative, they have been incorporated into the management of higher education at a number of levels. They are now far better understood and considerable investment has been made in their development by a range of key actors in the system. At the same time, uncertainties about their definition, their potential, and even their continuing identity have, if anything, intensified.

The development of PIs as instruments of public policy has increasingly come to be seen as a function of the interplay between technical advances and political interests and agendas. The framework we have developed for analysing the use of PIs in higher education derives from this observation (Cave and Hanney 1989 and 1992). Within this framework, differential usage of PIs can be explained in terms of four variables: technical development; the political decisions to create structures to permit and encourage their use; the adoption of policies which it is hoped PIs will be able to advance; and the influence of stakeholders who might use them.

Thus in the UK, as elsewhere, increasingly sophisticated techniques have been applied to the development of PIs. The levels at which they need to be aggregated and the problems entailed are being more clearly defined. In consequence, ambitions for PIs have become both larger and smaller. While technical advances have strengthened the hope that indicators can be made more robust and precisely targeted, they have also highlighted the complexities of achieving these ends. Partly but not wholly for these reasons, questions about the place of PIs in public policy have multiplied and become more pointed.

For the political as well as the technical context is changing. Governments striving to manage the mounting and competing demands made on them are increasingly embracing the ideologies and structures of the market in the form, for example, of 'new public management', quality assurance systems and consumerism. As knowledge comes to be seen as societies' prime capital asset, higher education systems are growing and becoming more differentiated and the stakeholders in them more numerous and varied: bigger and more diverse student populations; other consumers such as employers of graduates and users of research and other forms of advanced knowledge; parents; taxpayers.

If the initial drive to install PIs in countries such as the UK came from governments concerned to exert greater control over higher education and to establish a stronger and more publicly observable link between funding and performance in the context of economic stringency, gradually other values as well as economy, efficiency and even effectiveness have entered the arena. Many people within higher education can see the advantages of identifying usable forms of assessing or measuring its performance, as can other interested parties. But different perspectives may entail different priorities.

It is now widely conceded that there are likely to be few universally applicable PIs. Moreover, they are 'beginning to be subsumed under the larger managerial process of quality assurance and control' (Kells 1993; see also Banta and Borden 1994). They are regarded as one of the elements in the shift to a culture of self-regulation that is part of 'new public management' theory. As such, however, the distinction between them and other forms of information required for policy and management purposes is under question.

In some contexts the term 'performance indicators' has been abandoned. In the UK, for example, the Higher Education Funding Councils' Joint Performance Indicators Working Group (JPIWG) has been reconstituted under the title Higher Education Management Statistics Group (Committee of Vice-Chancellors and Principals 1995a). The JPIWG had concluded that of a range of stakeholders, including government, for whom their work would be of use, the principal were higher education institutions, 'their main concern being to use *management statistics* (our italics) to improve their own internal management' (CVCP 1995a para.2).

We now briefly sketch the policy background to what might be termed the initial cycle of the history of PIs in the UK.

1.2 Policy background

The explicit introduction of PIs into higher education in the UK was the product of a highly political process involving the government, the Committee of Vice-Chancellors and Principals (CVCP) and the then University Grants Committee (UGC). As such it exemplified a significant dynamic in the evolution of higher education policy in the 1980s. Government determined to bring to bear on higher education the principles it was seeking to install across the public sector: strong central direction; accountability for the economic, efficient and effective use of public money; the measurement of performance against outcome criteria and the substitution of the concepts and methods of management for those of administration or professionalism. University leaders and other elite academics, realising the strength of the Government's determination to impose new and explicit terms of its own choosing on the erstwhile predominantly implicit exchange relationship between the state and universities, strove to pre-empt or reshape government initiatives where it could not avoid them. At stake were issues of institutional autonomy, governance and control of the aims, objectives and evaluative criteria and mechanisms of higher education.

On 28 March 1984, the then Education Secretary, Sir Keith Joseph, announced that 'in response to my wish that there should be an efficiency study in the universities, the Committee of Vice-Chancellors and Principals have proposed, and I have agreed, that the study should be conducted under their aegis' (HC Debates Vol. 57, Written Answers, Col.205). The CVCP invited Sir Alex Jarratt, an industrialist, former civil servant and Chairman of the Council of Birmingham University to chair the steering committee that was to promote and co-ordinate the study. The Jarratt Report (1985) recommended that universities and the system as a whole must work to clear objectives and achieve value for money. It also made far-reaching recommendations about the governance and management of universities.

Universities had long been regarded as diarchies in which the power of the collegium, as represented by Senate and the academic autonomy of individual teachers, worked in tandem with the hierarchy embodied in the vice-chancellor, deans and heads of departments. The lay element represented by the university council played a primarily fiduciary and supportive role (Becher and Kogan 1991).

Jarratt now proposed that councils should 'assert their responsibilities in governing *their* institutions' (our italics). Vice-Chancellors would, in turn, become chief executives, overseeing the corporate management of the university. Given this proposed managerial metamorphosis, it was perhaps not surprising that the committee also advocated the introduction of PIs, and more specifically indicators which were calculable and usable by managers.

On 20 May 1986 Sir Keith Joseph told the House of Commons that the Government was to consider with the UGC and CVCP some further financial provision for the universities in 1987–88 and the following years but 'that the Government's willingness to make such provision depended crucially on evidence of real progress in implementing and building upon the changes that are needed' (HC Debates Vol. 98, Col.179). The areas identified were selectivity in the distribution of resources, the rationalisation and, where appropriate, the closure of small departments, better financial management and improved standards of teaching. Following this announcement, the UGC and CVCP came to accept what is known as the Concordat; if changes in university management as requested by the Government were met, further finance would be released to the universities. By November 1986 both committees were able to make a report of progress to Kenneth Baker, who by then had succeeded Sir Keith Joseph, and among the developments reported was the publication of the first of a joint working party's report on the use of PIs relating to both inputs and outputs in teaching and research.

During this period the binary line between the universities and the polytechnics and colleges was still firmly in place and the initiative was aimed, at least in the beginning, at the universities.

The universities had maintained a high degree of autonomy, despite the fact that their funding from UGC and home tuition fees increased from not much more than 30 per cent in 1939 to 76 per cent in 1980–81 (it subsequently dropped to 67% by 1984–85 and 60% by 1988–89 when the UGC was replaced by the Universities Funding Council (UFC)). This autonomy was reflected in the receipt of public money to be used in pursuit of purposes to be agreed with, rather than enforced on, them.

If universities in the UK acting through the UGC were free to negotiate their functions with government, even more were they the custodians of their own performance and standards. They made, and make, their own appointments, and ensure the quality of the degrees by the appointment of their own external examiners. They admit students on their own entrance criteria. But there has always been, even at the high noon of post-war autonomy, a form of institutional and subject evaluation. The UGC's main task was to distribute the financial allocations determined by the Government. To do so it made judgements through the use of largely informal evaluations by its expert subcommittees. These were, in effect, peer judgements made on a reputational basis, although framed by analysis of likely student demand for different courses and expectations of the resources to be made available by government.

By comparison, even by the 1980s the polytechnics and colleges were far from autonomous institutions. The allocation of their resources was in the hands of local authorities and they were still only gradually freeing themselves from dependence on the Council for National Academic Awards (CNAA) for the authority to make their own academic decisions. Their histories were embedded in external validation and review at both institutional and course levels. Despite the fact that peer review was at the heart of the CNAA's evaluation processes, many of the peers were from the universities and thus external to the sector, as well as to the individual institutions. In addition, polytechnics and colleges were subject to inspection by Her Majesty's Inspectorate (HMI). And by the middle of the 1980s various bodies, including the Chartered Institute of Public Finance and Accountancy (CIPFA) (1984), the Audit Commission (1985 and 1986) and the National Advisory Body for Public Sector Higher Education (NAB) (1987) had begun to pronounce on the development of performance measures in the sector.

However, the White Paper of 1987 signalled government's intention to reduce the distinctions between the universities and the polytechnics and colleges. The latter were to be taken out of local authority control and given corporate status. Funding arrangements for both sectors were to be reformed. The University Grants Committee was to be replaced by the Universities Funding Council (UFC) and a parallel body for the polytechnics and colleges, the Polytechnics and Colleges Funding Council (PCFC) created. Both were to be non-departmental bodies with a chairman and a chief executive appointed by the Secretary of State with membership incorporating representation from industry and commerce as well as from academe. The notion of grants was largely put aside. Institutions were to make contractual undertakings about their academic outputs with the councils in exchange for the resources allocated to them. Attention was drawn in the White Paper to the need for the development of national and institutional indicators of student achievements and of the value added to working life by the completion of a degree.

The Government's aim was to strengthen the concept of one national higher education system in which all institutions were required to work to objectives determined outside themselves and to demonstrate that they had met them. The statement of the aims of higher education in the White Paper reaffirmed the government's adherence to

> the Robbins Committee's definition: instruction in skills, the promotion of the general powers of the mind, the advancement of learning, and the transmission of a common culture and common standards of citizenship... But above all there is an urgent need... for higher education to take increasing account of the economic requirements of the country. [So] government and its central funding agencies will do all they can to encourage and reward approaches by higher education institutions which bring them closer to the world of business. (Department of Education and Science (DES) 1987e, paras.1.2–1.6)

This intention was backed up by the award of substantial grants to institutions by the Training Agency to mount projects which would embed enterprise into the curriculum.

These ambitions were linked by government with the need to increase student numbers. It announced its intention of substantial increases in the number of student places in the 1990s to yield an increase in the age participation rate from 14 per cent to figures varying between 20 per cent and 30 per cent. But it was also made clear that growth was to be achieved primarily by efficiency gains and the reduction of unit costs. Efficiency and the role of efficiency indicators in its achievement were highlighted in the White Paper (paras.3.23–3.30).

That performance measures were identified by government as tools central to its policies was underlined in the letter of guidance sent to the Chairman of the PCFC on its incorporation in November 1988. Two key expectations of the PCFC were stated.

> The first is a means of specifying clearly what polytechnics and colleges are expected to provide in return for public funds. The second is a systematic method of monitoring institutional performance. I attach particular importance to the latter since, without measures of performance, the Council will have the means neither of satisfying itself that institutions are providing what has been promised at acceptable quality, nor of making comparative assessments of institutions as a basis of future allocations of grants. (Quoted in Morris 1990, para.1.2)

Work on PIs was pursued in both sectors. But there were differences of emphasis. The Morris Committee set up by the PCFC focused on the function of both macro and institutional PIs. It drew attention to the potential role of macro indicators in protecting the interests of the whole sector in the annual public expenditure rounds. The White Paper itself had drawn attention to the superior performance of the polytechnics and colleges sector over the universities on two key measures in the first part of the 1980s: the increase in student numbers and the reduction in the unit of resource (DES 1987e paras.2.2, 3.3).

Second, while the Morris Committee endorsed the view of the CVCP/UGC working party of the potential value of indicators to institutions themselves and advocated that '"institutional performance indicators" should be chosen by and relate to the mission, aims and objectives of each individual college or polytechnic' (Morris 1990, para.6.3), it was in the context of advocating a strong role for the PCFC in individual institutional planning through the mechanism of triennial institutional reviews.

But the UFC and the PCFC were to be short-lived institutions. Under the Further and Higher Education Act, 1992, the binary line was abolished. All polytechnics and colleges that could meet certain criteria were given degree-awarding powers and the right to call themselves universities. New funding councils were now established on a country basis but with constitutions similar to those of the PCFC and UFC.

The Government took this opportunity to impose a more comprehensive system of quality control on the higher education institutions, a component of which was compulsory assessment by the funding councils of the quality of higher education. The longer-term intention was to link teaching resource allocation with quality of provision. The institutions were allowed to retain control of quality assurance and quality enhancement under the aegis of the Higher Education Quality Council (HEQC), established as a limited company in 1992, and owned and funded by the universities and colleges of higher education.

Quality assurance and quality assessment were to assume an increasingly important role in government's determination to impose some of the disciplines of the market on higher education, including competition, an increase in the power of consumer demand and the concept of universities as well-managed corporate enterprises. Since 1992 the work of the funding councils' JPIWG has to be seen in the context of this broader quality movement.

These developments are to be set against the background of a series of reports and policy proposals for performance measurement in the public services in general (Cave, Kogan and Smith 1990; Jackson 1995) that have emanated from central government and its funding agencies over the last few years.

The principal reports and policy proposals for higher education since 1984 are as follows.

- 1984. University Grants Committee. *A Strategy for Higher Education into the 1990s.* (UGC 1984b)

  Explained new approach to the determination of universities' allocations.

- 1985. UGC Circular Letter 22/85: *Planning for the late 1980s: The Resource Allocation Process.* (UGC 1985b)

  Letter to universities explaining the new resource allocation procedure. Referred to research PIs but stated that 'there are few indicators of teaching performance that would enable a systematic external assessment of teaching quality to be made'. If universities know how to do it 'the Committee would be glad to be told how they have done it'. A suitable methodology for taking account of teaching quality could be used in due course.

- 1985. CVCP. Jarratt Report. *Report of the Steering Committee for Efficiency Studies in Universities.* (Jarratt 1985)

  Universities and the system as a whole should work to clear objectives and achieve value for money. Made proposals for the functioning of the DES and the UGC. Recommended that the UGC and CVCP should develop PIs. Made recommendations on university policy and management structures, including: strengthening of role of council; rolling academic and institutional plans; Vice-Chancellor to be Chief Executive for the University; small planning and resources committee; budget delegation to appropriate centres; PIs; a more streamlined managerial structure.

- 1985. Green Paper. *The Development of Higher Education into the 1990s (Cmnd.9524).* (DES 1985)

  Rejected an 'over-arching' body for higher education. Revoked the concept of deficiency financing to universities (the system whereby universities were allocated funds sufficient to cover their costs), but conceded that for the foreseeable future the main source of income would be the taxpayer. Advocated development of PIs.

- 1985. Lindop Report. *Academic Validation in Public Sector Higher Education, Cmnd.9501.* (Lindop 1985)

  Made proposals for modes of validation to be adopted in the public sector, including stronger moves towards self-evaluation.

- 1986. UGC Circular Letter 4/86. *Planning for the Late 1980s: Recurrent Grant for 1986/87.* (UGC 1986)

  This letter gave details of the basis of the 1986–87 grant allocation and in Part III, Annex 3 published research gradings of universities' 'cost centres'.

- 1986. *Performance Indicators in Universities: A First Statement by a joint CVCP/UGC Working Group.* (CVCP/UGC 1986)

  Outlined a set of possible PIs, capable of realisation over different time horizons.

- 1986. CVCP. Reynolds Report. *Academic Standards in the Universities.* (CVCP 1986)

  Set up codes of practice on the maintenance and monitoring of standards, including external examining and postgraduate training and research.

- 1987. Croham Report. *Review of the University Grants Committee, Cm 81.* (Croham 1987)

  Proposed the reconstitution of the UGC as a university grants council with broadly equal numbers of academic and non-academic members, a non-academic Chairman and a full-time director general drawn from the academic world. UGC to have 'unambiguous powers to attach conditions to grant'. Other proposals for tightening up accountability of universities.

- 1987. White Paper. *Higher Education: Meeting the Challenge, Cm 114.* (DES 1987e)

  Stated aims and purposes of higher education. Student numbers to return to present levels in mid-1990s and then grow again. Age participation rate to increase to 18 per cent. Made recommendations for quality and efficiency including more selectively funded research, 'targeted with attention to prospects for commercial exploitation' (p.iv), and proposed improvements in management of the system. Favoured development and use of PIs. Proposed establishment of new Polytechnics and Colleges Funding Council (PCFC) and Universities Funding Council (UFC) and new contract arrangements for both sectors.

- 1987. Clayton Report on *The Measurement of Research Expenditure in Higher Education*. University of East Anglia. (Clayton 1987)

   Proposed a method for allocating costs between teaching and research and calculated average cost of research output.

- 1987. NAB. *Management for a Purpose: The Report of the Good Management Practice Group*. (NAB 1987)

   A report for the public sector somewhat equivalent to the Jarratt Report for the universities, but conducted by the National Advisory Body (NAB) rather than under the auspices of the institutions. Produced two lists of PIs for further consideration and selection. One for academic operations, the other for resource management.

- 1987. UGC. The Oxburgh Report. Report by E.R. Oxburgh. *Strengthening University Earth Sciences*. (Oxburgh 1987)

   Report on rationalisation of earth sciences from which proposals for grading of institutions on research potential have evolved.

- 1987. Advisory Board for the Research Councils (ABRC). *A Strategy for the Science Base*. (ABRC 1987)

   Identified a lack of purposeful direction in the deployment of university research effort. Recommended creation of three types of institution (R, T and X) and greater emphasis on programme grants. Emphasis on interdisciplinary research centres. Criteria for establishing priorities to be internal (timeliness, pervasiveness and excellence) and external (exploitability, applicability and significance for education and training).

- 1987. DES. *Changes in Structure and National Planning for Higher Education. Contracts Between the Funding Bodies and Higher Education Institutions.* (DES 1987c)

  Gave details of alternative proposals for system of contracting between institutions and the new planning and funding bodies to replace grants.

- 1987. CVCP and UGC. *Second Statement by the Joint CVCP/UGC Working Group.* (CVCP/UGC 1987a)

  Listed (with commentary) 39 PIs scheduled for publication later in the year.

- 1987. CVCP and UGC. *University Management Statistics and Performance Indicators in the UK.* (CVCP/UGC 1987b)

  Publication of 39 sets of comparative cost data and PIs for British universities.

- 1988. Education Reform Act.

  Created Funding Councils for Universities and Polytechnics and Colleges. Provided for incorporation of non-university institutions.

- 1988. CVCP and UGC. *University Management Statistics and Performance Indicators in the UK.* (CVCP/UGC 1988)

  Second edition. Included an increased number of PIs; up from 39 to 54. Became, with some technical amendments, an annual publication.

- 1989. UFC. Circular Letter 27/89. *Research Selectivity Exercise 1989. The Outcome.* (UFC 1989a)

  Published the ratings for units of assessment and cost centres following the research selectivity exercise. Ratings to be used to inform calculations of grant.

- 1989. CVCP and UFC. Performance Indicators Steering Committee. *Issues in Quantitative Assessment of Departmental Research.* (CVCP/UFC 1989)

  A consultative document from the Sub-Committee on Research Indicators setting out the issues surrounding the development of research PIs.

- 1989. PCFC. *Recurrent Funding Methodology 1990/91. Guidance for Institutions.* (PCFC 1989)

  Set out the funding method adopted by the PCFC following a consultative exercise on four options. The allocations to consist of two elements: core funding based on a percentage of the previous year's allocation – 95 per cent in the first year – and an element for which institutions bid competitively.

- 1989. CVCP. VC/89/160A. Sutherland Report. *The Teaching Function. Quality Assurance.* (Sutherland 1989)

  Proposals based upon the recommendations of a group chaired by Professor Stewart Sutherland to create a CVCP academic audit unit to monitor universities' own quality assurance.

- 1989. CVCP. Kingman Report. *Costing of Teaching in Universities.* (Kingman 1989)

  Report of the work of the group chaired by Sir John Kingman. Concluded that if allowance is made for that research and scholarly activity essential for teaching, almost all the cost of academic staff (except research staff) should be included in the teaching cost.

- 1989. UFC. Circular Letter 39/89. *Funding and Planning: 1991/92 to 1994/95.* (UFC 1989b)

  Explained how the Council intended to determine the distribution of recurrent funds in the four-year period from 1991–92. For funding on teaching-based criteria, universities were invited to submit offers of student places. Funding on research-based criteria to be increasingly selective based on the assessments contained in Circular Letter 27/89.

- 1989. UFC. *Report on the 1989 Research Assessment Exercise.* (UFC 1989c)

  Described the results of the consultative exercise prior to the 1989 exercise and how the ratings were derived in 1989.

- 1990. PCFC. *Recurrent Funding and Equipment Allocations for 1990/91.* (PCFC 1990)

  The results of the first round of the new funding methodology were announced along with a document, *In Pursuit of Quality: An HMI View,* explaining the inspectorate's approach to quality and context for its advice to the Council's Programme Advisory Groups on claims for 'outstanding quality'.

- 1990. PCFC. *Performance Indicators. Report of a Committee of Enquiry Chaired by Mr Alfred Morris.* (Morris 1990)

  Recommended PCFC publish four sets of 'macro performance indicators' relevant to national aims and objectives to illuminate the 'Public Expenditure Compact' it negotiates with the Government. Institutions should use a corporate planning process designed primarily by the institutions to their own specifications but involving the use of PIs. Institutions should publish some of their chosen institutional PIs in an annual 'performance report'.

- 1990. PCFC and CNAA. *The Measurement of Value Added in Higher Education.* (PCFC and CNAA 1990)

  Report of a joint project to test different approaches to the calculation of the value-added achieved by students, based on the comparison of entry and exit qualifications. Recommended the adoption of a comparative value-added method which looks at the difference between the actual and expected exit qualifications.

- 1990. PCFC. *Teaching Quality. Report of the Committee of Enquiry Appointed by the Council. (Warnock 1990)*

  Recommended six strategies to the Council designed to enable institutions to demonstrate the quality of their teaching. One strategy was to promote and develop quantifiable and other information relating to the quality of teaching. The report endorsed the finding of the Report on PIs (Morris 1990).

- 1990. UFC. Circular Letter 29/90. *Funding and Planning Exercise.* (UFC 1990)

  Announced that the Council was unable to accept 'the limited scale of economy' offered by the universities' bids over the four-year planning period.

- 1990. CNAA. Information Services Discussion Paper 4. *Performance Indicators and Quality Assurance.* (CNAA 1990)

  Considered the contribution which PIs can make to quality assurance. Not a policy statement. Contains a useful categorisation of the various lists of PIs proposed in reports produced for universities, polytechnics and colleges.

- 1991. White Paper. *Higher Education: A New Framework* Cm 1541. (DES 1991)

  Proposed: the end of the binary line; the establishment of new funding councils; research funding to be allocated entirely on a selective basis; quality audit to be the responsibility of the institutions and quality assessment that of the funding councils. Quality assessment was to inform funding and be based on two approaches – first, PIs and calculations of value-added, and second, external judgements on the basis of direct observations.

- 1991. CNAA. Project Report 30. *Performance Indicators: Observations on Their Use in the Assurance of Course Quality.* (Yorke 1991)

  Described as a project funded by CNAA that attempted to develop indicators of programme quality.

- 1991. CVCP. Academic Audit Unit: *Notes for the Guidance of Auditors.* (CVCP Academic Audit Unit 1991)

  Also defined the terms of reference of the unit, established in 1990.

- 1991. CVCP, Committee of Directors of Polytechnics (CDP), Standing Conference of Principals (SCOP). *Quality Assurance Arrangements for Higher Education.* (CVCP, CDP, SCOP 1991)

  Paper sent to the Secretary of State describing the quality assurance organisation that the three bodies planned to establish to help member institutions to monitor and improve the quality of their teaching and to develop access.

- 1992. *Performance Indicators: Final Report of the Conference of Scottish Centrally Funded Colleges/Scottish Office Education Department Working Party.* (SED 1992)

  Recommended that five broad indicators should be adopted: quality of learning and teaching profile; client satisfaction; unit costing; post-course success ratio; and student achievement rate.

- 1992. PCFC. *Macro Performance Indicators.* (PCFC 1992)

  Provided definitions for the macro PIs suggested in the Morris Report and where data were available the value of the indicators for 1989–90 and 1990–91.

- 1992. Further and Higher Education Act and Further and Higher Education (Scotland) Act.

  Created new funding councils: Higher Education Funding Council for England (HEFCE); Scottish Higher Education Funding Council (SHEFC); and Higher Education Funding Council for Wales (HEFCW). The Funding Councils were required to set up Quality Assessment Committees to assess quality in higher education. The CNAA was to be abolished.

- 1992. Letters of Guidance to the Funding Councils from their Respective Secretaries of State.

  Formally requested funding councils to work together with representatives from higher education institutions to build on earlier work and develop performance measures and indicators for both teaching and research. Joint Performance Indicators Working Group (JPIWG) established. Set out the HEFCE responsibilities for quality assessment. The Councils were free to determine the method of assessment and were to appoint assessors. The assessments should be in a form that could be used to inform funding allocations.

- 1992. UFC. Circular 26/92. *Research Assessment Exercise 1992: The Outcome.* (UFC)

  Announced the results of the third RAE that would be used to determine the allocation of research funds for 1993–94 by the HEFCE, the SHEFC and the HEFCW and the Department for Education in Northern Ireland (DENI).

- 1992. Letter to CVCP, CDP, SCOP.

  From Secretary of State encouraging them to set up the proposed quality assurance organisation.

- 1992. SHEFC. *Quality Assessment: The SHEFC Approach.* (SHEFC 1992)

  Outlined the Council's approach to quality assessment within a framework that included 11 dimensions. All institutions would be visited.

- 1993. HEFCE Circular 3/93. HEFCE *Assessment of the Quality of Higher Education.* (HEFCE 1993a)

  Outlined the purposes and methods of quality assessment. The purposes included: to ensure that higher education was of satisfactory quality or better, to encourage improvements in quality and to inform funding and reward excellence. Subject areas would be assessed within three categories, excellent, satisfactory and unsatisfactory. Assessment would comprise scrutiny of an institutional self-assessment supported by statistical indicators, together with an assessment visit in the case of all institutions claiming excellence, all whose self-assessment suggested they might be unsatisfactory and a sample of others.

- 1993. HEFCE. Circular 7/93. *Research Funding Method.* (HEFCE 1993c)

    Described the method for funding research in HEFCE institutions: the scores obtained in the 1992 RAE (one to five) would be translated into a funding scale of zero to four.

- 1993. HEFCE. Consultation Paper 6/93. *Research Assessment.* (HEFCE 1993d)

    Invited comments on the future conduct of RAE and enclosed an annex containing a report on the 1992 RAE which explained that consultation had produced a consensus that the 1992 RAE should be based on its predecessors, i.e. 'informed peer review', and it described the process by which the research ratings were derived.

- 1993. CVCP. *N/93/51. Research Performance Indicators: Annual Survey of Publications – First Annual Publications Survey: Calendar Year 1991.* (CVCP 1993)

    Circulated the national totals for publications for each cost centre (in 20 categories) and averages for three indicators. Institutional figures were not published and the exercise was not repeated.

- 1993. HEQC Division of Quality Audit *Notes for the Guidance of Auditors* (HEQC 1993.

    These make no mention of PIs in their guidelines for auditors.

- 1994. HEFCE, SHEFC, HEFCW and DENI. Circular RAE96 1/94. (HEFCE *et al.* 1994)

  Described how the 1996 RAE would be conducted in the light of the consultation process. The key change was that details of up to four publications per researcher would be requested but not the total number of publications.

- 1994. JPIWG. *Consultative Report – Management Statistics and Performance Indicators in Higher Education.* (JPIWG 1994)

  Invited comments on the indicators proposed in five categories: macro; teaching and learning outcomes and student achievement; research; financial health; estates.

- 1994. HEFCE and HCFW Commissioned Report. *Assessment of the Quality of Higher Education: a Review and an Evaluation (Barnett Report).* (Barnett 1994a)

  Proposed some changes to the HEFCE method of assessment, including universal visiting, summative judgement at the threshold level, and the framing of recommendations for improvement within a limited number of dimensions, so as to produce a 'quasi-profile'.

- 1994. HEFCE. Circular 39/94 *The Quality Assessment Method from April 1995.* (HEFCE 1994)

  Announcement following consultation of changes to the assessment method, including universal visiting, a framework based on six core aspects of provision, profiles structured within four grades, overall summative judgement at the threshold level.

- 1994. CVCP. *CVCP 11 Point Plan.* (CVCP 1994)

  Produced in reply to the Secretary of State's speech in April, inviting higher education to pay more attention to the broad comparability of academic standards. The plan centred on the intention to develop threshold standards for British higher education. Followed by the establishment by the HEQC of a Graduate Standards programme.

- 1995. CVCP. *University Management Statistics and Performance Indicators in the UK.* (CVCP 1995b)

  The ninth and final annual volume – still for the old universities only. Included substantially the same indicators as the second edition (1988).

- 1995. CVCP. *Higher Education Management Statistics: A Future Strategy.* (CVCP 1995a)

  Described the creation by the representative bodies of the institutions (CVCP etc.) of the Higher Education Management Statistics (HEMS) Group which was invited by the funding councils to take forward the work of JPIWG. The final JPIWG report forms an annex.

- 1995. HEMS Group. *Higher Education Management Statistics: Publication in 1996.* (HEMS 1995)

  A consultative document alerting institutions to the macro and institutional statistics (not PIs) it is planned the Higher Education Statistics Agency (HESA) will publish in 1996 in the student and finance areas. Invited suggestions on health warnings and caveats. It is not intended there should be a successor to the *University Management Statistics and Performance Indicators.*

- 1995. HEFCE. *Developing Quality Assurance in Partnership with the Institutions of Higher Education.* (HEFCE 1995b)

  HEFCE's response to the Secretary of State's request for proposals to bring audit and assessment together. Proposed that there should be no more institutional audits after the end of 1996. Instead the Council would introduce 'an integrated Process of Quality Assurance' in 1996–1997 as an interim measure through which the first cycle of quality assessments would be completed and some monitoring of quality assurance mechanisms continued, mainly through inquiry at programme or department level. A Joint Planning Group comprising staff from the HEFCE and the HEQC would then work out how a single

Quality Assurance Agency could be developed from that process.

- 1995. CVCP. *Developing Quality Assurance in Partnership with the Institutions of Higher Education*. (CVCP 1995c)

    CVCP response to the HEFCE proposals, with alternative recommendations for the functions and focus of a new single agency: it should incorporate scrutiny of standards as well as quality in institutions and the focus of inquiry would be at a higher level of the institution. More reliance would be placed on the institutions' own internal reviews.

- 1995. HEFCE Circular 29/95 *Fund for the Development of Teaching and Learning*. (HEFCE 1995c)

    Announced the establishment of a fund to stimulate developments in teaching and learning through projects designed to develop and disseminate innovation and good practice. Only those departments awarded an overall excellent grading or been commended for work coming within the scope of their project application would be eligible to apply. It therefore in a small way linked quality with funding, although this was not the prime aim of the initiative.

1.3 Defining and categorising PIs: input–output representation

Defining PIs

Despite the growing attention paid to PIs for higher education, there is no single authoritative definition or interpretation of their nature. In this section we first discuss the definitions in the literature and then propose our own framework.

In the survey carried out in the mid-1980s under the Organisation for Economic Co-operation and Development (OECD)'s Institutional Management in Higher Education (IMHE) Programme, an indicator is defined as 'a numerical value used to measure something which is difficult to quantify' (Cuenin 1986, p.6). Thus in the questionnaire sent out under the IMHE Programme, performance indicators were described as numerical values which can be derived in different ways. They provide a measurement for assessing the quantitative or qualitative performance of a system. For example, the ratio between output and input (i.e. benefits obtained and resources consumed) can be a performance indicator. Indicators need not be so strictly defined, however, and those which relate to quality should also be included for the purposes of this survey. (Cuenin 1986, p.71)

Cuenin drew a distinction between simple indicators, performance indicators and general indicators. This distinction is potentially particularly useful at a time when the space for PIs between the other two is under some pressure. Simple indicators, he suggests, are usually expressed in the form of absolute figures and are intended to provide a relatively unbiased description of a situation or process. This corresponds roughly to the UGC's and CVCP's use of the term 'management statistics' which was seen in the compilation of data published annually from 1987 under the title *University Management Statistics and Performance Indicators*. Sizer (1992) argued that when developing national databases it is important not to label management information and statistics as PIs 'since it implies that all management information and statistics are then apparently useful to measure the achievement of objectives' (p.158). Various authorities, including Sizer and Yorke (1991 para.17) had noted that the issue is complex because what appears as a management statistic at one level can become a PI at another. However, perhaps the JPIWG have taken things too far with their statement:

> During discussion it became apparent that the proposed indicators might be better described as management statistics rather than performance indicators. Institutions could, if they so wished, convert these statistics into performance indicators. Close attention must be paid to the missions of institutions before management statistics can be converted to relevant measures of performance. (CVCP 1995a, para.1.8)

PIs differ from simple indicators in that they imply a point of reference, for example a standard, an objective, an assessment, or a comparator, and are therefore relative rather than absolute in character. Although a simple indicator is the more neutral of the two, it may become a PI if a value judgement is involved. In order to avoid possible ambiguity, Cuenin proposed the general rule that performance indicators should have the following property: 'when the indicator shows a difference in one direction this means that the situation is better, whereas, if it shows a difference in the opposite direction, then this means that the situation is less favourable. The way in which the data are to be interpreted ought to be obvious' (Cuenin 1986, p.10).

CIPFA (1984) and others suggested that indicators are more tentative than measures or findings. Similarly, in 1986 the CVCP/UGC Working Group defined PIs as 'statements, usually quantified, on resources employed and achievements secured in areas relevant to the particular objectives of the enterprise' (CVCP/UGC 1986, p.1) and went on to suggest that the emphasis is 'on indicators as signals or guides rather than absolute measures' and that whilst indicators do not necessarily provide direct measurements of inputs, processes and outputs, they can offer valuable information relating to them.

There are in addition, Cuenin suggested, very general indicators which in the main are derived from outside the 'institution and are not indicators in the strict sense – they are frequently opinions, survey findings or general statistics' (Cuenin 1986, p.10). Although they may not conform exactly to the definition of an indicator they are used in decision making, and he argues, 'these general indicators could be converted into legitimate performance indicators, but it would seem there is no great desire to do so' (p.10). It could be maintained that the peer review exercise carried out by the UGC in 1986 into the quality of research in UK universities was just such an attempt to convert a general indicator into a PI (see Chapter 4.1). The Morris Report advocated that the HMI's database of inspection reports should be used as an indicator, at sector level, of the proportion of work in each PCFC Programme area, and overall, which fell within each of the five broad quality descriptors used by the HMI. Kells too in his 1993 definition claims PIs to be 'signals derived from factual databases or from opinion data' (p.5). However, the relationship between peer review and PIs is complex and will be examined further in later chapters.

Another property claimed for PIs when they are defined in their broadest sense is that 'they reduce a complexity of subjective judgements to a single objective measure' (Laurillard 1980, p.187). She questioned the validity of such an approach, but the point about reducing complexity is also made by Frackmann (1987) who concluded that 'performance indicators stand for simplified information that is needed for management and organisation. Performance indicators are always to be used by outside or higher levels of decision making, compared with the performing unit under review' (p.161).

Bringing these definitions and interpretations together, we define a PI as a measure – usually in quantitative form – of an aspect of the activity of a higher education institution. The measure may be either ordinal or cardinal, absolute or comparative. It thus includes the mechanical applications of formulae (where the latter are imbued with value or interpretative judgements) and can inform, and be derived from, such informal and subjective procedures as peer evaluations or reputational rankings.

Different categories of PIs and the input–output representation

There are a variety of intersecting attempts to categorise PIs. The Jarratt Report (1985) distinguished between 'internal', 'external' and 'operating' indicators. The first category includes variables which have the common features of reflecting either inputs into the institution (attractiveness of undergraduate or graduate courses) or valuations internal to the institution (award of degrees, teaching quality). External indicators reflect the valuations of an institution in the 'market-place' of its subjects – the employment of its graduates or acceptance of its publications. Operating PIs include 'productivity' ratios such as unit costs and reflect variables such as workloads or availability of library stocks or computing facilities.

The 1986 Report of the CVCP/UGC Working Party distinguished the more conventional categories of input, process and output PIs. Input indicators have to do with the resources, human and financial, employed by universities. Process indicators relate to the intensity or productivity of resource use and to the management effort applied to the inputs and to the operation of the organisation. Output indicators are about what has been achieved; the products of the institution.

Given the array of input, process, output and background variables how, Cullen (1987) asked: 'can they be assembled into performance indicators?' (p.172). He suggested that a conventional categorisation based on management concepts would distinguish three types of indicators – indicators of efficiency, of effectiveness, and of economy. Indicators of economy are defined as those which 'compare actual with target inputs' and thus measure input savings; indicators of efficiency are those which compare outputs with inputs – normally actual outputs with actual inputs. Effectiveness indicators show whether the objectives of policy have been achieved.

As an illustration of this distinction, the 1987 White Paper, in supporting the use of PIs, noted that the CVCP/UGC 1986 list covered both efficiency indicators including: 'student–staff ratios (SSRs) and a range of unit costs broken down by the main categories of expenditure'; and effectiveness indicators including: 'income from research grants and contracts, the number of research and sponsored students, submission rates for research degrees, the first occupation of graduates and the institution's contribution to postgraduate and professional training' (DES 1987e, para.3.27). Moreover, 'unit costs and SSRs are now accepted indicators of the intensity of resource use' (para 3.29).

The input–output representation

The input–process–output approach has always been associated with PIs and is increasingly being used in discussion about PIs in the USA (see, for example, Bottrill and Borden 1994). R. Richardson (1994) adopts the slightly different terminology inputs–outputs–outcomes which is quite frequently used and, as he notes, is favoured by the *Reinventing Government* movement. Using earlier editions of our book and other sources Bottrill and Borden (1994) identified over 250 PIs for higher education and classified each as either an input, process or output indicator.

The input–output approach can be explained in more detail by reference to a simplified conceptual framework which views higher education as a process which transforms inputs into outputs, and is itself part of a wider economic and social process. Figure 1.1 illustrates this framework. Higher education is seen as a process for transforming inputs (notably of students' time, academics' time, consumables and equipment and buildings) into outputs which can be broadly classified as relating to either teaching or research. The former includes the value-added of all those receiving instruction from the university or other higher education institutions – undergraduate students, graduate students and those taking short courses. It includes any increment in the knowledge of students, whether or not they complete their studies. Research is a shorthand for any increase in knowledge generated by the institution, in the form of publications, patents, development work, and the like. Figure 1.2 shows a fuller representation of the inputs, processes and outputs associated with research. Many higher education activities, notably the preparation of research degrees, combine 'teaching' and 'research' as joint products.

Some higher education outputs are used directly as consumption benefits. For instance, mastery of a discipline or completion of research may yield direct satisfaction. Others are intermediate inputs into other economic processes, or inputs which go back into higher education itself (for simplicity, this feedback is not shown in the figures). Thus both trained personnel and the results of research are used in all sectors of the economy, including the higher education sector. They are inputs into further transformation processes which generate other outputs, often in the form of consumption goods and services.

Historically, a number of techniques have been used to appraise the efficiency of public institutions in general (see, for example, Barrow 1990) and these can be applied to higher education. Typically they involve establishing some relationship between inputs and outputs. Where they differ is in the stage at which inputs and outputs are measured, the units in which they are measured, and the level of aggregation.

Figure 1.1 identifies four points at which measures or indicators can be recorded:

1. Inputs.
2. Process or productivity.
3. Intermediate outputs.
4. Final outputs or outcomes.

In many commercial activities, flows at all of these points would be measurable in money terms, and the measures ultimately be derived from the valuations of output made by final consumers. But this approach is not possible within higher education as many of the outputs are difficult or impossible to measure in monetary or even in physical units. Hence the emergence of PIs as partial and approximate 'surrogate' measures either of output or – in many cases – of inputs. But it is useful to review other techniques of measurement based on the input–output framework.

Cost-benefit analysis is one of the most ambitious techniques which has been applied (see Layard and Glaister 1994). It has been used to establish the rate of return to investment in higher education either for the economy as a whole (the social return) or for the individual student. In the former case the 'costs' are established by aggregating the teaching-related costs shown in Figure 1.1. Benefits are normally estimated as the discounted value of the increments in earnings associated with higher education, though it is difficult to separate these from other background or environmental effects. On fairly stringent assumptions about the operation of labour markets, they equal the increments in the individual's marginal product of labour. The calculation thus derives an output valuation from the operation of the economy as a whole. Studies of this kind (for example, Clark and Tarsh 1987 or, for a review, Weale 1992) typically distinguish between different disciplines or groups of disciplines (for example, social sciences or engineering) and between different levels of degree (for example, undergraduate degrees or postgraduate degrees). It is not, however, normally possible to distinguish between different institutions of higher education, because of problems of sample size. A similar approach is possible in principle in relation to research outputs, but the difficulties of establishing the economic benefits associated with research products (see Chapter 4.6) rule it out in practice.

A less ambitious technique is cost-effectiveness analysis. Inputs are measured in money terms and outputs in physical units (for example, number of graduates, number of research papers). The key difficulty here is ensuring that the physical unit adequately conveys the attributes of the output. When a homogeneous product is being produced, that assumption is reasonable. But the outputs of higher education differ substantially in quality. With cost-benefit analysis this is captured, in principle at least, by the increment in the market wage of graduates. In cost-effectiveness analysis this is not attempted, and the output measure is typically simply the number of students graduated.

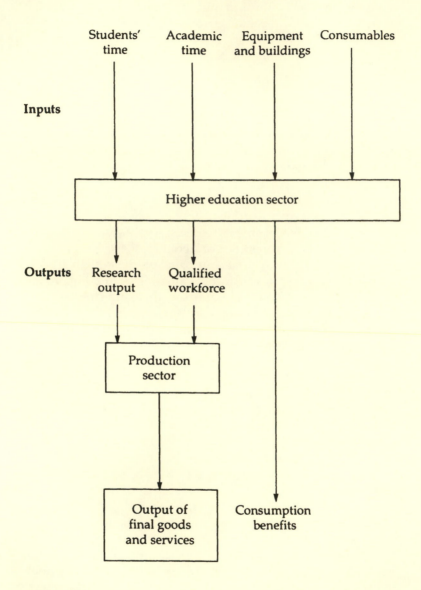

Figure 1.1 Inputs and outputs in higher education

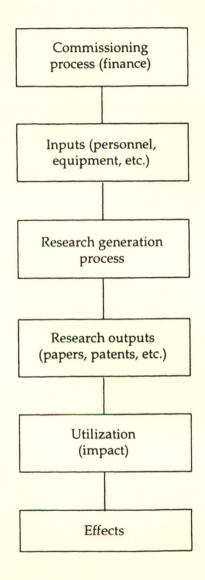

Figure 1.2 The Research Production Model

Cost-effectiveness analysis is a particular type of productivity measure, in which inputs are denominated in cost terms and outputs in some physical unit. Alternative output and input measures can also be combined to produce partial productivity measures – for example, output of graduates per member of academic staff (or, more conventionally, students undergoing tuition per member of academic staff – the staff–student ratio). In this instance both output and input are measured in physical units and there is no attempt to control for either the quality of output or the cost or quality of inputs. Such measures do however have the merit that they can be computed fairly quickly and on a disaggregated basis – for example, department by department in any given institution or across departments in the same discipline.

Measures of this kind are a form of PI – although in some treatments this term is reserved for cases where the evaluation does not pretend precisely to capture or measure the true variable which is sought. In other accounts, including the present one, the term is used more widely to convey a range of more or less precise measurements of outputs, inputs, productivity and other features of the process.

As noted above, the use of PIs within the UK non-marketed public sector has expanded significantly in recent years, as part of a central government programme to improve the planning, monitoring and evaluation of performance – to develop as far as possible analogues for the revenue and cost figures available in the marketed sector. As an illustration of this expansion at the level of central government, the 1990 Public Expenditure White Paper (Treasury 1990) contained about 2300 output and performance measures, compared with 1200 in 1986 and 500 in 1985. These include such indicators as the number of hospital in-patient and day cases treated, and the proportion of Ministry of Defence contracts subject to competitive tender. Higher education PIs listed in the 1987 White Paper included an index of unit costs in local authority higher education.

Both cost-benefit and cost-effectiveness analysis rely upon the assumption that particular costs incurred within higher education institutions can be associated with particular returns. For example, the cost-benefit study cited above (Clark and Tarsh 1987) assumed, in calculating the rate of return to society from undergraduate degrees, that alternatively 67 per cent, 80 per cent or 100 per cent of university costs were associated with teaching, the remainder with research. The distinction between research and teaching inputs and outputs raises a number of serious difficulties. On the output side, some products such as research degrees represent both teaching and research outputs. On the input side, many costs, in the form of academics' time, central services such as libraries and computer centres, and premises and equipment, are joint or common to both teaching and research.

This issue of cost allocation has been addressed in various ways. In 1985, the Department of Education and Science (DES) commissioned a study into the allocation of costs between teaching and research, published as Clayton (1987). The author asked a stratified sample of departments and central services in higher education institutions to complete a questionnaire allocating costs as far as possible between teaching and research. The results showed a much higher proportion of expenditure on research in the 'old' than in the 'new' universities (then known as polytechnics). There was also substantial variation from subject group to subject group.

A weakness of this original study was that institutions had a considerable amount of discretion in allocating costs, and difficulties arose in a number of areas. These related particularly to the allocation of staff time and of library expenditure. Experience in other areas, notably public utilities, shows that common conventions have to be established in cost allocation exercises for all respondents if the results are to be reliable (Cave and Mills 1992).

There is an alternative method for comparing inputs and outputs across a range of higher education institutions, known as the 'efficiency frontier' approach or data envelopment analysis. The efficiency frontier seeks to show the maximum combinations of level of outputs which can be achieved with a given level of inputs – if they are used perfectly efficiently. The frontier is estimated by comparing the performance of similar organisations, and establishing which of them outstrip their rivals in efficiency. The 'frontier' thus shows the limits of observable best practice.

Unlike cost-benefit analysis, which is capable in principle of establishing whether an activity should be undertaken, the efficiency frontier is only capable of identifying the most efficient method of doing it, and of showing how close to efficiency a particular institution comes.

As an illustration, suppose that a number of institutions with identical inputs are producing two homogeneous outputs only, 'arts' and 'science' graduates. Figure 1.3 shows the outputs of respectively institutions A to F. The 'efficiency frontier' is shown by line ABCD. On the assumption that an institution could be constructed which combines A and B in any given proportions, all points along the chord AB are possible. Similarly, combinations of B and C and of C and D would make possible any points on BC and CD respectively. It would not, however, be efficient to combine, for example, B and D, because the outputs made available could always be produced more efficiently by a combination of B and C or C and D. In the figure institutions E and

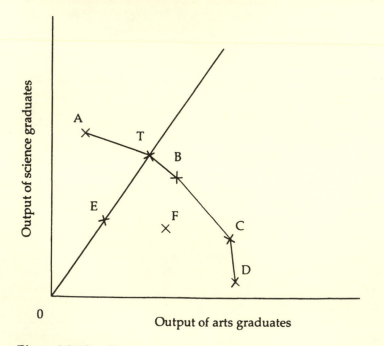

Figure 1.3 The efficiency frontier

F are inefficient, and their degree of inefficiency in the case of E can be measured as the ratio of ET to OT. This shows how much output has been lost as a result of failure to use 'best practice' technology – in this case a combination of those employed by institutions A and B.

The example in Figure 1.3 is a trivial one as it involves only two outputs and assumes uniform costs across institutions, measured in money terms. However, the model can be realised (though not, of course, drawn) in as many dimensions as are wanted. Different types of teaching outputs and of research outputs can be distinguished. Costs can be treated as 'negative' or 'inverse' outputs and disaggregated to any desired degree, by department and/or by type – for example, premises, equipment or lecturers' time. There is, however, a trade-off here, in the sense that the greater the degree of disaggregation, the less inefficient any institution will appear to be as its idiosyncratic cost or output profile promotes it to a point on the frontier. It is also possible to distinguish in the calculations between differences in productivity, arising from technical inefficiency, and those arising from economies of scale – the reduction in unit costs associated with higher levels of output.

Hitherto, little use has been made of this technique in higher education, despite its theoretical attractions and its widespread use in other areas of economic analysis. Sizer (1981) reported a single application and expresses doubt about its usefulness. Work has continued, however, aided by the availability of more consistent data collected in the course of the research assessment exercises (see Tomkins and Green 1988; Ahn, Charnes and Cooper 1988; Johnes and Johnes 1990; Johnes 1995).

It is disappointing that the efficiency frontier approach has not had a greater impact upon assessment in higher education. Probably what is required for more general acceptance is a run of studies showing consistent results when the inputs and outputs identified and other assumptions made are changed. But even now, the multi-input, multi-output approach adopted in efficiency frontier work is helpful in understanding the processes of higher education at a conceptual level.

The final technique for evaluating performance discussed here is regression analysis. This technique has been used particularly by a group of researchers at Lancaster University – G.

Johnes, J. Johnes and J. Taylor. Their detailed findings are described in the chapters which follow, and many are collected in J. Johnes and Taylor (1990a) and Taylor (1995). Later chapters also discuss how this approach influenced the thinking of the JPIWG but it is useful here to give a brief account of the principles underlying the technique. This is done on the basis of discussion of a hypothetical PI – research output per staff member.

Suppose that data are available on research output per staff member in a number of university departments within the same discipline. Suppose also that the size of each department is known. The data can then be represented as in Figure 1.4, where each point shown represents an observation of research output per staff member in a department of the indicated size. The average level for all departments is shown by the horizontal line in the figure. We may formulate the hypothesis that there are features of the production process for research which imply that larger departments produce more research per staff member. This hypothesis can be tested by fitting a line, using standard techniques of statistical regression, through the points in the figure. This line is shown by RR. The closer the fit of points to the line, the greater the proportion of variation in research output per staff member 'explained' by size. But it is highly unlikely that the fit will be perfect. Other factors than size will influence research output per capita; examples are the availability of research funding and equipment, the time and effort devoted to research, and purely random factors. A further application of regression analysis, discussed in Chapter 4 below, is to use it to investigate assessments of research. Here the dependent variable is the grading given in the research assessment exercise, and the explanatory variables are such things as research outputs, research income and size. Here regression analysis is used to infer the valuations of the assessors, rather than to explain the underlying determinants of research productivity.

How can regression analysis be used to improve or refine PIs? Given the data at our disposal, the simplest approach would involve comparing each department with the average. On this basis department A would be below average and department B above average. But we may wish to 'correct' our measure of research output per staff member for the size of department. On this basis, department A will have performed better than expected, while department B will have performed worse than expected. Running the regression of research output per staff member on size has enabled us to identify departures above and below the expected output level for a department of any given size.

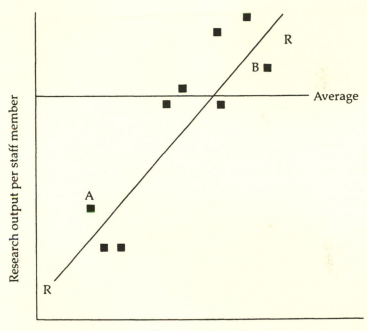

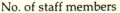

Figure 1.4 Regression analysis in a hypothetical example

Regression analysis thus offers two advantages. First, it makes it possible to test hypotheses concerning factors which affect the production process in higher education. Second, it provides a more refined basis for evaluating the performance of an individual department by comparing the actual outputs with the expected outputs for a given level of inputs. However, it is important to avoid drawing the wrong policy conclusions from the second approach. In Figure 1.4, A's performance is better than expected and B's worse. In certain circumstances we might

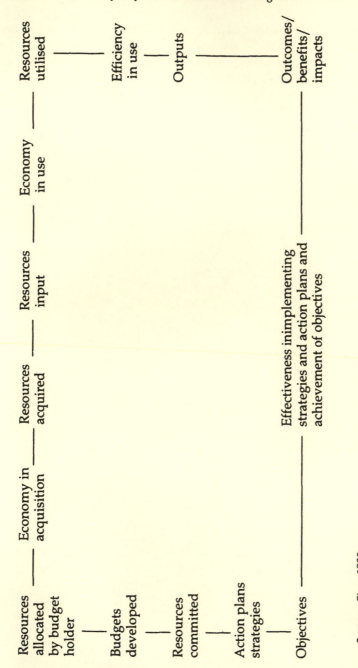

Source: Sizer 1989
Figure 1.5 Value for money – the three Es

be prepared to describe A's behaviour as praiseworthy and B's as blameworthy. But it still remains true that department B has a higher research output per staff member than department A. If the purpose of performance measurement in higher education is not so much to reward and blame but to achieve an efficient allocation of resources, then the (hypothetical) lesson that large departments have a higher research output per staff member is the more significant one.

Despite its apparently reductionist nature, and criticisms, for example by Elton (1988a), the production model approach is useful not only for shedding light on particular techniques, but also in illustrating the classification of PIs. The issues surrounding the various classifications of PIs in general are well discussed in Beeton (1988) and with particular reference to higher education, many of these points are brought together in the sequence developed by Sizer (1989) – see Figure 1.5. The figure also illustrates the interactive relationship between objectives, measurement and indicators of economy, efficiency, and effectiveness.

1.4 Developing frameworks for the application of indicators to policy

When a system of PIs is being devised a proper framework for analysis and application to policy is necessary otherwise problems will arise. Mayston (1985) showed, on the basis of early American experience with PIs in general, that if PIs lack 'decision relevance' they are ignored. Alternatively, the introduction of PIs may have an impact but a dysfunctional one. It could lead to less easily measured activities being given lower priority and it may affect in unanticipated ways: the pattern of working relationships between decision-making units and individuals within the organisation; relationships with clients and sponsors; the responsiveness of an organisation to the demands made upon it; and the scope for discretion in the use of resources.

Within the field of higher education and research these dangers can be illustrated by a number of examples:

1. The greater emphasis being given in universities to research, where funding is linked to performance rather than to teaching.

2. A change in the pattern of publications.
3. The greater pressure to publish, irrespective of the state of the material.
4. The greater emphasis given to types of research where performance can be measured bibliometrically, at the expense of other objectives.

Two further dangers can be noted. First, the partial nature of most indicators leaves ample scope for strategic behaviour on the part of the unit being appraised. This fact has been widely recognised in other contexts: for example in the health service, where use of such indicators as average length of stay of hospital patients is widely believed to have a distorting influence on the pattern of treatment. Clearly, similar opportunities exist in higher education, where departments or institutions have considerable scope for determining their input and output mix, and where in many cases members of the institutions themselves largely determine the 'quality' of their output by determining students' degree classes or the completion rate of research degrees – however assiduous external examiners, accrediting bodies and quality assessment organisations may be.

Second, there are obvious difficulties in using PIs as an input into the resource allocation process. Because of their partial nature, individual PIs often provide potentially misleading impressions even of average productivity. For example, two departments may appear to have an equal output of publications per staff member, while one may have a substantially greater amount of complementary inputs. Equally important, resources should be allocated so that contributions of resources are equalised at the margin. The fact that one department may have a lower average level of performance than another does not imply that resources should be taken from the poor performer and given to the good performer. Unless we know about the two departments' relative ability to convert inputs into outputs at the margin, we can make no such claim. Thus the problem of interpretation and use of PIs is quite as complex as that of measurement itself. It is important, however, that the qualifications are not simply recorded and then ignored as, in the words of Bud (1985), 'disappearing caveats'.

A way of reducing the dangers is not only to develop a framework showing the production function represented by

PIs, but also a frame showing how the PIs can be applied to policy. Moravcsik (1986) has usefully proposed a 'methodology for finding a methodology' for the assessment of science, though its potential sphere of application is wider. The framework includes:

1. Identifying the relevant objectives of the organisation.
2. Specifying the parts or levels of the system to be analysed and specifying the uses to which the assessment will be put.
3. Listing the PIs to be used.
4. Devising simple strategies for their application to the organisation and predicting the implications that their application might have.

Along similar lines, and to tackle the need identified for PIs to be 'decision relevant', Jesson and Mayston (1990) identified three conditions for the successful use of PIs:

1. A clear conceptual framework within which the indicators are derived, and the associated set of purposes that they are intended to serve.
2. A selection process to determine which indicators are to be applied, and how.
3. A specification of how the indicators fit into the management and decision process.

Banta and Borden (1994, p.96) provide a list of standards or criteria for judging PIs for higher education that could also be used to form a framework for applying them. They suggest PIs should:

(a) have a clear purpose
(b) be co-ordinated throughout an organisation or system (vertical alignment)
(c) extend across the entire range of organisational processes (horizontal alignment)
(d) be derived from a variety of co-ordinated methods
(e) be used to inform decision making.

Clearly an overlapping range of classifications and frameworks can be applied to PIs. In Chapter 5 we shall draw upon the above frameworks and other literature to suggest a three-level analysis which includes: a classificatory scheme for individual PIs; an analysis of the conceptual and structural issues surrounding the use of PI systems; and an assessment of the broader policy context within which the set of PIs is to operate.

1.5 Plan of the book

In this chapter we have sought to explore, in general terms, some of the key issues in the development of PIs. We have noted how the Government has radically changed the assumptions upon which higher education is to be conducted, and that the introduction of PIs forms part of a general shift from academic control over objectives and evaluation to control by the system and its managers. We have briefly enumerated the different definitions and categories of PIs, and have related them to the measurement of inputs and outputs in higher education.

These themes are taken up in Chapter 2 through an overview of recent experience in the UK, the USA and other countries. Chapters 3 and 4 attempt a closer and more technical survey of the components of PIs of both teaching and research. These chapters rely upon surveys of research undertaken in a range of countries. It will be clear that our approach relies heavily on the distinction between research and teaching outputs and thus implicitly on a division of research-related and teaching-related costs, although we recognise that this involves serious difficulties.

In Chapter 5 we put some of our descriptions and conceptualisations to work by reflecting on the different models of PIs and their modes of application. We thus move from analysis of what is now being proposed in different systems to our own proposals of how they might be used within the UK context, both by funding bodies and within institutions.

Chapter 2

An Overview of Recent Experiences and Current Perspectives

2.1 The United Kingdom

Background

Although some PIs had always been used in higher education they had been unsystematically applied and their systematic use was perceived as a threat to the traditional and highly valued autonomy of the institution, the department and the individual. This is partly because the application of PIs, or at least their proper use when policy decisions are being made, depends, it is widely claimed, on the establishment of agreed objectives for higher education. Academics have not been prone to participate in the making of consensus about objectives. Whilst there are philosophical objections to the concept of objectives-led higher education, without them, however, the successful implementation of PIs is doubtful: 'performance indicators are only useful if clear priorities have already been established. Sadly there are no such priorities in higher education policy today. So PIs may be misused' (*Times Higher Education Supplement*, 20 February 1987).

As recently as 1985, the Jarratt Report asserted that 'objectives and aims in universities are defined only in very broad terms' (para.3.30). The development of objectives for a non-profit-making sector such as higher education is immensely difficult. Bourke (1986) claimed that:

> One notable feature of recent British experience... is the absence of specification of goals for single institutions and for the higher education system as a whole. It is a serious

problem for British higher education that there is now pressure for quality controls and for evaluation but no agreed
statement of system-wide or institutional objectives. (p.11)

These factors help explain 'the lack of the systematic use of PIs'
(Jarratt 1985, para.3.31). Practical difficulties will be elaborated
in later sections but it is a commonplace in higher education that
institutions may be characterised by 'goal conflict rather than
by striving towards goal congruence. They have joint inputs and
multiple outputs and outcomes, the ultimate impact of which is
extremely hard to measure' (Sizer 1979, p.53).

Despite the scepticism voiced in many academic quarters, the
pressures for change from the government and some institutional leaders in higher education in the UK were considerable
and PIs acquired a higher profile.

The pressures for change

Some of the key pressures behind the international introduction
of PIs have been identified as: value for money concerns at times
of financial constraint; demands for greater accountability; and
an interest in the strengthening of institutional management
(Cave and Hanney 1989 and 1992). These themes emerge in the
account below of the development of PIs in the UK but once
performance assessment starts various interests argue also for
the introduction of the PIs most favourable, or least unfair, to
them.

Education standards and costs have been increasingly under
scrutiny since the 'Great Debate' on education from 1976 onwards. At that time, institutions of higher education, like other
non-profit-making organisations, were being asked to justify
their activities and account for their use of resources and their
performance to external funding bodies in terms of their efficiency and effectiveness (Sizer 1979). Attempts in the 1970s to
apply non-profit performance evaluation techniques, such as
programme planning budgeting systems (PPBS) and cost-benefit analysis, to the institutions of higher education were not
found to be feasible because of their complexity. Nevertheless,
Sizer (1979) thought it might be possible to build on the legacy
of PPBS in the development of PIs for the various activities that
take place within institutions rather than at the level of the
system of higher education.

He further argued that, 'while it may not prove possible to agree objectives, measure outcomes and develop performance indicators for an institution as a whole, it should be possible to do so for parts of the organisation' (p.56). Sizer suggested that a whole range of PIs should be considered when establishing indicators for research, teaching and central services and that the following standards should be applied to these partial PIs: relevance, verifiability, freedom from bias, and quantifiability.

The OECD's Institutional Management in Higher Education (IMHE) Programme turned its attention to PIs in the 1970s (Sizer 1990). It did so because of both the financial constraints being imposed on higher education systems and the other pressures for their application considered here. Despite this and the work of Sizer, when the Society for Research into Higher Education (SRHE) asked in 1979 for papers on PIs they were 'disappointed by the dearth of contributions at institutional and, in particular, at national level' (Billing 1980, p.1).

Jarratt (1985) listed some of the PIs that were used and claimed much information was collected by universities. The apparent contradiction between the reports in 1985 of much information being collected and the dearth of interest in 1979 can be explained. First, Jarratt reported that much of the information was used for 'administration and not for management' (para.3.33), and that there was a lack of systematic use of PIs. Second, as Bourke pointed out, the PIs being pursued in the UK 'derive ultimately from the crisis of 1981 and from the need to preserve standards in the face of declining real resources... and following the UGC's realisation of the difficulties associated with the application of quality/performance judgements that are confidential and unspecified' (Bourke 1986, p.16).

In 1981 the information that was thought to have influenced the UGC included the amount of income universities received from research councils and the quality of the students on entry. Considerable debate about quality followed the 1981 decisions and the *Times Higher Education Supplement*, in the absence of any tradition of research in the area, launched a controversial series of surveys of the reputational standing of various departments in British universities.

In its Green Paper (DES 1985), *The Development of Higher Education into the 1990s*, the Government made it clear that it saw the development of PIs as the key to value for money. It is perhaps worth quoting at length:

> The essential purposes of performance measurement in education are to introduce into considerations of policy and the management of the education system at national and institutional level some concrete information on the extent to which the benefits expected from education expenditure are actually secured, and to facilitate comparisons in terms of effectiveness and efficiency as between various parts of the system, and as between different points in time. The pursuit of value for money in higher education can only be successful if it is based on an analysis of benefits and their related costs in different activities. There are significant difficulties in measuring performance in higher education... But the effort has to be made if the government is to pursue its objectives of controlling public expenditure and of making the most effective use of the taxpayer's money; and if institutions and others concerned with higher education planning are to be fully informed in taking their decisions on the allocation of the resources available. (p.49)

As noted in Chapter 1, Sizer (1989) set out how the Thatcher Government's demand for greater accountability and value for money in performance in terms of economy, efficiency and effectiveness could be modelled. The Jarratt Report elaborated a requirement for the development of strategic plans to underpin academic decisions and structures, which brought planning, resource allocation and accountability together into a corporate process linking academic, financial and physical aspects.

In the 1985 Green Paper the DES welcomed the Jarratt Report's suggestions for the use of PIs at institutional level, and discussed their application to evaluating the national system of higher education. It saw the three main outputs of higher education as being highly qualified manpower, research, and other social benefits; it discussed some of the performance measures developed for these outputs but noted that at the national level significant progress was limited to research. Even if the difficulties of constructing these measures could be overcome, there would still be no adjustment for quality of output and no satisfactory measure of a major output of higher education – the impact of highly qualified labour in the economy. The Green Paper suggested that some aspects of these variables could be captured by indicators such as wastage rates, entry standards and graduates' first destinations. The PIs discussed included: student numbers and participation rates; unit costs; recurrent costs; the number and costs of successful students. One measure which, according to the Green Paper, attempts to conflate some of the indicators into an overall index of value for money is the 'rate of return' of higher education. The 'rate of return' is the annual flow of benefits, such as contribution to the economy, which are reflected in higher earnings, expressed as a percentage of the initial cost of education. The DES put considerable effort into the development of PIs to measure the extent to which higher education was serving the needs of the economy for highly qualified manpower (Cullen 1987). Particular emphasis was given to a broader definition of 'consumer' to include groups such as employers in addition to the previous implicit emphasis on students.

Mainly as a result of the Jarratt Report and of government concern about the preservation of academic quality the Committee of Vice-Chancellors and Principals (CVCP) established a committee under Professor Philip Reynolds (1986) which listed the data that might be, and in many cases already were being, collected by universities and which could be used to monitor academic standards. Many of the points were incorporated in the CVCP/UGC 1986 list of proposed PIs.

The University Grants Committee likewise had to be actively involved in judgements of quality (Harris 1986). Sir Keith Joseph, when Secretary of State, had in fact threatened to remove research funding from the UGC to the research councils unless the UGC launched a selectivity exercise. Better evaluation of the quality of existing research has also become more necessary as reduced funding has limited the proportion of 'alpha' quality research proposals that can be supported.

Even in an era of steady state funding, the unparalleled growth in scientific opportunities and ever more expensive equipment means that emphasis is placed on the search for more 'objective' decision aids, rather than relying solely on peer review because the research funding decisions become inevitably more controversial (Gibbons and Georghiou 1987; Ziman 1987; Phillips and Turney 1988). Irvine (1989) suggests that the UK was the first to experience these research pressures. Although such pressures impinged particularly on the research councils they had an impact on higher education in general.

Generally, at a time of financial restrictions the pressures on the funding bodies – both at national level and within the institutions – to justify their decisions become greater. The lack of debate about, or announcement of, explicit criteria by which the 1981 cuts were made by the UGC was vigorously attacked. Many academics felt it essential to ensure that 'future judgements, while certainly selective, would be carried out on the basis of criteria as far as possible known in advance to the university community' (Harris 1986, p.2).

By 1986 the universities knew that the UGC was taking the research rankings (see Chapter 4) into account when deciding about resource allocations in a further period of constraint. However, the ways in which the research rankings were produced were not entirely clear and strengthened the case for more explicit, objective PIs (for example, Sheppard, Last and Foulkes 1986; Rogers and Scratcherd 1986; Evans and Clift 1987).

Financial constraint not only leads to demands for a clearer identification of the criteria on which decisions on resource allocations are made but also encourages institutions to develop, or accept, PIs to show that they deserve a bigger allocation. Such pressures might be resisted by those institutions doing best under the current methods of allocation but the more likely result is an increase in the number of PIs advocated as the most suitable ones upon which to base resource allocations.

In its 1987 proposals that higher education institutions be required to seek funding on the basis of specific contracts the DES noted that measures of performance would be needed to ensure that institutions met their contracted output targets and suggested that more research would be required in this area.

Just as individual institutions have an incentive to gain a larger slice of the higher education cake, so the higher education system, at a time of financial constraint, has an added incentive to show that the system deserves a larger slice of the nation's resources than might otherwise be intended for it. According to the second statement from the CVCP/UGC working group, 'several universities suggested that the development of performance indicators should be undertaken with an eye to strengthening the public image of the university system'

(CVCP/UGC 1987a, p.5). Ewen Page, a member of the working group's technical committee, thought that universities must adopt PIs because, 'if universities wish to receive increased sums of public money – and they must receive more – they must exhibit evidence that what has been received has been well applied' (Page 1987).

As was noted earlier, the proposals of the Jarratt Committee entailed a strengthening of the role of the management of institutions and PIs were advocated as one of the tools of management. Although evaluation has always been present in higher education, the introduction of PIs changes both how it is done, and who does it. Academics undoubtedly fear that evaluation may be taken out of their hands and used for purposes which they do not themselves determine. Moving the criteria from those of excellence determined by 'internalist' criteria intrinsic to the academic profession towards criteria related to discernible economic or other social outcomes inevitably moves the control of evaluation away from the academics towards the managers (Kogan 1989).

Once the development of PIs had been accepted, albeit reluctantly, anxiety concentrated on choices of PIs and the use to which they might be put. Furthermore, some critics were concerned that as full a range as possible of PIs be used rather than a limited, possibly damaging, one.

We have already seen that critics of the methods used in producing the UGC research rankings argued for more objective PIs to be developed. With the UGC basing some funding decisions on its research rankings, pressure began to mount for the difficult task of assessing teaching quality to be tackled, to meet the danger that academics would devote more effort to research and less to teaching (Harris 1986).

Sizer foresaw some of these problems when, in 1979, he suggested that a wide range of PIs should be used because there might be a danger that 'in using short-term output indicators of performance, such as cost per full-time equivalent student or cost per graduate, sight will be lost of the long-term measure of the effectiveness of institutions, i.e. their contribution to the needs of society' (p.62).

Some other issues which have always been of concern to certain people illustrate the point that once consideration of PIs begins pressures can build up for further (or alternative) development and use of PIs. It was argued that the interests of consumers were given insufficient attention in the PIs of the 1980s (Pollitt 1987, 1988). Pressures to pay more attention to the perspective of students has been a feature of the further development of PIs in the 1990s in several directions (Cave, Hanney and Henkel 1995). The role of student evaluation of teaching and of student guides such as *The Times Good University Guide* (O'Leary and Cannon 1995) will be examined later. Discussion of the developmental or enhancement role that PIs can play in quality assurance was given impetus by CNAA funding for various projects (see, for example, Allsop and Findlay 1990; Yorke 1991 and 1995).

The development of PIs

The case for the development of PIs was then building up throughout the 1980s. Furthermore, as we shall see in relation to research PIs, one of the factors behind their development was the technical advances in bibliometrics spearheaded by the Institute for Scientific Information (ISI) at Philadelphia. This section examines the evolving relationship between technical developments, the political impetus behind the adoption of PIs and the policy uses to which they could be linked. It provides an essentially historical account of developments over the last decade.

Considerable work was necessary before PIs could be adopted. In response to the recommendations of the Jarratt Committee, and the terms of the Concordat reached with the Government in return for the settlement of pay anomaly (see Chapter 1.2), the CVCP and UGC set up a working group on PIs. Its first statement, *Performance Indicators in Universities* (CVCP/UGC 1986), was published in July 1986 but it recognised that further work was required before the PIs could be fully implemented. It had been pressed to produce PIs during 1987 and could use only the information already available within the Universities Statistical Return (USR). Chapter 4 discusses the way in which the UGC started using some PIs to help implement the policy of selective funding of research.

The 1986 CVCP/UGC statement claimed to have sought to establish PIs which would assist universities in the internal management of their affairs and help the UGC and DES monitor university performance and the control of public expenditure. Teaching and research were said to be the major focus and the main aims were better accountability and the provision of management tools. The group found that all universities already had available information, much of which could be used effectively as PIs. The 16 most commonly used indicators were listed and over 70 others were used. Some of these, however, would not fall within the definitions of PIs discussed in Chapter 1. The statement recommended a range of PIs to cover inputs, processes and outputs and stressed that some PIs could play a particularly useful role in the identification of trends in performance.

The working group saw its principal task as being 'to standardise existing practice by formulating common definitions and developing an agreed list for use by all universities' (p.4). The need to introduce common PIs on a national basis as soon as possible caused them to look at some aspects of universities' work, in addition to teaching and research, where data were available for immediate implementation of valid and useful information. Each proposed PI was tested against a range of agreed questions including:

- was it relevant to the objectives of the organisation?
- could it be quantified precisely and in an objective manner?
- would it be of practical value to management of the organisation and to others outside the institution?
- would it be acceptable?
- were the data already collected satisfactorily?
- what would be the cost in relation to benefit?

These questions were based on the earlier standards proposed by Sizer (1979) although Pollitt (1987) has described such lists as being 'next to useless' because they describe 'a state of grace repeatedly envisioned in the managerial scriptures but unknown in the untidy reality' (p.88). Whilst this warning is useful, it remains a fact that PIs are being introduced and it is of value to have these standards against which to test them.

Table 2.1 Initial range of Performance Indicators proposed in first statement by CVCP/UGC working group

	Implementation time scale		
	1986/87	Near future	Future
Teaching and research			
Cost per FTE student	X		
Research income	X		
Contribution to PG and professional training	X		
Submission rates for research degrees	X		
Number of research and sponsored students	X		
Occupation of graduates after 12 months	X		
Undergraduate wastage rates		X	
Occupation of graduates after 5 years			X
Analysis of publications/patents/ agreements/copyrights			X
Citations			X
Peer review			X
Editorship of journals/officers of learned bodies			X
Membership of research councils			X
Costs per graduate			X
FTE students to FT academic staff	X		
Equipment costs per FT academic staff	X		
Others			
Administrative costs per FTE student	X		
Premises costs per FTE student	X		
Library costs per FTE student	X		
Careers services costs per FTE student	X		
Medical services costs per FTE student	X		
Sports facilities costs per FTE student	X		
Other central costs per FTE student	X		
Ratio of support staff to academics	X		

Where the relevant information was already available, some PIs were suggested for possible introduction in 1986–87. Another group was listed which could be implemented in the future and for which the information could be collected – see Table 2.1.

An interesting omission from the list was standards of entry to higher education (i.e. A level scores) with the statement acknowledging that 'it is known that the relationship between entrance score and degree class is weak'. This suggests a change of opinion from 1981 when A level entry scores were one of the main criteria used by the UGC. Harris, a member of the working group, took the argument a step further by suggesting that however difficult value-added was to measure, it, and not entry standards, was the relevant factor that should be used in judging university departments. An era of wider access subsequently made entry scores less justifiable as a PI.

The first statement advocated the development of teaching appraisal in all institutions and supported the use of student questionnaires but, apart from brief references to costs and wastage rates, did not specify which PIs related to the teaching function. The working group claimed that 'this first statement has concentrated on creating an operational framework and on determining the mechanisms necessary for the implementation of performance indicators. There is still much work to do in devising specific indicators for a wider range of universities' work' (CVCP/UGC 1986, p.8).

In 1987 Cullen (a DES official) discussed a number of PIs that might help the government decide how far higher education was achieving its objectives but which had yet to be formulated in operational terms. He concluded that despite the difficulties, 'perhaps the most striking development has been the growing and widening acceptance of it [performance measurement] at all levels in the HE system' (Cullen 1987, p.178).

Inevitably interwoven with discussions of PIs are the policy and funding initiatives pursued by the government. The 1985 Green Paper stated that 'an important thrust of research policy over the next few years will be towards selectivity and concentration' (DES 1985, p.5). The UGC research rankings were being used to implement this policy and many were looking to the development of more adequate research PIs to improve the reliability and validity of the UGC's research ranking exercise and, as happened in the USA, the production of reputational rankings stimulated work on PIs that were claimed to be more objective. In its 1987 White Paper *Higher Education: Meeting the Challenge* (DES 1987e) the government welcomed the progress made by universities (including the CVCP's promotion of the development of PIs) to reassure the public about the ways in which they controlled standards. The contracts system, however, implied continued determination to monitor outcomes.

In the second statement (CVCP/UGC 1987a) the technical committee set up by the CVCP/UGC working group proposed that the 1984–85 and 1985–86 statistics could constitute the data for the 39 PIs published in the autumn of 1987. Of the 16 PIs that the first statement had suggested could be implemented in 1986–87, seven were omitted. Some of them could be not implemented because there were inadequate means of collecting the information. This problem is not peculiar to the UK.

In most cases, for example library costs per student, several of the 39 PIs identified by the technical committee related to one of the 16 proposed in the first statement for initial implementation. The statistics were published under the title *University Management Statistics and Performance Indicators*. This was a better title than *Performance Indicators* because, Page claimed, the term PIs 'is an abbreviated way of referring to all those numerical data which are useful in managing a university, assessing its operations, costs and performance' (Page 1987). The working group noted that further work was required and that even the 1986 list was felt by some 'to emphasise inputs and quantitative measures as opposed to outputs and qualitative results' (CVCP/UGC 1987a, p.4). The technical committee also stressed 'the need to be aware of the dangers of concentrating solely on the measurable and to neglect the wide range of qualitative factors which are impossible to quantify' (21). Nevertheless, the working group accepted that government pressure had created 'an imperative to produce a suite of indicators which could be published at the end of 1987' (15). This meant producing a list which overwhelmingly contained measurable input items and which was inevitably open to the question raised above about the validity of a list of PIs which does not give adequate attention to outcome measures. The list provided a good example of the point made by Carter (1989) that most PI systems in the UK are 'data driven' i.e. they are based on information already collected for other purposes. Similar criticisms have been made of the PIs used in the NHS (Allen, Harley and Makinson 1987).

Many of the PIs included also seemed open to the criticism that they failed to meet the point, hinted at in the statement, and noted in our discussion of the definition of a PI (Chapter 1), that the way in which the data are to be interpreted ought to be obvious. The working group's approach implied, although this was refuted, that lower costs of higher education were desirable and there was a danger of ignoring PIs concerned with the quality of the output. Thus, as we shall note in the next section, this approach is at odds with that sometimes adopted in the USA, at least until recently.

Despite these reservations and the pressure under which the work was completed, the second statement contained some sound analysis. The suggestion that PIs helped to stimulate intelligent questions was important, as was the stress on trends rather than on a 'snapshot'. Such analysis was in line with general conceptualisations about the role of PIs within the public services as in, for example, Beeton 1988. Because of a redefinition of cost centres in 1984, a consistent data series was available only from 1984–85. The repeated warnings that PIs needed to be used carefully as an aid to judgement and not a replacement for it were also helpful and in particular the warning that 'uncritical use of these indicators may seriously damage the health of your university' (CVCP/UGC 1987a, p.15) has been frequently quoted. The working group praised the technical committee for so rapidly producing PIs for publication in 1987. They could, however, be criticised on the ground that emphasis may have been given to certain PIs simply because information was readily available. More significant PIs did not appear because of data collection difficulties. The result was a somewhat unbalanced list. It was noted that there was 'a radical change of direction in the aims of the working group between its first and second statements' (Elton 1987b). This claim was disputed by Page who went on to accept, however, that 'of course, there was an imperative to publish some useful figures by the end of 1987' (Page 1987). The prime reason, he made clear, was the need, already discussed, to illustrate that universities were properly spending the money they had already received and should therefore receive increased funding.

The list became an annual publication and the management statistics and PIs appearing in the ninth volume, published in spring 1995, are given in Table 2.2. The list has been both extended and improved since 1987 but most of the changes were made in the early years. For example, as is explained in Chapter 3, the first destination indicators were improved to take account of the differences between universities in terms of their subject balances. Undergraduate success rate indicators were introduced as were indicators for entry qualifications.

Table 2.2 University management statistics and Performance Indicators, 1995

Expenditure in academic departments (by cost centre)
FTE academic staff
J1   Expenditure per FTE student
J2   Expenditure per FTE academic staff
J3   Expenditure on support staff per FTE academic staff
J4   Expenditure on equipment per FTE academic staff
J5   Research income per FTE academic staff

Students and staff (by cost centre)
FTE student load
J6   Research postgraduates as a percentage of FTE students
J7   Taught postgraduates as a percentage of FTE students
J8   All postgraduates as a percentage of FTE students
J9   Ratio of FTE students to FTE teaching staff

Expenditure on central administration
J10   Central administrative expenditure as a percentage of grand total expenditure
J11   Pay expenditure as a percentage of central administrative expenditure
J12   Central administrative expenditure per FTE student
J13   Central administrative expenditure per FTE academic staff

Expenditure on Libraries
J14   Library expenditure as a percentage of total general expenditure

Table 2.2 University management statistics
and Performance Indicators, 1995 (continued)

J15   Publications expenditure as a percentage of library
        expenditure
16   Library pay expenditure as a percentage of library
        expenditure
J17   Library expenditure per FTE student
J18   Library expenditure per FTE academic staff
J19   Expenditure on books per FTE student
J20   Expenditure on periodicals per FTE student

Expenditure on computer services
J21   Computer services expenditure as a percentage total of general
        expenditure
J22   Computer services pay expenditure as a percentage of total
        computer services expenditure
J23   Computer services expenditure per FTE student
J24   Computer services expenditure per FTE academic staff

Expenditure on premises
J25   Total premises expenditure as a percentage of total general
        expenditure
J26   Premises pay expenditure as a percentage of premises
        expenditure
J27   Heat, water and electricity expenditure as a percentage of total
        general expenditure
J28   Cleaning and custodial services expenditure as a percentage of
        total general expenditure
J29   Repairs and maintenance as a percentage of total general
        expenditure
J31   Total premises expenditure per FTE student
J32   Premises pay expenditure per FTE student
J33   Heat, water and electricity expenditure per FTE student
J34   Cleaning and custodial services per FTE student
J35   Repairs and maintenance expenditure per FTE student

Expenditure on careers services and student organisations
J37   Careers services expenditure per FTE student
J38   Grants to student organisations per FTE student

Table 2.2 University management statistics and Performance Indicators, 1995 (continued)

First destinations of first degree graduates by subject

J39   Destinations as at 31 December after graduation, UK totals by academic subject

First destinations of first degree graduates by university

J40   Total graduates with known destinations
J41   Graduates with destination 'unemployed or short-term'
J42   Predicted value indicator of J41
J43   Difference between indicators J42 and J41
J44   Difference per hundred graduates

First destinations: national proportion of 'unemployed or short-term' by subject 1992 to 1995
Undergraduate success (by academic subject group)

J45   Number of successful leavers
J46   Successes as a percentage of those ending their studies
J47   Proportions on three- and four-year courses
J48   Terms of attendance per success
J49   J48 relative to expected value

Qualifications of full-time undergraduate entrants, 1992 to 1994 (by academic subject group)

J50   Entrants with three or more A levels, numbers
J51   Entrants with three or more A levels, scores
J52   Entrants with five or more Scottish Highers, numbers
J53   Entrants with five or more Scottish Highers, scores
J54   Entrants with other qualifications

Source: University Management Statistics and Performance Indicators in the UK, CVCP, 1995b

The list was still open to many criticisms. In the Foreword of the 1989 Edition (CVCP/UGC 1989) it was admitted that 'the title "University Management Statistics and Performance Indicators"' continues to be used despite critical comments that 'arrays of numbers do not become performance indicators just by being called so'. The inclusion of, for example, telephone expenditure as a percentage of total general expenditure and per FTE student (indicators 30 and 36) was open to obvious criticism as in Ron

Johnston's (1989) review article, 'Do You Use the Telephone Too Much? A Review of Performance Indicators, Evaluation and Appraisal in British Universities.' They were subsequently dropped from the list as the last major change. Moreover, as was admitted by Sizer (1989), a member of the Performance Indicators Steering Committee which produced the list, only two could be identified as being output or outcome measures and the set was more useful in assessing efficiency than effectiveness.

There was the usual general warning in the 1990 Foreword (CVCP/UGC 1990) that users of the volume need 'knowledge, understanding and intelligence' and that 'careful interpretation' is vital if 'the data are to be the aid to good judgement which we intend'. The various editions included an illustrative commentary on the interpretation of some of the indicators along with the usual list of caveats.

Under the auspices of the steering committee, the technical work was undertaken by an editorial and development group and a Sub-Committee on Research Indicators (SCRI). SCRI was part of the growing network of groups developing research PIs in the UK and it considered the introduction of various research PIs into the CVCP/UFC list. Following the Oxburgh Report in 1987 on earth sciences, similar reviews into a number of subjects were undertaken by the UGC and are described in Chapter 4.

Another research assessment (or selectivity) exercise was conducted by the UGC/UFC in 1989 (UFC 1989a) (see Chapter 4). Although the procedure used was described as 'informed peer review', it was supported by a more systematic collection of research PIs than in 1986 and was subject to less criticism.

Ministers had been pressing the universities over a long period to give greater attention to teaching quality, and in 1988 the CVCP established a standing group under Professor Sutherland to create an academic standards unit to monitor universities' implementation of procedures for teaching quality assurance. Following a report from the Sutherland Group on academic audits, a unit was established. It was proposed that before visiting a university the 'audit team would *receive* an initial briefing based on performance and other quantitative indicators' (Sutherland 1989, p.2) – (our emphasis). As Sizer (1989) argued, the unit 'cannot be expected to assess the comparative quality of teaching by subject areas in all universities. There is an important distinction between *minimum quality assurance* and *comparative quality judgements'* (p.10). Publishable PIs of institutional teaching quality are difficult to develop (Sizer 1989). Apparently the joint CVCP/UGC PIs steering committee considered possible indicators but concluded that some used within institutions, such as classification of honours degrees, were inappropriate for making comparisons between institutions. It took the view that universities should undertake formal self-evaluation and appraisal of teaching as a matter of good practice, including the development of systems of individual teacher appraisal and student questionnaires.

PIs for UK higher education were mostly developed systematically, initially in the university sector. A report produced for the Committee of Directors of Polytechnics (CDP) in 1987–88 was not fully adopted. However, the Performance Indicator Project (PIP) at Nottingham Polytechnic resulted in a quarterly publication, *Print Out* (Pettifor). It provided information on questions such as: recent trends in cost, size and SSRs in polytechnics and colleges, and how far cost was explained by variations in size and SSR; how far student attainment indicators were explained by variations in expenditure (teaching and nonteaching), size and SSRs.

The political imperatives behind the development of PIs in the public sector were explicit. The Secretary of State sent a letter of guidance to the chairman of the PCFC at the time of its incorporation in which he stated: 'I look to the Council to develop further indicators of both quality and quantity of institutions' teaching and would be grateful if it could consider how these might be used as an input to its funding policies and decisions' (Morris 1990, para.1.2). The PCFC established a committee of enquiry, chaired by Alfred Morris, to suggest a range of indicators that might be used to assess the performance of institutions and advise how they might be used by the PCFC and the institutions themselves. The committee stated that it was in the interests of colleges and polytechnics to encourage the use of PIs because 'this will help the PCFC to champion the interests of the sector, particularly in the context of its annual negotiations with the Secretary of State and the Treasury over the future scale of public expenditure on higher education in colleges and polytechnics' (Morris para.1.3). A more explicit example of the partisan use of information would be difficult to find.

It was stressed that information only becomes a PI when it is used to illuminate or measure progress relative to stated objectives. PIs are, therefore, 'the spotlights of a form of "management with objectives" in which a planning process provides the integrating framework for a system of institutional self-critical appraisal and review' (para.1.5). Having identified the limitations of PIs the Report reviewed the experience of the universities and the work on PIs by CNAA, NAB, CDP, the Business and Technician Education Council (BTEC), and the Unit for the Development of Adult Continuing Education (UDACE), together with the recent reforms in the health service and the experience of the Scottish Education Department (SED). On some topics, for example, in recognising that PIs are desirable but limited, the Morris Committee endorsed the work of the CVCP/UGC. However, its key findings about the use of PIs in universities were that 'the CVCP performance indicators are of limited value to institutional managers; and that the best practice is found at institutional level when institutional comparisons are made using performance indicators which are integrated into the decision making processes of the university' (para.2.5).

The Report noted that HMI suggested the judgements in their reports could be informed by the use of PIs. HMI drew several general conclusions about PIs from their inspections: institutions vary in how far PIs are used and seen as useful; the cost and difficulty of collecting and using information inhibits developments; SSRs are the most commonly used indicator; and there is little evidence of the systematic use or development of indicators relating to the quality of teaching and learning.

Having outlined the key objectives of the Government and the PCFC, the committee described the levels and purposes for which the PCFC needed PIs. At the sectoral or macro level they supported the Public Expenditure Survey (PES) submission to the Secretary of State, and illuminated progress towards the stated objectives of the Government and the PCFC. At institutional level indicators were required by the PCFC to assist decisions on institutions' bids for recurrent funding and to form the basis of discussions with institutions on progress towards any particular objectives which may form part of the funding agreement between PCFC and an individual institution. The committee was conscious of the Government's eagerness to 'stimulate competition between institutions and stimulate relevant aspects of a regulated market in higher education' (para.3.19). In stressing the importance of reconciling autonomy with accountability the committee highlighted its belief that it should be for each institution to determine which PIs were most appropriate to its own internal management purposes, in the light of its distinctive mission and characteristics.

The outcome of the annual PES negotiations could be regarded as a collective 'public expenditure compact' between the sector and the Secretary of State. In the negotiations the PCFC 'needs to be able to illustrate that the sector is well managed, accountable, performance conscious, a good investment and that its claims for resources are credible' (para.3.34). Therefore the committee recommended that the aims and objectives underlying the public expenditure compact should be made explicit and they might be illuminated by four sets of 'macro performance indicators' relevant to the stated aims and objectives of the government and the PCFC (para.4.3). These were:

1. Scale and effectiveness indicators
   Student population
   Course completion
   Student achievement
   Value-added
   Employment and client satisfaction profiles
   HMI and BTEC quality profiles

2. Level of resourcing indicators
   Index of revenue resource
   Index of capital resource (equipment)
   Index of capital resource (buildings)

3. Efficiency indicators
   Index of output cost
   Ratio of students to staff

4. Source of funds indicators
   Ratio of public to total income
   Ratio of private fees to public funds

Each PI was explained in detail. At institutional level, the committee believed that to be effective, evaluation of performance must be rooted in its corporate planning process, through which the institution has set out its mission and objectives in terms which allow actual and planned performance to be compared. Institutions should share with PCFC 'a confidential Executive Summary of the institution's corporate plan as the contextual basis for the PCFC's processes of monitoring, review and of competitive bidding for funds, contracting and performance monitoring' (para.6.5). It was also suggested that the institutional funding agreement with PCFC might be reflected in an annual performance report.

The PCFC was recommended to introduce a rolling system of triennial institutional performance review visits. They would be the final stage in a process of institutional self-evaluation, the purposes of which would include 'to review with the institution, its self-critical appraisal of performance in relation to its mission statement and corporate plan and as illustrated by the institution's chosen performance indicators' (para.6.10).

In many ways the PCFC Report (Morris 1990) followed the frameworks outlined in Chapter 1.4, with the stress on the importance of objectives and the use to which PIs should be put. In welcoming the Report the *Times Higher Education Supplement* (15 June 1990) said that one way to misuse PIs was to devise a set 'which fail to bite on day-to-day management... This sadly seems to be the outcome of the joint effort of the former University Grants Committee and the Committee of Vice-Chancellors and Principals to design appropriately discreet performance indicators for universities. The Treasury was suitably unimpressed.' It was suggested that the approach adopted by the Morris Committee should ensure a sensible context within which PIs would be used.

The PCFC agreed to endorse ten of the macro PIs and asked the steering group on statistical information chaired by Professor David Legge to refine them. The remaining three, where further development work was required, were: value-added, quality profiles, and employer/client satisfaction. Even for the ten some reformulation was necessary but in 1992 values of the indicators for which data were available were published (PCFC 1992).

With the end of the binary line much of the previous work on developing PIs was brought together and built upon when the funding councils followed the letters of guidance from their respective Secretaries of State and created the Joint Performance Indicators Working Group (JPIWG) chaired by Professor Michael Sterling. With the retirement of Page, he became chairman of the PIs Steering Committee responsible for the final two editions of *University Management Statistics and Performance Indicators in the UK.*

The JPIWG's terms of reference were broad:

1. To propose a range of institutional PIs of the efficiency and effectiveness of the use of public funds for teaching and research distributed by the Funding Councils. In particular this should cover:

    (a) output measures

    (b) measures of the quality of teaching and research provided to be used in conjunction with the research assessment and teaching quality assessment exercises and to inform an assessment of value for money.

2. To propose a range of indicators of the financial health of institutions.

3. To provide a range of sector-wide (macro) performance indicators.

4. To advise the Funding Councils on the arrangements for publication of institutional and sector-wide indicators.

5. To consider how the range of information which institutions are requested to publish under the further and higher education charters might be presented to make it as informative as possible.

The group stated that the main purpose of the indicators was 'to inform institutional managers about the performance of their institution in its various aspects, and particularly in relation to other institutions' (CVCP 1995a para.1.15). The requirements of others, such as funding councils, were claimed to be secondary. This seems to represent something of a change from the initial view stated by funding council officials: 'the White Paper of 1991 stated that the Funding Councils will be responsible for the development and monitoring of performance indicators in higher education. These indicators will be used to monitor quality within the institutions and will be incorporated in the funding process' (Nandy, Brown and Woollard 1993, p.118). Furthermore, the development of PIs for research and teaching inevitably overlapped with the wider debate on the RAE and quality assessments of teaching.

The work of the JIPWG was given to various subcommittees (teaching, research, financial health and estate management) and *ad hoc* groups considered recommendations in relation to the higher education Charters, performance against mission and macro indicators. The development of macro indicators drew heavily on the work of the PCFC, and the subgroup on indicators of financial health reviewed the existing CVCP/UFC indicators of financial health and agreed they should be retained with some additions. Various estate management indicators were devised covering space utilisation, maintenance and capital expenditure. The thorough deliberations of the subgroups dealing with teaching and learning, and with research, will be discussed in detail in the following chapters. It is worth noting that although, as mentioned in Chapter 1, the report suggests the proposed indicators might be better described as management statistics than PIs, in the various sections, especially the one on research, the term PI is at times used. In the research section not only is the relationship between PIs and the continuing RAEs of 1992 and 1996 analysed but also the CVCP's 1993 first Annual Publications Survey is referred to under the important heading, given the JPIWG's terms of reference, of 'value for money'. The JPIWG had some difficulties with the survey's indicators such as publications per £1000 of external research income and per £1000 of UFC research grant. There are problems with this approach and presumably the JPIWG's objections were similar to those of the institutions which prevented the publications survey being published again. However, we shall see that the JPIWG's proposals for normalising the indicator for publications went to the opposite extreme and would present an exaggeratedly favourable picture of those institutions receiving most funding council money for research because they proposed just using the other PI in the publications survey – publications per academic member of staff. This approach can be criticised as being unfair because whereas before 1986 the notional research element in the allocation of funds per university academic did not vary between institutions, there are now enormous differences following the RAEs.

Several interesting themes emerge in the work of the JPIWG. Two of its principles were that the proposed statistics 'should be sufficiently flexible in their construction and application to reflect the wide diversity of institutional missions and objectives' and that the data 'should, wherever possible, be available from existing sources' (CVCP 1995a para.1.24). The latter is a continuation of a point noted earlier about indicators often being 'data driven'. There were attempts, to be described later, to incorporate the lessons from Johnes and Taylor's regression analysis more deeply into the PI set than they had been in the CVCP/UFC list. This meant trying to take more account of the variations in inputs that are thought to account for much of the difference in output by establishing benchmarks of 'expected' output levels given the relevant institution's inputs. Furthermore, there was some attempt to suggest different research indicators are appropriate for different subjects.

In 1994 the JPIWG issued a consultative document describing their work and listing 88 proposed indicators in five categories: 10 teaching; 14 research; 23 financial health; 4 estate; and 37 macro. This explicitness about the various categories of indicators was something never achieved in the *University Management Statistics and Performance Indicators* and reflects the considerable level of technical development work undertaken by the JPIWG. There was a generally favourable response from institutions; most criticism was levelled at the teaching section.

The funding councils decided publication of the final JPIWG report (with its slightly amended and extended list of indicators) should lie with the CVCP and it was published as an annexe to the first report from the newly created Higher Education Management Statistics (HEMS) Group which took over responsibility in this field from the JPIWG. It is chaired by James Wright, vice-chancellor of Newcastle, and was created to take the work forward and publish the data. It took the JPIWG's report as its starting point and initially reviewed and refined the suggested macro (i.e. sector-wide) statistics in the student and finance areas and the corresponding institutional statistics with a view to the data for them being published in 1996.

HEMS Group published a consultation paper on this stating that 'It is not intended that there should be a successor to the University Management Statistics and Performance Indicators volume' (HEMS Group 1995, para.5). Instead it was planned that the institutional statistics should be published alongside HESA's main publication of institutional data from the corresponding record and the macro statistics would be published separately: 'This will be a relatively small publication aimed at publicising the sector' (para.5). In the specific fields for which it thought statistics could be published the HEMS Group developed the JPIWG indicators, added a few but backed away from adopting the full benchmarking approach. The four sets of management statistics proposed for publication in 1996 are shown in Table 2.3.

Table 2.3 Higher education management statistics – publications in 1996

Macro statistics for teaching
Applicants and admissions
A1   Applicants
A2   UK domicile applicants by age and gender
A3   UK domicile applicants by subject
A4   UK domicile applicants by ethnic origin
A5   UK domicile applicants by social class
A6   Successful applicants
A7   Successful UK applicants by age and gender
A8   Successful UK applicants by subject area and gender
A9   Successful UK applicants by ethnic group and age

Participation
B1   Participation rates
B2   Student participation by mode

Table 2.3 Higher education management statistics – publications in 1996 (continued)

B3   Student participation by gender
B4   Participation by ethnic group

Student population description
C1   Student population
C2   Student population by programme area
C3   New students by programme area
C4   Student disability

Progression
D1   Completion of year in good standing by gender
D2   Completion of year in good standing by age group

Costs
E1   Index of revenue resources
E2   Cost per student year in good standing
E3   Total costs incurred by HE institutions

Length of HE experience
F1   Length of HE experience

Reverse qualifications
G1   Completion with qualifications by gender
G2   Completion with qualifications by age group
G3   Students gaining qualification by subject group
G4   Students gaining qualification by type of qualification

First destinations
H1   Leavers reported as being employed or studying overall by gender
H2   Leavers reported as being employed or studying overall by programme area
H3   Leavers reported as being employed or studying overall by age group

Impact on population
I1   Percentage of the UK population with higher education qualifications by age and gender over time

Macro finance statistics
1.   Index of public funding of HE
2.   Ratio of all public funds to total income

Table 2.3 Higher education management statistics – publications in 1996 (continued)

3. Ratio of Funding Council and TTA teaching grants to total income
4. Ratio of Funding Council and TTA research grants to total income
5. Ratio of Research Council research grants to total income
6. Ratio of overseas student fees to total income

Institutional statistics for teaching
Student progression rate
1. Proportion of students who are assessed as being unable to progress
2. Proportion of students who are assessed as being able to progress but who do not progress

Exit qualifications
3. Leavers defined by reason for leaving
4. Proportion of students who qualify that achieve a particular qualification

Employment destinations
5. Proportion of new qualifiers who are in employment
6. Proportion of new qualifiers who are unemployed
7. Proportion of new qualifiers who are in short-term employment
8. Proportion of new qualifiers entering further study or training
9. Proportion of new qualifiers who are not available for employment
10. Proportion of new qualifiers of unknown destination

Institutional financial profiles
1. Ratio of liquid assets to current liabilities
2. Days ratio of net liquid assets to total expenditure
3. Ratio of current assets to current liabilities
4. Days ratio of increase/decrease in cash and cash equivalents to total expenditure
5. Days ratio of net cash flow from operating activities plus returns on investment and servicing of finance to total expenditure
6. Per cent ratio of total payroll costs to total expenditure

**Table 2.3 Higher education management statistics –
publications in 1996 (continued)**

7. Per cent ratio of surplus (deficit) for the year (before transfers)
    to total income
8. Days ratio of general funds to total expenditure
9. Per cent ratio of total general funds to total expenditure
10. Per cent ratio of long-term liabilities to total general funds
11. Per cent ratio of interest payable to total income
12. Per cent ratio of premises maintenance expenditure to total
    expenditure
13. Per cent ratio of grants from HEFCs to total income
14. Per cent ratio of 'T' grant from HEFCS to total income
15. Per cent ratio of 'R' grant from HEFCs to total income
16. Per cent ratio of home/European Union (EU) fees to total
    income
17. Per cent ratio of overseas fees to total income
18. Per cent ratio of income from research councils and charities to
    total income
19. Per cent ratio of income from other research grants and
    contracts to total income
20. Per cent ratio of income from other services rendered to total
    income
21. Per cent ratio of residences and catering income to total income
22. Per cent ratio of miscellaneous income to total income

Source: HEMS Group 1995

It is significant that, although lengthy, the statistics listed in
Table 2.3 are not very broad and the HEMS document states:
'obviously this is all only the beginning of a long process'
(para.6). This statement is symptomatic of developments over
the last decade which have seen various bursts of political
pressure including the Green Paper of 1985, the letter of guidance to the PCFC, and the letters of guidance to the funding
councils in 1992. Each was followed by a period of technical
work which, whilst making advances, tended to throw up difficulties that resulted in each of the three main attempts
(CVCP/UGC in 1987, PCFC in 1992 and HEMS Group in 1996)
producing a narrower list of indicators than had been initially
proposed. Overall the list of indicators to be published in 1996

is narrower (though longer) than the list proposed in the first statement by the CVCP/UGC working group in 1986.

However, as noted before, the development of PIs in the UK is not limited to the work of the official bodies. The new commercially produced league tables and some of the student guides are based on a plethora of PIs with varying degrees of validity and reliability. Morrison, Magennis and Carey (1995) mount a strong critique of the validity of the league table of universities published in *The Times* on 27 May 1994: 'The Table is technically incapable of producing a rank order of universities on some meaningful measure. This central failure renders inferences based upon the table invalid' (p.142). *The Times* league table was based on the weighted combination of scores on 14 PIs and improvements were made in the 1995 version (O'Leary and Cannon 1995). Morrison *et al.* argue that not only are some of the PIs, especially value-added, flawed, but most importantly the attempt to combine them into a single table is invalid because the 14 points are not indicators of a single construct. They suggest universities should abandon the stance of having nothing to do with league tables and instead use the measurement literature to demand that the tables meet a set of measurement standards. Writing the Foreword to the 1995 edition of *University Management Statistics and Performance Indicators in the UK*, Sterling commented: 'In these days of league tables, the publication of this volume will inevitably facilitate the construction of spurious as well as informative comparisons. Those who would like to prepare derivative tables are encouraged to seek advice from HESA in order to avoid statistically dubious or misleading comparisons.' (CVCP 1995b, p.5).

Despite all the technical development the use of PIs within the UK thus remains controversial and we shall explore these issues in greater depth in later chapters. In the reviews of both teaching and research PIs the issue now has to be addressed of how far PIs inform the peer review assessments and then whether the peer review judgements can themselves become PIs.

2.2 The United States of America

The contrast between the HE systems in the UK and the USA helps to explain the differences in the nature of the development of PIs in the two countries. Although prestigious American institutions have high entry standards, the majority do not. Nor are the courses necessarily of the quality that was traditionally guaranteed by external examiners and common assumptions of standards in the UK. In America, therefore, some measurements that could be called PIs were developed in order to judge standards and differentiate high ranking from lower ranking institutions. There was such diversity, even among the doctorate programmes that, according to Cartter (1966): 'Just as consumer knowledge and honest advertising are requisite if a competitive economy is to work satisfactorily, so an improved knowledge of opportunities and of quality is desirable if a diverse educational system is to work effectively' (p.3).

The basis of student funding and the pressure on public institutions from state legislatures might also contribute to this more consumerist approach in the USA. However, as noted later, there are doubts about how far PIs supply information that is used by consumers of HE.

The American 'non-system' of higher education 'is an extremely large, highly diverse patchwork of institutions that differ greatly in quality, in character, and purpose, in size and complexity, in fiscal stability, and in sources of funding' (Gardner 1985, p.5). In such a diverse system, which includes some major private universities, and with state agencies more influential than Federal in most cases, with undergraduate and graduate programmes often considered separately, and with a long and varied tradition of academic research into the quality of departments, describing the development and current use of PIs is a complex task as has recently been acknowledged by Borden and Bottrill (1994). Most of the measures included in the original CVCP/UGC list of PIs for the UK had been collected in the USA, but although, as we shall see, it has become very important in the 1990s, the term 'performance indicators' does not seem to have been used consistently by Americans. The term was fairly popular in the early and mid-1970s but then for all practical purposes dropped out of the higher education literature (Miller 1987a). Bourke noted that US policy use in this area 'is of relatively recent origin but it occurs in a context of extensive and long standing academic research in the field of quality/performance measures' (Bourke 1986, p.12). Probably more research is carried out at the technical level of developing equivalent measures to PIs in the USA than elsewhere. Thus Hüfner and Rau (1987, p.6) note that

> the US market type of interaction in higher education has led to extensive and long-standing academic research activities in the field of performance indicators... the experience gained in the US in developing, applying and modifying quality/performance indicators/measures in higher education... [serves] as a methodological-theoretical starting point for similar attempts in Europe.

This remark illustrates the freedom with which outsiders can apply the term 'PI' to the US. It suggests that its absence in local discussion was merely a question of terminology rather than a result of the difference between the characteristics of US higher education and those of other systems. Such an interpretation was challenged by Kells (1989). He pointed out that although quantitative data were collected in the USA they were not akin to Western European PIs because they were used to inform peer review and to assist internal management and formative self-assessment rather than related to government goals and published in league tables that might have influenced funding decisions. Nedwek and Neal (1994, p.80), however, claim that 'Performance indicators are a specialised subset of system indicators... while introduced to higher education far earlier in the United States than in Europe, several common characteristics exist regardless of the setting'. There has recently been much more explicit use of the term with an issue of *New Directions for Institutional Research* being entitled 'Using Performance Indicators to Guide Strategic Decision Making' (Borden and Banta 1994). In the introductory chapter of this Borden and Bottrill compare developments in the USA with those in Europe: 'Although this terminology has only recently become popular here, in many ways PIs have a longer and more complex history of development in the United States' (p.6). Furthermore, a federally funded assessment of the role of PIs in ten states of the USA that has almost been akin to some of the official reports launched in other OECD countries with a detailed analysis of the concept and applications (Ruppert 1994).

Hundreds of quality rankings of American institutions of higher education and their various departments have been published since the first in 1910. These rankings have employed dozens of methodologies, many of them only used once. Whilst a clear chronological picture does not always appear some general points emerge.

Although only a small proportion of the attempts to assess quality has been carried out as national reputational rankings, they have been the best known, have created a number of spin-offs, and provide an interesting contrast with the UK. Unlike the UGC research rankings they have not been linked to specific policy initiatives. However, inevitably they have had an influence on funding and have improved the knowledge of students when making their choice of colleges. It was hoped that the information would be 'useful in strengthening graduate education across the country' (Cartter 1966, p.118).

The best-known national reputational rankings include those of doctoral programmes published by the American Council on Education in 1966 (Cartter) and 1970 (Roose and Andersen) and the Carnegie classifications (for example, of 1976, 1979 and 1987) concerned with institutional rankings. Cartter provided a few objective correlates (e.g. publications, institutional backgrounds of faculty, faculty salaries, national graduate fellowships) for some of the departments and institutions but his was primarily a reputational ranking. Cartter found generally high correlations but, as is explained in Chapter 4.2, other researchers produced work suggesting 'no objective measure is linearly, or even monotonically, related to the Cartter ratings across fields' (Drew and Karpf 1981, quoting Beyer and Snipper 1974). The Cartter, and the Roose and Andersen studies generated a large amount of work on objective indicators of quality. Jordan (1989) suggests that the role of reputation in ratings is influential and the rating reports contribute further to the mystique of higher education, but not to its serious appraisal.

Objective indicators of quality

The USA has a much more extensive tradition in this field than has the UK. Much of the work concentrated on developing refinements to, or new versions of, bibliometric measures of research, i.e. publications and citations. Other objective indicators developed include: faculty awards, honours and prizes; scores at entry of undergraduate students on standardised tests, e.g. Scholastic Aptitude Test (SAT) and the American College Test (ACT) and student fellowship awards; years taken to complete; students' achievements in later life; the academic background of the faculty; faculty salaries (see for example Adams and Krislov 1978); institutional resources, e.g. expenditure per student, library holdings, physical plant, endowments, student-faculty ratios, research income earned.

The advantages and disadvantages of each of these, and the best way of measuring them, have been discussed at length elsewhere and Tan (1992) lists many articles covering various of these areas specifically in relation to just the quality of doctoral programmes in sociology. However, several general comments might be made. In various combinations they have been discussed as part of the academic research tradition – the use of these indicators for policy making is discussed later. When the lists are discussed in general by some American authors such as Webster (1981) and Astin (1982) the natural inference is that the more generous the resources, the better the institution is doing. As we saw in Chapter 2.1, UK policy makers seem to take a different view, for at least some of the items such as staff–student ratios, although the recent league tables produced in the UK share the traditional USA approach.

The significant development in the USA in the 1980s and 1990s has been the growing preoccupation with one area of objective indicators, namely the quality of outcomes of undergraduate education. There has been a shift in professional research from ranking inputs to the study of effects. It has become increasingly clear that the measures used in the different studies reflect different constituencies with different stakes in higher education. Whereas peer evaluation and publications and citations rankings have come to be seen as expressing the producer's interest, outcomes research reflects the realisation of the range of expectations held by different clients of the system – students, parents, employers, taxpayers, policy makers. There is a growing belief that it is important to attempt to discover the benefits conferred by inputs and processes thought to be of high quality. There is widespread agreement that there is a growing concern with the assessment of quality and outcomes (see for example, Adelman 1986; Dill 1995b; Ewell 1985; Jordan 1989; Kells 1986; Nedwek and Neal 1994) and with inter-institutional evaluation (Brinkman 1987; Ewell 1994). Brinkman and Teeter (1987, p.6) suggest that one area for inter-institutional comparison is analysis of input and output data including: 'output patterns such as degrees awarded by field and level, research expenditure per faculty, percent of students graduating or dropping out; relative efficiency measures (or surrogates thereof) such as expenditures per credit hour or per student; and relative effectiveness indicators such as measures of value-added or quality rankings.'

Jordan also notes that empirically generated data on outcomes could permit comparisons of campuses which use similar measures. After discussing how such comparisons might be used in, for example, 'a legislative debate on getting value for the investment of public funds' (p.43) he notes that 'in some respects the matter is predetermined by the locus of authority... The term "performance indicators" may be used to bring to bear on students' learning econometric idioms and cost/benefit ratios. Such an approach may be methodologically driven when several institutions must be evaluated and the metric is not so much individual learners as aggregates in the thousand' (p.44).

In 1986 the Council on Post Secondary Accreditation issued new guidelines which required an assessment of outputs by institutions of higher education. Rogers and Gentemann (1989) show that in fact the six regional accrediting agencies that cover the USA had already begun to add criteria that examined institutional effectiveness as measured by outputs. However, a survey they conducted in 1987 suggested 'an alarming lack of preparedness to demonstrate institutional effectiveness amongst colleges and universities' (p.352). Only 44 per cent of their sample had defined expected outcomes, and only a third had recommended or selected ways of evaluating the achievement of educational outcomes. More recently Nedwek and Neal (1994) show how, for example, one of the six agencies, the North Central Association, 'has shifted its focus from the institution's capacity to achieve its mission to accomplishments as expressed by student achievement' (p.77). No longer would visiting teams be preoccupied with resources such as books in the library and number of PhDs on the staff; the emerging questions for the assessors focus on 'what the students have done or achieved as a result of having experienced the institution' (p.77). Dill (1995b) suggests that the accreditation process generally utilises 'a combination of performance indicators, self-study and peer review' (p.6). The PIs might include funding levels; facilities and libraries; students' profile and admissions selectivity indices; and student attainment rates.

Multidimensional approaches and league tables and value-added

Major authorities in the field now maintain that even more than might have been the case previously a multidimensional approach should be used, whether for objective indicators, reputational rankings or a combination.

Solmon and Astin's major reputational study of undergraduate education (1981) asked respondents primarily in private colleges to rate each listed undergraduate department on six criteria. They then collected a range of objective data (e.g. student–faculty ratios, total enrolment size, percentage of graduate students, per student expenditure for various purposes) and correlated them with reputational rankings.

In the early 1980s a major multidisciplinary ranking of the quality of doctoral programmes was carried out through a multidimensional approach. In addition to the usual reputational rankings it included rankings of the programme's size, characteristics of its recent graduates, the size of its library and, in all fields bar the humanities, the research support and the recent journal articles produced by the faculty (Jones, Lindzey and Coggeshall 1982). According to Fairweather (1988) this 'reputational rating of faculty quality has found widespread acceptance as a proxy for doctoral program quality' (p.346). Dill (1995b) describes how the study was recently replicated with faculty asked to rate research-doctorate programmes. The study also used information on: number of faculty and percentage of full professors participating in the programme; the percentage of faculty with research support; the number of full- and part-time graduate students enrolled; the number of PhDs produced; the median time lapse from entering graduate school to receipt of the PhD; the proportions of women, minorities and US citizens among the doctoral students; and, for engineering and science, publications and citations using data from the Institute for Scientific Information. Tan (1992) criticises quantitative correlate studies that rely on reputational rankings as the dependent variable and believes his study represents a start towards the use of a multivariate approach. However, because of the difficulties of finding an appropriate theory of quality, 'whether or not the clusters identified in the study were adequate indicators of quality remains a topic for further analysis' (p.218).

In the USA, as in the UK, there has recently been an upsurge in the publication of league tables by commercial publications such as *US News and World Report* and *Money* magazine. These league tables of the undergraduate level use a multidimensional approach – including in some an assessment of 'best buys' – and are controversial. Not only has their validity been questioned (Schmitz 1993) but also their rationale. Dill (1995b, p.14) argues 'that even in the most market-oriented system of higher education, quality ratings do not decisively influence student undergraduate college choices'.

One potential PI that did not seem to feature much in the traditional discussion of multidimensional criteria is student evaluation of teaching. This has been a feature of American higher education as is discussed further in Chapter 3 but such approaches do not easily lend themselves to comparative judgements between institutions and still do not appear in many of the statewide PI developments discussed later. However, Astin (1982, p.14) argued that institutions could be tested and scored on a series of developmental questions such as:

1. Do students regularly evaluate their teachers? Are professors given student feedback in a non-threatening context that will maximise learning?
2. Do faculty members receive critical evaluations of their teaching from peers?
3. Do academic advisers regularly receive student feedback?

One criticism of these approaches is that even they do not relate the inputs to the outputs with sufficient precision. It is suggested that to do so a value-added approach is necessary (see Chapter 3.6). Astin, one of its long-term advocates, claimed in 1982 that his 20 years' experience as a researcher conducting value-added studies had convinced him that

> funding agencies have never had much interest in support-ing value-added studies and what little support there is seems to be waning. The argument here is not that these national studies have not proved useful or that they should not continue... However, such studies frequently take a long time to produce useful results, and the results are often so general that they are difficult for individual institutions to apply to their particular problems. (p.13)

This situation has now changed somewhat, and throughout the 1980s a number of states (for example, Tennessee) have been or are attempting to make use of value-added (McClain, Krueger and Taylor 1986; Bogue 1982). A value-added scheme was intro-duced in Northeast Missouri State University with quantitative measures used to gain qualitative improvements (T. Taylor 1985). It is increasingly recognised that 'approached in a com-prehensive fashion, the issue of value-added to human lives by college can become the basis for claiming support from the polity' (Jordan 1989, p.30).

Policy use

PIs traditionally played a limited role in influencing policy makers in American higher education. This was despite the mission statements that provided institutions with objectives necessary for proper use of PIs and despite the amount of research on assessments of quality.

More recently, however, there has been greater use of PIs. Faced with unlimited demand for service on one side and the harsh realities of public accountability on the other, the state colleges and regional universities are moving away from the rhetoric of education and towards the rhetoric of administration and management. In these colleges, 'student credit hours per full-time equivalent faculty becomes a term heard as often in the faculty lounge as in the president's office; fiscal exigency, layoff, and retrenchment become parts of the argot as well as the environment, and discussion of access, quality and other core values is displaced by contingency planning, new management systems, and the need to collect data for external accountability purposes even though they may have little campus utility' (Birnbaum 1985, p.21).

Furthermore 'the quality control of higher education is also moving outside the academy' (Boyer 1985, p.159). He suggested that accreditation, which had always been a feature of American higher education, was increasing. A typical list of items used in an accreditation process in the State of New York was cited by Gevers (1985). A comprehensive judgement, he suggested, was based on: the quality of the staff (PhDs, etc.); the amount of external grants; the number of publications and citations; the membership of professional associations; the quality of students (SAT scores, etc.); the content of the curriculum; the employment of graduates; the library and computing facilities; the policy and support of top management for teaching and research; the interaction with other departments; and the centrality of the concern.

There were developments in various states in the 1980s. In Ohio policies developed by the Board of Regents enhanced the use of PIs. Funding had been based on uniform payment for standard service and designed to encourage access to higher education. The early 1980s saw financial constraints but a new policy in 1983 aimed at increasing the quality of higher education so that it would provide a resource for stimulating economic revitalisation. To find the centres of strength that were to receive the extra resources through competitive challenge grants the full range of PIs were used: reputational; inputs; outcomes; and value-added (Coulter and Moore 1987). Such add-on funds are, however, vulnerable and in various states, including Ohio, challenge programmes have been reduced or eliminated (R. Richardson 1994).

According to Dill (1995b) by 1990 about two-thirds of states had adopted assessment requirements. But it is the 1990s that has seen an emphasis on PIs: 'Across the nation, state leaders are showing increasing interest in the development and use of state-level performance indicators for higher education' (Ruppert 1994, p.iii). As with the development of quality assurance systems in the UK, accountability policies were sometimes designed to forestall a legislative mandate. Ewell claims:

> Performance indicators as tools for state higher education policy have many roots... Approximately one-third of states

now have such indicators in place, the vast majority of which have been developed and implemented within the last three years...the conversation accompanying the recent emergence of performance indicators differs considerably from its counterpart around assessment some 10 years ago... While the emergence of state interest in assessment in the early 1980s signalled a new concern with quality as opposed to more traditional issues of access and efficiency, current initiatives embrace both. (1994, pp.147 and 149)

In most cases these PIs are published in a higher education annual report, or report card, which allows for institutional comparisons and provides the broad range of stakeholders, including students, employers, parents and the general public, with information in a readily available format (Ruppert 1994; Ewell 1994). The reference to the wide range of stakeholders, and the need for greater accountability to them, provides one reason why this development of state-based PIs has been added to the earlier state efforts to promote assessment of student learning which were 'decentralized and institution-based' (Ruppert 1994, p.2). Other, linked reasons for the emphasis on greater accountability include the decreasing state resources for higher education at a time of rising costs, growing demands for access and increased recognition of the role played by higher education in international competitiveness (Ruppert 1994; Dill 1995b). Given these circumstances, 'The challenge to manage the higher education enterprise effectively in a manner consistent with public purposes has never been greater.' (Ewell and Jones 1994, p.6).

The detailed case studies in Ruppert (1994) describe the development of PIs in higher education in ten states. They reveal a variety of motives and uses for state systems of PIs and demonstrate the complexity of analysing the position in the USA. In one of the general chapters in Ruppert the PIs from the ten states are organised in two different ways. First, as was mentioned in Chapter 1.3, they are categorised into inputs, outputs and outcomes; then they are organised according to five categories of quality (R. Richardson 1994). Furthermore, different actors emphasise different definitions of quality and thus are oriented towards certain sets of quality indicators. This identification of multiple stakeholders is compatible with the mode of analysis for PIs described in Chapter 1.1 and, indeed, the other three elements of that analysis also seem to be present in the accounts in Ruppert.

There are references to the technical development of PIs. In the majority of case study states, according to Ewell,

> performance indicator initiatives contain many of the same elements despite their diverse origins... This convergence in context is due more to circumstances than consensus: because only a small body of available state-level data is available and since there are limited technical possibilities for manipulating it, indicator initiatives, often end up alike. (1994, p.154)

Perhaps because most research funding does not come from the states, only one research PI appears in the lists, and even then in fewer than half of the ten states. It refers to the levels of sponsored research.

Clearly there has been a state policy that PIs should be introduced – or the system has reacted to pre-empt legislation – but the linking of PIs to specific planning or budgeting initiatives has often proved more difficult to implement. Partly this is because of the 'data-driven' nature of many of the indicator proposals which 'arose extremely rapidly and rely heavily on existing information or readily available data. As a result, few have been guided by prior analysis of statistics that would identify those most appropriate for systematic decision making and public reporting' (Ewell 1994, p.150). One of the major exceptions to the generally low level of linkage between the PI initiatives and budgeting or statewide planning is provided by Tennessee where the longer history of statewide PIs has provided an opportunity for the measures used, and the manner of presentation, to be refined and there have been several initiatives in the last two decades. There is considerable experience with performance funding in Tennessee. A particular aspect of some of the Tennessee developments in the 1980s was that the public authority did not make evaluative judgements but up to five per cent of the annual allocation was awarded on an institution's ability to demonstrate performance in a range of areas to which different weights were attached. These included: the proportion of programmes which had received accreditations and value-added testing in the area of general education scores at the point of graduation (Bourke 1986). The developments in Tennessee have been the focus of international attention, for example being visited by a team from Sweden.

In addition to activities initiated by various states Dill (1995b) examines the role of the federal level.

The 1992 reauthorisation of the Higher Education Act required the creation of State Postsecondary Review Entities which were charged with developing quantified performance standards in five basic areas: graduate rates, withdrawal rates, occupational placement rates for vocational and professional programmes, licensure and certification pass rates for applicable programmes, and the degree to which tuition and fee charges in vocational programmes were 'excessive'. The congressional elections in 1994 and other pressures resulted in a move away from federal involvement in both the SPRE initiative and the attempt to set national standards for academic accreditation.

However there is still considerable activity at state level and as is now argued in the UK and elsewhere the policy requirement for state or nationwide PIs to be developed is generating information which might be of primary use at the institutional level:

> state mandates for performance indicators are now making available to colleges and universities reliable outcomes data... common performance measures such as those in New York and Tennessee, can introduce into universities data on student attainment after college and employer satisfaction, that are more likely to be utilized in the internal assessment and program review process. (Dill 1995b pp.11–14)

Despite the long history of interest in measures which can be thought of as being PIs, and all the recent activity, Ruppert refers to the development and use of PIs as being 'preliminary in most states' (1994, p.3). Furthermore Ewell (1994) argues that to be effective PIs should be seen as a tool to shape the future, not a collection of statistics to report the past, but few states have yet been able to achieve that because the higher education leadership has been unable to develop a clear state consensus on policies and priorities. Consequently 'the question of what kinds of data and performance measures are appropriate to guide future development has not been systematically addressed. Well beyond the technology of indicators themselves, this is a task requiring systematic attention on the part of all state-level stakeholders' (Ewell 1994, p.165).

2.3 Other countries

Introduction

In the UK themes such as value for money, accountability, and strengthening institutional management have been seen to be important. Such concerns exist about other public services in the UK and in other countries. These concerns have led to the emergence of the 'Evaluative State' (Neave 1988). The rise of the Evaluative State involves a consolidation of previous evaluative activities and a shift towards a posteriori evaluation, which seeks to elicit how far goals have been met, not by setting the prior conditions, but by discovering the extent to which overall targets have been reached through the evaluation of the product: '*A posteriori* evaluation works then through control of product, not through control of process' (p.10). This development involves, amongst other things, the 'multiplication of indicators of performance' and 'the judicious application of the econometricians' art' (pp.11–12). The move towards expenditure-driven as opposed to demand-related budgeting has promoted performance related funding and encouraged PIs or quality assessments which permit finer targeting of resources (Neave 1987). The way that this has been applied in Holland is described by Maassen and Van Vught: 'The proposed use of PIs is an example of the way government wants to replace the former *ex ante* control mechanism of the performance of higher education institutions by an *ex post* evaluation mechanism' (1988, p.73). PIs are also one of the elements of 'new public management' (Pollitt 1995).

Despite the existence of these general themes, systems of higher education vary in many ways including the degree of autonomy for institutions and individual academics. Furthermore within any one country different policies might be pursued for different sectors of higher education (as happened in the UK) or for different activities. Thus in Finland PIs were used to allow greater autonomy to the undergraduate level of Finnish higher education, but to bring greater central co-ordination to the postgraduate level and research activities (Höltta 1988). It is also possible to identify life cycles of interest in PIs within different countries and public services (Pollitt 1989).

These factors mean that the development of PIs within countries varies greatly, as is confirmed in recent OECD studies (Kells 1990 and 1993) which provide a thorough analysis of the development of PIs in the context of each country's higher education system. In general the discussion about PIs occurs at two main levels; a policy-making level and a technical level. Laying the groundwork in the former is critical. Thus Frackmann (1987), having explained the failure of attempts in the Federal Republic of Germany (FRG) to introduce competition and selectivity by using PIs, concluded that before PIs are composed and structured, the conditions that are prerequisite for their use should be established: this would be likely to involve political decisions. Similarly Kells (1983) suggested that quality control was a two-stage process involving first, measuring quality and second, steering on the basis of the measurement recorded. As we saw in Chapter 1.1, therefore, three main elements or variables emerge and were used by Cave and Hanney (1989 and 1992) when analysing the development of PIs in different countries: technical development; the political decisions to create structures to permit and encourage the use of PIs; and the adoption of policies which it is hoped PIs will be able to advance. A fourth variable was also seen to be important – pressure from a range of stakeholders including consumers and from those wishing to use PIs in a developmental way. Countries differ markedly in respect of the variables.

The countries selected for discussion below illustrate many of the above points. The drive towards the Evaluative State is most advanced in Finland, the Netherlands, Sweden and the UK (Neave 1988). The two European countries identified by Teichler (1988) where performance or outcome measures have had most impact on policy and research are the UK and the Netherlands. Ten lessons for governments and intermediate funding agencies which it was hoped would facilitate debate on the development and use of PIs in government – institutional relations were drawn from an OECD study of the role played by PIs in Denmark, the Netherlands, Norway, Sweden and the UK (Sizer 1992; Spee and Bormans 1992; Sizer, Spee and Bormans 1992).

Jongbloed and Westerheijden claim that 'A consensus seems to be growing in Western Europe regarding their applicability, suggesting that PIs are powerful tools that nevertheless need to be complemented by non-quantitative judgements' (1994, p.37). They examine this proposition in relation to the contrasting systems in three countries: Germany, the Netherlands and the UK.

Segers, Wijnen and Dochy (1990) suggest that 'three countries took a leading position in the development of sets of performance indicators and pragmatic management technologies based on performance indicators: the United Kingdom, the Netherlands and Australia' (p.2). They go on to suggest that in all of these three countries there were two important government papers, released almost at the same time and with a content that is surprisingly similar: the English and Australian Green and White Papers and the Dutch Higher Education and Quality (HOAK) and Higher Education and Research Plan (HOOP) reports. It seems, they believe, 'there has been an extensive communication on these matters between government managers' (p.2).

An examination of PIs for the Commonwealth Higher Education Management Service focused on the three countries where information was readily available: UK, Australia and Canada (Davis 1996).

The Netherlands

The Netherlands has seen one of the most comprehensive debates about plans for the introduction of PIs, but implementation has proved difficult. The Chairman and Secretary of the Dutch Technical Working Party on PIs reported that 'the actual results of all the thought and discussion devoted to this subject in recent years is not, in fact, impressive. There has been a great deal of talk but very little has been achieved' (Mertens and Bormans 1990, p.95).

Similarly, Dersjant suggests, 'Although a rather comprehensive debate about plans for the introduction of performance indicators in higher education took place in the Netherlands, their implementation has proved to be quite a different story' (1993, p.90). It was also suggested that the use and life cycle of PIs are limited because 'the practice under consideration will change as a consequence of intelligent behavioural reactions of the organisation and people involved' (In't Veld, Spee and Tseng 1987, p.11). They also believed that more progress had been made in developing and applying indicators for academic research than for education in general.

Changes in the funding of research around 1980 at Leiden University forced departments 'to develop research performance criteria and, subsequently to apply these criteria in a sort of self-evaluation, in order to avoid a considerable decrease in research support' (Moed *et al.* 1985, p.186). Subsequently the national system for university research financing changed from a 'dual support' type system to a 'conditional funding' system which was very similar to the Leiden scheme. According to Moed *et al.* both the Leiden system and the national policy 'expressed a need for more objective, quantitative research performance indicators' (p.186). As a result a research project into bibliometric indicators started at Leiden in 1981. Some of its work is described later in Chapter 4.3.

The project showed that indicators could be used in several ways by different levels of university management. They could be fitted into the conditional funding system which involves research programmes being funded on condition their quality is guaranteed by the institution and favourably assessed by independent, external committees.

Developments in research form only a part of wider changes in Dutch higher education forced largely by economic pressures. In 1985 a government paper entitled Higher Education Autonomy and Quality (HOAK) (Ministry of Education 1985) proposed self-regulation and autonomy as the new mechanism for steering higher education, and the development of a formal quality control system was regarded as an important condition for the transition from central control to self-regulation (Maassen 1987). In this move from *ex ante* control to *ex post* evaluation the representative bodies of the institutions played a role. The Association of Co-operating Universities in the Netherlands set up a steering committee which examined the development of various PIs and proposed their adoption. There was, however, opposition and the Association did not go ahead in the manner of its UK equivalent and introduce PIs.

The new quality control system being developed in the Netherlands involved a number of stages: self-evaluation by the faculties; comparison between faculties made by visiting review committees, and a response by the institution to the committee's findings. The development and use of PIs within this quality control system has been controversial and difficult. Several commentators (see, for example, Bormans *et al.* 1987) stress the importance of PIs in the dialogue between the Higher Education Institutions and the government. The HOAK scheme was being implemented in the Higher Education and Research Plan (HOOP) (Ministry of Education 1988). Dialogue was important in HOOP and In't Veld *et al.* (1987) argued that PIs

> can stimulate a dialogue that is precise and fruitful because PIs can back statements with the relevant facts... we also expect that PIs will not only make the dialogue more to the point, but will also provide an incentive to make the qualitative reasoning more precise, because the qualitative reasoning has to compete with supposedly objective facts, which seem to be a priori convincing. (p.13–14)

This role for PIs is further discussed in Chapter 5.

The Government, according to Maassen and Van Vught (1988), attempted to establish a major role for PIs in HOOP. It set out structures for the deployment of PIs and proposed a number of policy uses for them within the system of internal and external evaluation being established. According to the government PIs would serve as operational instruments for: evaluation (to show to what extent government goals had been achieved); monitoring (to signal relevant developments and trends); dialogue (to provide an objective basis of information); and funding. Maassen and Van Vught questioned the extent to which the new system would enhance the autonomy of institutions and suggested that 'the ways these indicators are intended to be used make it very clear that this new system of quality control is as invasive for the institutions as was the [former] system' (p.73).

In 1988 a tentative matrix of 26 indicators was published in HOOP. For each of the 26 a ranking order between the universities was given. There were many criticisms of the indicators, especially the fact that for those where a time series was given, account was taken of only the changes per institution in their relative position compared to others. This reflected badly on the universities which were performing well initially. There were also doubts about what some of the PIs were intended to measure.

The PIs Research Group of the University of Limburg was appointed by the Minister to define quality, establish the conditions for quality assurance and to establish which indicators and variables were valid operationally (Dochy, Segers and Wijnen 1990). The research included sending a questionnaire to a range of stakeholders asking for opinions about which out of a number of indicators and variables identified were considered to be valid measures. The findings were intended to be used as the starting point for an attempt to develop a shared language.

Kells (1989) stressed that it was the government which had been pushing for the introduction of PIs and doing so in relation to government goals for higher education, but that concentration on this by some British commentators had underestimated the main thrust of policy which was the establishment of the systematic, cyclical, developmental self-assessment and regular site visits by subject matter peers and lay citizens.

Writing in 1993, Dersjant, a ministry official, explained, 'At the moment at central level there are no longer any talks about performance indicators as such. Instead there are talks... about the basic needs for quantitative information' (1993, p.91). In the first round of discussions a set of major information types was defined which included items such as student success rate and research outputs. In 1993 a new system for funding the core of teaching in each institution relied on a formula in which two PIs played an important role – the number of students in their first to fourth years and the number of degrees awarded. Core funding of research is determined in part by the number of postgraduate degrees awarded. These developments lead Jongbloed and Westerheijden to comment, 'In general, very little use is currently being made of PIs in Dutch higher education policy. However, the ones that are used explicitly – student numbers and degrees awarded – are crucial to institutions in determining the amount of core funding' (1994, pp.41–42).

As elsewhere there has been the development of a consumers' guide published by a private company – but in this case initially using a grant from the Ministry.

Australia

Although four Australian institutions took part in the OECD survey in the mid-1980s, Bourke referred to 'the virtual absence, in the very considerable literature of higher education research in Australia, of any sustained work on performance indicators, quality measures and the like' (1986, p.3). However, following a Government Green Paper the bodies representing leaders of higher education institutions – the Australian Vice-Chancellors' Committee (AVCC) and the Australian Committee of Directors and Principals (ACDP) – set up a joint working party on PIs 'to develop a set of PIs which would be acceptable to the Government' (AVCC/ACDP 1988, p.i). In its White Paper of the same year the Government stated that 'as soon as practicable, indicators which are agreed to be useful and appropriate will be incorporated into the Commonwealth's general funding arrangements for higher education' (quoted in AVCC/ACDP 1988, p.1). The joint working party thus had the incentive to conduct the technical work to develop a list of PIs that could be tested and then used. Their report opposed the use of PIs by the Government 'in any purely mechanical fashion as in formula funding (p.2) but recognised that they have a place in financial matters and that given the need for institutions to be made accountable and transparent by a process of expert review 'performance indicators form part of the necessary raw material of evaluation and assessment' (p.1).

The working party set limits on what should be regarded as a PI. Although it listed some indicators of institutional context it reserved the term PI (in respect of teaching and research) for: students' evaluations of teaching and curriculum; completion rates; destination and acceptance of graduates; and research grants and publications.

A Higher Education Performance Indicators Research Group was established to define in operational terms, and conduct an empirical trial of, the indicators identified in the working party report. It was intended that those considered feasible and appropriate would be applied system-wide (Linke 1990). The comprehensive but controversial report of the research group chaired by Russell Linke, identified PIs relating to teaching and learning, and research and professional services in addition to indicators of institutional context, and participation and social equity (Linke 1991). Although the indicators were related as closely as possible to existing data sources only a few could be calculated reliably from such sources. The most striking proposal was to use the Course Experience Questionnaire to enable a PI to be developed for use at national level from student evaluations of their courses. This is analysed in more detail in Chapter 3 but approval was given for it to be incorporated in the national graduate employment survey and it is used by some institutions, including the University of Queensland.

Linke claimed, however, that 'By the time the Report of the Research Group was released in 1991, Government policy on the use of performance indicators had been subsumed by broader concerns with quality improvement in higher education and the development of quality assurance mechanisms at both institution and system level' (1993, p.15). There have been a range of developments at various levels.

A National Quality Assurance Committee was established with a dual function of 'auditing institutional mechanisms for quality assurance, and assessing the quality of output of the institutions' (Linke 1995, p.55). Exactly how the funding was to be linked to the quality assurance was a matter of intense political debate and lobbying by the various institutions with the details changing on several occasions (Marshall 1995). There was argument about the resources that should be involved but these started at about two per cent of the total grant. Institutions, on a voluntary basis, make an annual submission to the committee and are then visited. Writing in 1993 Linke argued: 'While this approach to quality assurance does not prescribe the use of any specific performance indicators, nor assume their use by institutions, there is an implicit expectation that more reliance will have to be placed on quantitative measures of performance' (p.16).

In relation to research, PIs are being used directly to influence funding in a way Linke (1995) claimed had previously been ruled out. About six per cent of the existing grant was defined as the research quantum and the Government decided this should be distributed according to some form of composite index reflecting the relative success of institutions in attracting external research grants and research higher degree students. In 1995 a measure of publications was added. League tables of institutions based on competitive grants earned have been established for some years (Baldwin 1995).

There has been considerable work in institutions on the development of PIs and management information systems which could be used internally and to enhance comparability. In Monash University, for example, the faculty share of the research quantum is determined by a formula incorporating both research grants and publications. At a national level Linke (1995, p.53) reports that the government published in 1993 'a selected range of comparative measures covering all institutions as a way of providing a public profile of the system as a whole'. There is a new national framework for institutional data systems, CASMAC, which incorporates 'the capability for producing a considerable range of standard indicators relating to institutional context (student background, staff profile, finance and physical resources etc.) as well as student and staff performance, defined in a consistent way to allow at least some level of comparison across the system as a whole' (p.59).

In an era of greater competition between institutions various media organisations have begun publishing independent guides to institutions. Some of them use a variety of quantitative and semi-quantitative indicators when comparing institutional performance in teaching and research, and in the provision of resources and student support (Linke 1993).

Germany

Any review of PIs in German higher education faces similar problems to those posed by the USA – a federal system and traditional university autonomy (Alewell and Göbbels-Dreyling 1993). The first pilot study of PIs in West Germany was in 1975–76 and the idea for the original OECD survey followed proposals from a German research team. In 1983 the Federal Minister for Education and Science introduced a new policy in a document entitled *Competition Rather than Bureaucracy*. It demanded less state intervention and more market mechanisms and stated: 'the higher education institutions have to acquire an interest in the specific performance they offer in the competition' (quoted in Hüfner 1987b, p.136). The influential Science Council published detailed suggestions in 1985 for introducing competition. Internal judgements of individual institutions based on a list of proposed PIs were to be followed by an evaluation by the scientific community, the results of which would be the determining factor in the resource allocation process (Hüfner and Rau 1987). Partly as a consequence of these debates many surveys were published on differences of quality and reputation between universities or within disciplines (Teichler 1988).

When the OECD survey was conducted in the mid-1980s only limited use was being made of PIs beyond those 'operating' PIs required by the *Länder* for state planning mechanisms (Hüfner 1987a; Frackmann 1987). Further, some of the measures that might have been in use were not recognised as PIs.

Therefore despite some developments in techniques and ideas for policy use in West Germany, Frackmann is probably correct in arguing that the attempt in the 1980s to introduce competition and selectivity by using PIs failed because the structures for the use of PIs were not adopted or imposed. In contrast to the UK and Australia, the organisation representing the heads of institutions did not feel under sufficient political pressure to introduce a recommended list of PIs. Hüfner (1987b) concluded that 'the willingness of universities to develop systems of performance indicators which go beyond those prescribed by the state is almost zero because further financial cuts and/or a further narrowing of institutional autonomy might occur... The actual application of different sets of PIs between and within institutions of higher education remains primarily a political decision' (pp.140–1).

It is perhaps significant that Germany was not one of 12 countries surveyed in the 1990 OECD Compendium of PIs in higher education (Kells 1990). In the 1993 Compendium, however, Alewell and Göbbels-Dreyling start by explaining that 'The diversity of data collected (and partly published) by quite different institutions with different goals on three levels (institutions, *Länder* and federal government) make it difficult to present a clear survey of indicators' (p.62). They analyse each of the four main types of indicators relevant for Germany: inputs, outputs, expenses and revenues. The most developed aspect is quantitative input analysis including staff and space. These indicators, along with quantitative output analysis concerning student numbers and statistics of examinations, are well developed for planning and short-range management. Input–output ratio indicators including staff–student ratios (which have been published for a decade) and student–space ratios are important. There has been less development with the qualitative analysis, especially of the output of teaching. Some magazines, for example *Der Spiegel*, have published ranking lists based on student opinions about teaching quality.

The German Rectors' Conference eventually overcame the institutional scepticism about the development of a PI system to be published covering institutions: 'The opinion about performance indicators has changed within the last year, maybe as a result of the international discussion, maybe as a result of the financial situation of the state and of higher education institutions. There are a lot of interested institutions which want to join the project' (Alewell and Göbbels-Dreyling 1993).

Finland

Recent experience in higher education in Finland is that of a determination to expand and sustain a higher education system that will support the needs of an economy under duress, and which is concentrating strongly, therefore, on both expansion and on improved efficiency.

Its public expenditure on education as a whole rose from six and a half per cent of GDP in 1990 to over seven per cent in the early 1990s. Savings in education and a new economic upswing will probably eventually bring education spending to around six per cent which is still above the OECD average. After an attempt in the late 1980s to protect annual increases in higher education, spending was cut by 16–17 per cent between 1991 and 1994. Plans for the future therefore aim at diversifying the basis of education institutions, including the recruitment of resources from business and industry and external financing for research from both Finnish and international resources (Ministry of Education, Finland 1994).

Before, however, economic difficulties set in, there was an awareness of the importance of the information in management and planning as well as awareness of cost. Their intentions in all public administration have included reviewing steering mechanisms, delegating authority and shifting emphasis to performance. For some while now, the Finnish Ministry of Education has sought to make education socially more relevant and economically more efficient, both by increasing direct public accountability through formal evaluation systems and by encouraging institutional leadership and academic self-regulation (Hölttä 1988).

Quality was assured in the past through standards and qualifications at entry, that is input measures, and through the national co-ordination of study programmes. They have thus moved from legal prescription and detailed rules-setting to control by outcomes and evaluation. From the early 1990s, a new and formidable set of arrangements for evaluation have been created:

- Outcome measures which have been developed over the last ten years. From 1987, the Ministry of Education began to maintain a database (KOTA) for evaluation and planning purposes. This provides data on the numbers of students, teachers and staff, the number of degrees awarded, different cost measures and information about physical facilities, all classified by fields of study for each university.

- On the basis of these data it is possible to administer the allocative system known as *budgeting by results*. In this system, institutional performance is judged by such indicators as the numbers of students graduating as a ratio to the numbers of staff employed and the rate of employment of graduates.

- Disciplinary reviews of teaching administered under the guidance of a Ministry Committee and concerned primarily with the quality of teaching. The reviews are largely conducted by foreign experts and review the state of the subject throughout the country and by institution. These have taken place in 12 subject areas between 1991 and 1994.

- Of the FIM 130m performance-based allocations in the 1995 budget, FIM 20m was allocated to centres of excellence in teaching. The Council for Higher Education selected ten such centres on the basis of written proposals put in competitively. FIM 48m was allocated to centres of excellence in research. The

Academy of Finland selected 12 such units on the basis of written proposals, using seven criteria based mainly on international estimation and visibility.

- Disciplinary reviews of research conducted by the Academy of Finland. These are based on peer review and on definable outcomes of research in the different areas. Fourteen subjects had been covered by the end of 1993 and the results are available for national research planning and funding. In addition there is the normal assessment of research proposals by the separate research councils which operate under the aegis of the Academy.

- Institutional self-reviews. Seven institutional evaluations were supported by the Ministry between 1992 and 1994. Many other self-reviews are being conducted on their own initiative by universities and *ammattikorkeakoulu* (i.e. non-university institutions). Six reviews were to be subject to external evaluation in 1992–95 by international and national expert groups.

The new budget system has moved from an emphasis on input norms to outcome-oriented budgeting; a key instrument in controlling the decentralised system. The Ministry negotiates broad goals, such as the total numbers of who should graduate, with each university. The areas and volume of teaching and research to be achieved are determined in an agreement be-tween the state and each university and these constitute the general goals for each faculty. Managing by results can start with performance criteria which may be of several kinds. It can enumerate the number of degrees awarded as a ratio of the number of teachers, or it can be based on qualitative judgements arrived at by peer evaluation or on other criteria such as dem-onstrated innovation. The responsibility for reaching these goals, and finding the means to achieve them, rest with the universities.

Performance affects the size of the next budget. The element of the budget available for rewards affects only a margin of resources. In 1993–94 FIM 130m out of a total of FIM 3.900m., or little more than three per cent, was distributed in this way. Evaluation and allocation on the basis of results are also intended to introduce the competitive psychology of the market into the public sector.

There is thus an enormous amount of evaluative activity throughout the system. Nor has the Finnish Government spared itself the pains and pleasures of being evaluated. There have been several external reviews including one on the functioning of the Academy of Finland and, in 1994, an OECD review of higher education policy began with an extensive self-report (OECD 1995).

Sweden

The Swedish higher education reform of 1977 initiated a process of decentralisation, part of a general shift in public sector strategy, in which self-evaluation, process orientation and the capacity for self renewal were key concepts (Furumark 1981). However, progress since then towards a system of 'management by objectives has also created greater demand for systematic follow-up and evaluation' on a national level (Bauer 1993, p.102).

The movement to emphasise greater institutional autonomy and system diversity rather than inter-institutional equivalence and central control in higher education was accelerated by the conservative/liberal government elected in 1991. It abolished the National Board of Universities and Colleges and replaced it with three institutions, whose roles were to be service to the institutions, the development of evaluation systems, and methods and appeal. Responsibilities for basic data collection were split from those for evaluation, including the development of PIs in this system. In 1992 the Act introduced under the banner 'Freedom for Quality' substantially enhanced the independence of higher education institutions in the organisation and deployment of resources, in the name of educational diversity and the role of higher education and research in promoting national participation in the global economy. The broad direction of reform has been sustained under a switch back to social democratic government in 1994. But there is now a greater emphasis on equality values, such as the promotion of equal opportunities for women, and some reassertion of the need for central control, in the creation of a single new higher education agency.

From 1993, funding allocations, now made on a three-year rather than an annual basis, were to be based on the criteria of quantitative performance, student demand and, to the tune of five per cent, quality. The bulk of resources were to be allocated on the basis of student admissions at the programme level and annual undergraduate student progression. A committee was appointed to develop the system of funding allocation, part of which was to be made on the basis of predetermined PIs.

National PIs are therefore seen as an instrument of resource allocation policy and the government wanted initially to extend their potential through developing quality indicators. However, they concluded that the consequences would harm rather than benefit higher education and abandoned this approach. The indicators already built into resource allocation are seen as vulnerable to manipulation in a way that could lower standards. Others proposed, such as the number of higher-level undergraduate courses in an institution, intended to indicate the depth of knowledge acquired by students, are seen as easily met and not necessarily achieving their purpose. The concept of value-added, while recognised as relevant in a system geared towards diversity and the inclusion of an increasingly high proportion of the population, has so far been felt to be too technically complex.

On the other hand, a great deal of investment has been made at the institutional level in the development of quality assurance systems. The first results of this investment are now emerging and will be audited by the new higher education agency. As yet it is too soon to tell whether or not they can become embedded in institutions and contribute to a concept of institutional autonomy that brings together academics and institutional management. Early indications are that that would require major change in academic conceptions of institutional governance and development (Bauer 1995).

Developments since 1977 seem to have reflected a high degree of commitment at national level to self-evaluation that incorporates concern for input and process and internalist conceptions of quality in the quest for greater diversity and decentralisation. The reforms of the early 1990s sought to superimpose upon these some of the disciplines of the market in the forms of measures of output and consumer demand, while at the same time reinforcing values of institutional autonomy. They have brought some more emphasis on PIs but little systematic development. It seems likely that indicators will be incorporated into larger systems but what the balance in these systems will be as between the state, the market, management and the professionals is uncertain.

Norway

The use of PIs in Norwegian higher education has been promoted by general public sector reforms from the mid-1980s onwards. The reforms have been based on 'new public management' ideas shifting the emphasis of public planning procedures from *ex ante* control to *ex post* evaluation. Following the 1984 report of a public commission (The Haga Commission) and a parliamentary decision to implement its recommendations in March 1985, public institutions were requested as part of their budgetary procedures to formulate clear goals for their achievements the coming year and report on last year's performance from 1986 on. In the university sector this new budgetary system, 'Activity Planning', was formally introduced in 1990, but the universities almost immediately tried to implement budgetary procedures in accordance with the new system. Although PIs are developed by the institutions themselves, they are supposed to indicate the number of students they can process and to report on the number of students, the production of candidates and the production of research publications. A number of subsequent civil service and higher education reforms have further promoted the use of PIs in the Norwegian higher education system.

First, the use of PIs has been promoted by the introduction of performance pay in the civil service in 1991. As civil servants, university employees are included in these arrangements. The criteria by which performance is measured are agreed upon at the individual institutions in negotiations with the unions. A study from the University of Bergen indicates that performance pay in its current form is unlikely to be an effective incentive in the future. It has been used to a limited extent, and the employee unions have managed to negotiate a rather comprehensive list of performance criteria. Consequently, as it has worked till now, seniority appears to be the best predictor of extra performance pay.

Second, as part of the national higher education reforms following the report of a public commission on higher education (The Hernes Commission) education policies now include an element of performance-based budgetary allocations according to the production of candidates and research at the individual institutions. Thus the Ministry of Education annually puts a 'price tag' on Master's and PhD candidates and research contributions that are allocated to the institutions according to production output. A sum of money is also given according to the improvement of results measured in credits per student at the universities. A small percentage of the university budgets have been allocated on the basis of such measures in recent years.

The new emphasis on efficiency and productivity has promoted a variety of valuation procedures in addition to the use of quantitative measures for budgetary purposes, most important among which are peer reviews. The Ministry of Education has stated that quality evaluation is a responsibility for the institutions, or their own boards of co-ordination and co-operation, such as the Norwegian university council. Institutional evaluation may take many different forms. A very complex evaluation process has been carried out at the Faculty of Social Sciences at the University of Bergen including self-evaluation and peer reviews of all individual departments and an overall international evaluation of the Faculty. However a number of national disciplinary reviews have been arranged by the Norwegian Institute for Studies of Research and Higher Education. These reviews include all national programmes and departments in specific fields such as business administration, informatics and sociology.

2.4 Some comparative points

The uses of PIs in the eight countries described in this Chapter are at different stages and, despite some common general themes, occur within the settings of different political and educational objectives. There is, however, no clear correspondence between characteristics of systems and the use of PIs. When some of the developments are compared, paradoxes emerge which lead to the conclusion that the introduction of PIs reflects the interaction of complex and imperfectly understood forces, and that they may be used in different places to advance quite different ends. Furthermore, there seem to be life cycles of PIs with different countries experiencing pressures to develop and use PIs at different times.

Thus, in the UK, PIs were seen as a way in which a hitherto liberally administered system could enforce higher standards of academic performance and more economic use of resources. They are clearly tied to notions of public accountability and form part of a major reconstruction of relationships and modes of decision making between the state, the central funding agencies created by the state, and the management of individual universities.

By contrast, in Finland, the legislation incorporates PIs as part of a revised structure for financing universities but, starting from a system in which central control has been detailed and prescriptive, the authorities believed that PIs will enhance rather than reduce the freedom of universities. This claim was echoed in proposals made for Germany and for the Netherlands. The argument is that to apply objective indicators will both free universities from detailed and subjective processes of making a case for funds and establish clear rules of the game and a structure of incentives within which they can operate. PIs thus create a system of incentives akin to that conveyed by a market. Hüfner (1987a) argues similarly that 'in theoretical terms, it can be said that the more decentralised/less government-controlled and the more competition/market orientated a national university system is, the larger the necessary number of performance indicators will be' (p.145).

Analogies with the operations of the free market also apply at another level. Bourke (1986) made comparisons between the USA and the UK. In the USA, there was prolific provision offered by a wide range of institutions in which state control of public institutions went alongside a strong regard for the rights of consumers to have information about the institutions for which they were paying fees or taxes or both. Thus Bourke maintained that in the USA the primary impulse towards using quality

indicators was a market pressure to provide consumer information, although there was also pressure from the economic desire
to be internationally competitive. The mixed private and public
market there, too, constituted in his terms 'a very substantial
free market of institutional preferences and choice' (p.16) in
which information is valued. Whilst the pressures for accountability have increased in the USA since the mid-1980s there has
also been a transformation of consumer information into highly
controversial (commercially published) league tables. These are
now found in many other countries.

A further strand is the use of PIs for purposes of professional
development. Bourke advocated this in Australia and this
theme was taken up by the 1988 AVCC/ACDP Report. It is also
important in Sweden.

PIs have also been linked in a number of countries with moves
towards increased selectivity in research flowing from a concern
to enhance the competitiveness of the economy. The balance has
shifted from 'indirect' funding of research, where an institution
employs its general funds or block grant for research in areas
chosen by its own staff, to 'direct' funding where particular
projects are funded on the decision of external bodies, with a
greater or lesser degree of immediate governmental influence
or control (M. Taylor 1989b). In countries including the UK, the
Netherlands and Australia there is a debate about the role PIs
can, and should, play in the implementation of such a process.

It will thus be seen that PIs, as other managerial devices, are
tied up with systems rather than individualistic thinking, but
are not necessarily shaped by a particular style of policy concern. The enhancement of managerial control, the opening up
of institutions to consumer review, the strengthening of professional judgements, and assisting the introduction of research
selectivity, are all motives that have been advanced. However,
a major policy development common to most countries has been
an increased concern with quality. As we have seen in various
countries the debate about PIs has become subsumed within the
wider quality debate.

The picture is further complicated by the fact that a policy
such as increasing the role for institutional management may, as
with the general rise of the Evaluative State, take place both in
systems where the central government previously had consid-

erable influence over higher education and in systems where there had traditionally been considerable autonomy for the individual academic. Similar policies may be viewed very differently in different systems. Nevertheless, a common thread – for example in the UK, Australia, Finland and in various states of the USA – is that the development of improved information bases at the national or state level may provide indicators or statistics that can be useful for the management of institutions even when doubts are being expressed about their usefulness as comparative PIs.

Furthermore, policies might not achieve what the government suggests they are intended to achieve or they might be open to various interpretations. This is recorded as happening in Holland (Maassen and Van Vught 1988). Van Vught's (1988) wider analysis covered other countries and suggested that moves towards greater autonomy for institutions were somewhat spurious; instead, with the development of PIs, governments were attempting to use new methods to steer the higher education system towards its desired goals.

The situation in the UK is also the subject of a debate in which some see the development of PIs as part of a move towards centralisation and others (for example Sizer 1989) see it as giving greater autonomy to institutions. This is one of various points from this section that is further discussed in Chapter 5.

Everywhere the introduction of PIs is controversial. There have been various attempts at an 'official' national state level or at the level of an individual institution to test the validity and/or acceptability of different PIs by assessing the attitude of lecturers and other stakeholders towards them. In addition to the Limburg project in Holland there have also been projects in Australia – see Moses (1985) and more recently at the University of Queensland; and in the UK at Birmingham University (Rutherford 1987 and 1988).

In many countries, especially where proposals have been made for PIs to be linked to funding, the intense political debate and lobbying by institutions (or groups with a common interest) has resulted in the original plans being overturned and in some a move away from the concept of national PIs being used at a national level. 'Over the last few years few subjects relating to higher education have received more attention in the debate internationally. This is all the more striking when we consider that indicators themselves have to date played a relatively minor role in actual policy of national governments or of the institutions' (Spee and Bormans 1992, p.139). In similar vein, Jongbloed and Westerheijden conclude: 'In general, the role of PIs at the national policy level no longer seems to be growing in Europe: doubts about the validity of what is measurable, especially if the object is quality, have led to some disenchantment with PIs' (1994, p.48). It might be that the greatest interest in developing PIs is now coming from the USA.

Chapter 3

Performance Indicators of Teaching and Learning

3.1 Introduction

We first identify some of the key factors which seem to make it particularly difficult to determine appropriate performance indicators of teaching or education. We then note the political pressures in the UK to find ways of measuring the quality of higher education, and the responses of higher education. The relationships between PIs and government quality policies are then analysed. In Sections 3.4 to 3.9 we examine developing thinking and practice in the following indicators: costs; value-added; student progression and exit qualifications; employment destinations; and student and peer ratings. The main focus of the chapter is on the development and use of PIs at the level of the institution, although indicators of the performance of the sector as a whole in its educational function are of growing interest.

3.2 Difficulties in applying PIs to teaching

We have seen in Chapter 2 that the teaching and research functions of institutions were early on perceived as the main targets for the development of PIs in higher education in Britain (CVCP/UGC 1986). However, in Britain, as elsewhere, it has been conventional wisdom that it is much more difficult to establish indicators of teaching than of research performance. Early work by Birch, Calvert and Sizer (1977) did not at first have much impact on this convention.

They had claimed that even if the inevitable generality and vagueness of the objectives of higher education were accepted, it was possible to move directly to the measurement of output, or perhaps more exactly, the outcomes of higher education: 'enrolments, pass and attrition rates and information on graduate employment by course are all indicators of society's response to the institution's provision of learning opportunities, i.e. they are outcome measures' (p.135) Although value-added was seen as a more sophisticated measure of output, they were not able to use it. As a measure of the input–output relationship, i.e. of efficiency, they suggested that one possible approximation of unit cost was the student–staff ratio and that a number of variables needed to be considered when working this out. Despite their work, in 1985, the UGC, in a Circular Letter, told universities: 'Research can be assessed through peer judgement and a variety of performance indicators, but there are few indicators of teaching performance that would enable a systematic external assessment of teaching quality to be made' (UGC 1985b)

The reasons for the persistence of this view are both technical and political. Given that the development of valid PIs depends on determining the goals of the system or institution concerned, one source of the problem is clear. The period covered in this book has been one in which the educational goals of higher education in the UK have become contentious and political. While it might be broadly conceded that 'conceptually, higher education has moved from a type of "public utility" to a "strategic investment"' (Nedwek and Neal 1994, p.75, quoting from Ewell 1991), goals are multiple and contested. Competing ideologies of higher education are informed by competing conceptions of knowledge (epitomised in Britain by, for example, the competence debate (Barnett 1994b)), and conflicting economic and social values. An increasing emphasis on the instrumental importance of higher education has meant that individual consumption benefits are increasingly tied to the needs of the economy and the nature of the workforce required to meet them. The claims of government and employers rather than the providers of higher education to define them have recruited more support. At the same time, consumers are being given a stronger voice and policy statements emphasise the importance of sustaining a diverse higher education system.

In this context, the challenge of identifying relevant and generally accepted PIs intensifies, most notably at the institutional level. As Schmitz has shown in the USA, it is all too easy for indicators to be maintained that effectively discriminate only between institutions of a particular (in this case, élite) type (Schmitz 1993; cf. Tan 1992). Arguments for the identification of families of institutions for the purposes of comparative performance measurement are gaining ground.

A second problem is the definition of what it is that teaching PIs are required to measure, a question linked closely to the levels of aggregation. At the levels of the sector and the institution, teaching stands for their educational functions or, in an arena in which production models insinuate themselves, for their conversion of inputs into graduate outputs. At the levels below these, the department, the programme, the discipline and the individual, the focus is more strongly on teachers, teaching activities and, more recently, on teaching and learning and on students. At all levels there has been increasing recognition of the range of activities and provisions apart from teaching that constitute education and of the problem of determining the key variables affecting educational output. In the context of the USA, Dill (1995a), notes that recent research (Terenzeni and Pascarella 1994) emphasises the value of educational cohesion for student learning, the role of student interactions with faculty and peers and the capacity of institutional structures to 'promote cohesive environments that value the life of the mind' (Dill 1995b, p.11).

Such developments have also been due partly to sustained attention to the technicalities of producing PIs. We have seen how a combination of political pressures and lack of technical expertise results in PIs that are data driven and determined by quantifiability. A combination of political responses to pressures and more rigorous technical analysis may in turn shift concerns to issues of validity and 'the need to have a conceptually defensible system of indicators' (Nedwek and Neal 1994, p.79). As Sizer, Spee and Bormans (1992) point out, where indicators are, or are expected to be, used for any form of selective funding, the debate on them 'is often coloured by the distaste for the underlying concept of selectivity operated by government. The discussion, however, frequently focuses on the issues of validity and reliability' (p.134). Demand builds up for evidence and also theory of the relationship between outputs such as student progression rates or exit qualifications and the goals, the inputs and the processes of education systems. Absolute and one-dimensional concepts of excellence are challenged by relative concepts, such as 'value-added', as diverse institutions find that indicators do not reflect their own perceptions of their achievements.

The ending of the binary line in the UK brought together two different educational cultures. Traditionally in universities teaching goals and teaching quality have been framed almost entirely in terms of disciplinary knowledge and the concepts and skills required to master that. The emphasis on induction of students into disciplines, and on research and scholarship as the basis of good teaching, combined with the value of academic autonomy, have resulted in the relative neglect of thinking about educational process. On the other side of the binary line there was a rather different culture. Various reasons have been suggested for this: the accreditation procedures of the CNAA; the role of HMI; the more widespread development of interdisciplinary, domain-based and vocational studies; and the fact that 'research is not a primary concern for the majority of academic staff' (Sizer 1989, p.9).

But far more than the coming together of these cultures, increases in student numbers, the introduction of modular curricula and credit accumulation and transfer systems, and the introduction of quality audit and quality assessment have focused attention on teaching methods and educational theory. A particular focus of such theory has been student learning: how students learn, how different kinds of learning can be promoted and how students can be enabled to take more responsibility for their learning. The influence of such thinking can be seen in the development of teaching PIs and the language in which they have been couched. The CVCP/UGC teaching PIs have become the JPIWG indicators first of the quality of teaching and then of 'teaching and learning outcomes and student achievement' (CVCP 1995a, para.2). (Similarly, the quality assessment committees of the funding councils emphasise student experience and achievement in their documents and the UK Higher Education Quality Council's (HEQC) focus is on teaching and learning.) Interest has grown in the fields of both quality assessment and PIs in student evaluation, alongside peer evaluation and management statistics, as potentially fruitful sources of measurement.

A further factor contributing to the problems of determining PIs of teaching is that the purposes for which they are used are proliferating: for example, 'monitoring conditions, measuring progress, forecasting problems, diagnosing problems, allocative decision making, and political symbolism' (Nedwek and Neal 1994, p.89); monitoring, evaluation, dialogue, rationalisation, resource allocation (Sizer *et al.* 1992, p.137). At all levels, but perhaps particularly those of the sector and the institutions, the use of PIs in image management and the protection of interests is increasingly evident.

A key issue is the distinction between the use of evaluation for external and internal purposes. Initial political pressures for economy, efficiency and accountability, linked with policies of differential funding, stressed the need for means by which external comparative measures could be made. Aspirations for universal, system-wide teaching PIs usable in this way have been dampened by the technical and political problems outlined and anyhow run counter to a serious commitment to a policy of diversity. The other initial drive, to find PIs that would aid institutional management, has, however, been strongly reinforced.

We therefore have a context for the development of teaching PIs over the three decades covered by this book: higher education systems with multiple goals and multiple stakeholders, indicators required at multiple levels, increasingly rigorous definitions of validity and a proliferation of the uses to which PIs can be put. There are, however, two further factors which impinge particularly on their development and use: the relative status in policy and practice of teaching and research and the development of quality policies.

There is evidence from a number of countries of increasing pressure to appraise teaching, and yet, in practice, increased emphasis on performance in research. The previous chapter showed that in a number of countries funding for research has become increasingly selective. This has created the danger that unless similar policies are adopted for teaching, effort is diverted to 'grant earning' research activities, to the detriment of teaching.

Now that effectively all the research funding by the funding councils in the UK is allocated selectively on the basis of the four-yearly research assessments, the issue has become more sharply defined. There is mounting evidence (Jenkins 1995; Bauer and Kogan 1995) of anxiety in universities that research selectivity has reinforced the precedence given to research records in academic recruitment and reward systems. This is despite the counter-pressures of teaching quality assessment and quality audit, neither of which, however, carry funding implications apart from in the exceptional circumstances when provision is found to be unsatisfactory in an assessment and the problems are not rectified in the year before a reassessment of such provision occurs. In that case funding would be withdrawn. Moreover, in some new universities there is a feeling that their previously strong teaching culture is being undermined by their admission to the competition for research funding.

As long ago as 1986, in the USA Miller showed that performance in research had become increasingly more important than teaching performance when promotion and tenure decisions were being made.

In 1990 the Chairman of the Australian Research Council, Don Aitken, claimed that teaching in Australian universities needed to be restored to a place of honour and taken much more seriously by academics. Universities were essentially funded as teaching institutions, yet research was given much more status and priority. The reasons for this included: 'the best research advances knowledge; research is easier to evaluate than teaching; research is an international activity while teaching is local; excellence in research will get you promotions faster than excellence in teaching' (Aitken 1991).

However, as we have seen in Chapter 2, Australia has been the source of some of the most systematic attempts to address this problem. The trial evaluation study of PIs commissioned by the Commonwealth Department of Employment and Training incorporated six indicators of teaching performance, including that of perceived teaching quality based on Ramsden's Course

Experience Questionnaire which we shall consider in detail later in the chapter (Linke 1991). Other developments are reported by Moses (1989).

In Britain there was a short-lived attempt by the PCFC to incorporate quality into funding allocations at the margin. Institutions seeking to provide additional places in programmes deemed to be of above average quality were specially favoured in the tendering arrangements. Quality judgements were made by HMI and converted into broadly defined quality bands. The criteria embraced dimensions of teacher performance, student learning and educational environment (HMI 1989). A system depending on the authority of HMI could not survive the ending of the binary line but the government did not abandon the principle towards which it could be said to have been moving slowly since 1987.

The 1987 White Paper (DES 1987) endorsed the view that the quality of teaching should be evaluated. It suggested that the maintenance of high standards of teaching could be helped by 'systematic arrangements for: staff training and development; staff appraisal; evaluation of the results achieved, including analysis of external examiners' reports and students' employment patterns; involvement of professional practitioners in vocational courses; and feedback from students themselves' (para.3.12).

The White Paper went on to suggest that the quality of teaching needed to be judged by reference mainly to students' achievements. Items that provided some measure of teaching quality included: non-completion rates; the subsequent employment patterns of students; and students' achievement compared with their entry standards. A similar list of PIs appeared in the Report from the NAB's Good Management Practice Group (NAB 1987). In 1988 the then Secretary of State for Education, Kenneth Baker, stated that 'effective teaching needs to be identified, highly prized, encouraged and rewarded' (Baker 1988).

The pressure from government on universities for increased accountability in the whole range of their work and specifically in terms of the efficiency and effectiveness of their teaching was taken up by the CVCP under the heading of academic standards, a matter considered to be incontrovertibly the preserve of academics themselves. The Academic Standards Group, chaired first by Reynolds and then by Sutherland, concerned itself with identifying and trying to secure cross-sector adoption of procedures through which academic standards could be assured, for example, a code of practice for the external examiner system and the establishment by institutions of systematic monitoring of students' progress and eliciting of student views. It did so within an explicit reassertion of the values of university autonomy, individual creativity and responsibility and the belief that the maintenance of academic standards depended essentially on university teachers, 'themselves engaged in research [and]... in touch with the movement and advance of knowledge in their fields' (Reynolds 1986). There is no evidence that a definition of academic standards was considered necessary.

The Academic Audit Unit established by the CVCP in 1990 and its successor, the quality assurance division of the HEQC set up under the Further and Higher Education Act, 1992, extended this approach. However, in 1994 the issue assumed a higher political profile and in his speech to the HEFCE annual conference in April the Secretary of State invited the sector 'to give greater attention to broad comparability of standards in UK higher education' (HEQC 1995c, para.3). The immediate context was the raising by some overseas countries of the issue of comparability between UK undergraduate degrees and more generally the size and diversity of the newly constituted higher education system and the development of modularisation. The CVCP's response was to set up a programme of investigation to be undertaken by the HEQC 'to examine the desirability and feasibility of defining threshold standards for undergraduate degrees in the UK' (HEQC 1995b, para.1).

The definition of academic standards adopted by the graduate standards programme was output-centred: 'explicit levels of academic attainment which are used to describe and measure academic requirements and achievements of individual students and groups of students' (HEQC 1995c, para.9).

A series of consultative seminars organised by HEQC in conjunction with the Quality Assurance Enhancement Network (QAEN) to help formulate their approach to their task revealed substantial divisions within universities as to the feasibility of establishing threshold standards. 'There was a widespread recognition that explicit standards were hard to disentangle both from the disciplinary practice of academics (in which implicit judgements were deeply embedded...) and from the processes by which students learned to master what they were studying' (HEQC 1995b, para.9). However, it was agreed that three main approaches would be adopted either separately or in combination: to establish specialist, subject-based definitions; to attempt to characterise the nature of 'graduateness' in terms of a series of generic qualities that must be demonstrated for the award of a degree; to identify a typology of degree programmes for which threshold specifications could be established (HEQC 1995b, para.10). The programme is seen by many as a long-term venture, although further clarification of the issues was made in the interim report of the programme (HEQC 1995c).

The establishment of this graduate standards programme serves as a reminder that standards of output did not play a significant role in either HEQC's quality audit or even the funding councils' quality assessment systems.

3.3 Quality policies and PIs

By the beginning of the 1990s the language of efficiency, effectiveness, performance and standards had begun to be incorporated into the broader concept of quality in the development of the Evaluative State. Higher education, as we have seen, was no exception.

The establishment of systems of quality audit and quality assessment raises the question of their relationship with PIs. Both audit arrangements and those for the assessment of the quality of education have relied primarily on a combination of self-assessment and peer assessment, based on documentary analysis, together with institutional visits. Potentially, PIs might have a range of functions in relation to their work. They might provide background or contextual information; they might be used by themselves or in combination with other information to help formulate an agenda or a set of key questions. They might be a distinct component of the judgements formed. Alternatively, at least in the case of the assessment exercises, the judgements reached might themselves be converted into PIs.

One problem for the relationship is that there are multiple concepts of quality and the relevance of particular PIs might vary according to the concepts informing the quality systems. Joss and Kogan (1995) distinguish between specialist, generic and systemic concepts of quality, each of which might, however, have a place in organisations reliant on professional expertise. The idea that quality is essentially customer or consumer-defined is a dominant feature of total quality management. Harvey in his discussion of the relationship between quality and standards in higher education identifies five perceptions or notions of quality discernible in higher education: quality as exceptional (linked with excellence or elitism), as perfection or consistency, as fitness for purpose, as value for money and as transformative (interpreted as 'the enhancement or empowerment of students or the development of new knowledge') (Harvey 1995, p.9; see also Harvey, Burrows and Green 1992).

The White Paper (DES 1991) in which government stated its intention to impose a system of quality assurance on higher education institutions subsumed the ideas of quality control, quality audit and quality assessment under the broad heading of quality assurance but it did not define quality itself. Both the HEQC, charged with quality audit, and the funding councils, charged with quality assessment, have adopted the definition, 'fitness for purpose', and explicitly linked that with the principles of institutional autonomy and system diversity. Each has developed a generic framework of aspects to be examined and some criteria of assessment but these are intended to allow institutions to pursue different goals which might entail different concepts of quality. Whether they themselves have also in practice adopted particular meanings of quality has been a matter of some debate, particularly in the case of the funding councils. Neither has seen its role as being to define or to evaluate standards of output. The HEFCE quality assessment process concerns itself with, among other things, student achievement but 'neither the establishment of "standards" in an absolute sense nor the monitoring of the comparability of "standards" between institutions, is part of the HEFCE quality assessment brief' (HEFCE 1994, para.49).

PIs figure little in the methods or approaches to quality audit of either the CVCP Academic Audit Unit or the successor quality audit division of the HEQC. The emphasis is on the need for institutions to develop procedures and systems of, for example, peer and student evaluation of teaching, codes of practice, more rigorous methods of determining academic standards and assessing students. We have noted that the intention from the beginning was that audit teams would receive 'an initial briefing based on performance and other quantitative indicators and descriptive material' (Sutherland 1989, p.2). However, the notes for the guidance of auditors (HEQC 1993) contain no suggestions as to the use of PIs by them and refer only to three possible statistical indicators (student numbers, drop-out rates and classified degree results) that might be part of institutions' mechanisms for quality assurance in teaching and communications methods monitoring.

The annual report of the CVCP Academic Audit Unit (1992) suggested that quantitative PIs in use related to issues of resource allocation and financial management. While it commended the idea of developing qualitative indicators it had no suggestions as to their purpose or nature. HEQC criticises the use of outcome indicators of the quality of teaching and learning, such as degree classifications, numbers of firsts, non-completion rates and examination performance. These 'might be regarded as narrow, failing to capture the overall "quality of learning"' (HEQC 1994, p.15). It commends those who use a variety of indicators but no examples are offered.

The key differences between the HEQC audit and the funding councils' role in quality assurance are those of ownership, function and focus. The funding councils are external to the institutions and they are making assessments which cut into the world which academics have traditionally regarded as their own: assessments of the quality of education at the level of the subject. These entail scrutiny not only of curricula and methods of assessment, but also of the interaction between teachers and students. For the former polytechnics who came within the remit of the CNAA and of HMI inspectors, this is not wholly new but the import of the judgements made is. They are making 'an explicit connection between government and the student experience' (Yorke 1995, p.15). As we have seen, the remit given to HEFCE by the Secretary of State requires them to produce assessments in a form usable in funding allocations.

There are differences between the funding councils as to their chosen modes of operation. For example, institutional visits have been a universal feature of assessments in Wales and Scotland but not until 1995 in England, when the HEFCE made significant changes to its quality assessment framework. So far, however, PIs have no mandatory role in the process. The HEFCE position is that 'statistical indicators (SIs) contribute contextual information to the assessment process' (HEFCE 1993a, para.23). In 1994 they reiterated their view that 'statistical indicators generated by the Council from currently available data sets will play no further part in quality assessment', given the weakness of those data sets (HEFCE 1994, para.40a). However, they invite subject providers to include in the annex to their self-assessments data that they have on four SIs: student entry profile, progression and completion rates, student attainment and post-graduation employment and further study.

The main independent analysis of the funding councils' quality assessment has been that of Barnett (1993, 1994a). Some of his criticisms of the HEFCE initial methods are also relevant to the task of developing PIs for the British higher education system. In particular, they concern the problems of defining quality in a system which is committed both to diversity and to the maintenance of some core standards and principles. Barnett noted the HEFCE's statement which represents its attempt to manage the tensions and elaborates its chosen concept of quality as fitness for purpose. In the context of diversity, 'there can be no one set of criteria... no gold standard against which to assess quality. It is nevertheless possible and necessary to identify those features of student learning experience and student achievement which are valid across the sector' (HEFCE 1993a, para.10).

Barnett argued that these core or universal criteria needed to be more clearly stated. As it was, institutions were forming their own perceptions of hidden emphases and values in the assessment process. 'Our inquiries lead us to conclude that the greatest weighting is given to teaching performance, [followed by] the student experience (within timetabled sessions) and physical resources' (Barnett 1994a, para.5.12). The Council's own analysis of the assessors' reports sought to refute this conclusion by showing that there were examples of provision graded excellent that had a poorer profile of class observations than some of those graded overall as satisfactory and that gradings of excellent had been achieved by subject providers with less than a quarter of their observed classroom sessions judged as excellent (HEFCE 1995).

Other concerns derived from the need to decide on and articulate universal quality criteria. 'There is sufficient literature on teaching and learning to suggest that there are matters of course design and presentation which can... be said unambiguously to count towards course quality' (HEFCE 1995, para.5.13), such as the importance of the quality of student learning (as distinct from HEFCE emphasis on students experience) (para.5.15).

However, the Council's finding that of the 26 per cent of all judgements resulting in a grade of 'excellent', over 77 per cent went to institutions in the former UFC sector caused it to raise some questions of its own – as did the relationship that emerged between the research assessment ratings and the assessments of teaching quality. In the first two rounds of assessment, 71 per cent of those subject providers with a research grading of five also achieved a rating of excellent, while in the third round 97 per cent of grade five departments were rated excellent. Although assessors rarely referred to the research gradings explicitly, it was noted that the relationship between research and teaching was commended in over 75 per cent of 'excellent' reports in the first two rounds, most often in the case of former UFC institutions, where this was a feature in 88 per cent of reports (HEFCE 1995, para.95). More generally, although the Council found that reports cited a wide range of criteria of excellent teaching, they were led to ask whether the peer assessors' own values and expectations or conceptions of quality were leading them to 'cut across the framework of criteria they were asked to apply' (para.69).

Both Barnett and HEFCE's own analysis raised a number of other important questions. Both reports made a contribution to understanding how the system was working in practice. Patterns of criteria and judgements and also patterns of institutional responses were beginning to emerge that require better understanding. Three particular issues might be highlighted here. All are relevant to PIs. One was how far it is possible to construct a clear framework of criteria that is neither narrowly prescriptive, constraining institutional distinctiveness, nor vulnerable to manipulation. A second concerned the evidence, theories, beliefs and values that inform evaluative processes or performance measures and the nature of their authority. It is necessary to distinguish between the authority of criteria that are deeply embedded in disciplinary cultures and practices or historic concepts of higher education (Humboldtian doctrines of the interconnections between research and teaching), those that derive from educational practice wisdom, those grounded in educational theory and those grounded in research evidence. And if authority is evidence-based, is the evidence of correlation or causation? Another way of formulating this issue is in terms of the choice between connoisseurial (Rossi 1982) or theory-driven (Chen 1990) evaluation (see also Elsworth 1994).

The third issue is rather different. It is sharpened by one of the main changes made by HEFCE to its quality assessment framework following the review set in motion by the Barnett Report (Barnett 1994a). In consultation with the higher education sector the Council identified six core dimensions of educational quality: curriculum design, content and organisation; teaching, learning and assessment; student progression and achievement; student support and guidance; learning resources; quality assurance and enhancement. The original three categories of judgement (excellent, satisfactory and unsatisfactory) were replaced. Assessors are now required to score subject providers on each core quality dimension on a scale of one to four points. Providers must score a minimum of two points on each to be deemed to have reached the threshold of satisfaction. Thus an overall peer judgement is superseded by a profile, in which at the threshold, there can be no compensatory weighting. And the assessment of the quality of education, as of research, is now expressed in numerical scores or grades. Both may now explicitly or implicitly themselves be used as PIs.

As we have noted, teaching quality assessors rarely explicitly mentioned subjects' research assessment grades. There is no evidence that implicitly they were being used as a PI in the teaching quality assessment process. But logically if the trend noted towards high correlation between teaching and research continued or even became more marked, that might be precisely what they come to mean for various groups of stakeholders. We would then be back to the position obtaining before there were assessments of teaching quality and one that echoes the peer evaluations of departments in the USA. Departmental quality is judged primarily in terms of the research record of its staff and the link between good research and good teaching is taken for granted (Schmitz 1993; Tan 1992).

The Council has sought to hold assessors more tightly to the concept of quality as fitness for purpose and thus to the values of the subject providers under scrutiny by requiring them and those writing the self-assessments to be more rigorous in ensuring that their judgements and their reports are consistently shaped by course aims and objectives. The judgements of the assessors are structured and, to some extent, shaped by the protocol. But the essence of peer evaluation is that it is connoisseurial: evaluators apply their own values, knowledge and beliefs formed within their own practices and experience to the judgements that they make. Moreover, although they are making educational judgements, their professional reputations and their expertise are likely to rest on their achievements within their discipline. Certainly, because educational theory and training have had a relatively low profile in academic work, these are most unlikely to provide a common framework for their work. Thus although their conclusions are expressed ultimately in numerical scores there is room for substantial variety in what these scores represent – or in other words in the nature of the performance of which they are indicators.

However, the quality movement and quality assurance policies and institutions, in Britain as elsewhere, have had implications for the use of PIs more far-reaching than what has been described so far. They are profoundly implicated in the adoption of broad and holistic definitions of the quality of education, the realisation of which requires understanding of the complex processes involved. Such definitions have raised new questions about the nature and use of PIs, at the same time as the complexities of their development have been increasingly recognised.

3.4 PIs in use: introduction

We have seen in Chapter 2 that the increasing level and scope of technical knowledge available to those charged with the development of PIs have tended to induce greater caution in their selection of PIs. In the UK, this was given clear expression in the final report of the JPIWG (CVCP 1995a). While maintaining its interest in developing robust statistical output measures, it warned against assuming that these could in isolation provide reliable evidence of the quality of teaching: 'inputs and processes must also be considered to provide a credible blend of qualitative and quantitative indicators' (para.2.2). It also decided to redesignate as management statistics indicators for teaching as well as for other dimensions of higher education performance.

However, despite the fact that some measures, including that of value-added, have, at least for the time being, been dropped on the grounds that more work on them is needed, there is some degree of continuity and progression from those indicators originally proposed by the CVCP/UGC in 1986. And there is a wider level of concurrence with international trends on the range of indicators which are potentially of use and on which more work should be done.

The indicators to be examined in the remainder of this chapter are either the subject of firm proposals or under discussion in the UK.

3.5 Using cost measures as PIs

What do measures of average cost mean?

Average cost per student, per graduate or per completed credit unit is a natural PI. It combines measures of inputs and of outputs. It is available by cost centre in statistics, and it lends itself naturally to comparative analysis by calculating the average cost per student in a discipline in one university and comparing it with a national average or average of similar institutions. In some ways, average cost per graduate or per credit unit is the more satisfactory variant because it is a true output measure rather than a process measure. In practice, however, average cost per student is more widely used. The two will diverge when there are differences in progression rates between institutions. One particularly simple variant of the cost measure is the staff–student ratio. This measure ignores all inputs other than labour supplied by lecturers, and may therefore encourage inefficient substitution of other inputs – for example, equipment or secretarial and administrators' time – for inputs from lecturers. It also makes no distinction between teachers of different seniority and income levels. This, too, may lead to distorted measurement and distorted incentives.

All average cost measures (whether expressed in monetary terms or in the simplified form of staff–student ratios) are subject to a number of difficulties in the measurement of both inputs and outputs. As far as inputs are concerned the allocation of an institution's costs to a particular department or cost centre raises many practical difficulties, and consistency of treatment must be attained if inferences are to be drawn from comparative data. It is also inappropriate to assume that all costs are teaching costs, or that teaching costs are the same proportion of costs in all universities.

Traditional procedures for allocating costs rely upon the distinction between costs which can be attributed on a causative basis to particular outputs (for example, teaching or research in general, or a cohort of students taking a particular course), and unattributable or overhead costs. The latter includes such things as the costs of shared premises, facilities such as libraries used for both research and teaching and managerial overheads. Conventional methods of cost allocation simply determine the fully allocated cost of any product by adding to the attributable cost some, often arbitrarily chosen, proportion of overheads. The resulting unit cost measures are thus rather suspect, because they depend critically upon the formula used to allocate overheads.

More recently, a new approach to costing has been developed, known as activity based cost or ABC (Rimson 1991). Under this approach, the analyst first establishes what activities are required to generate particular outputs, then establishes what inputs are required for each activity, and then costs the inputs. For example, producing a graduate in a particular discipline will require expenditure on recruitment, lectures, seminars, laboratory work, assessment and administration. By identifying and costing each of these activities, a more soundly based unit cost can be established.

Although ABC in higher education has been examined in the general context of the development of PIs it is still in its infancy (see DeHayes and Lovrinic 1994). But according to Mitchell (1996) one-fifth of respondents to a survey on the usage of ABC in UK universities in autumn 1994 reported that they had made use of this costing method, and were overwhelmingly positive about its benefits. However, the results of activity based costing still remain sensitive to the techniques adopted, and the results of studies employing different detailed approaches are not strictly comparable. This problem continues to bedevil the collection of consistent data on unit costs.

There are problems, too, of measuring output. One of these is that of aggregating undergraduate, postgraduate taught and postgraduate research students into a single measure. Traditionally the weights adopted in the UK were chosen fairly arbitrarily, rather than based on an evaluation either of relative costs or of relative benefits. Moreover, universities often used for internal resource allocation purposes a set of weights different from those adopted by the funding bodies. In the next section we shall consider the case for adopting value-added as the measure of output rather than number of students graduating or receiving instruction. On this basis, even if entry standards were uniform across institutions there is still the question of whether output standards are identical – whether a degree in a given class is of uniform value across all institutions.

Uncertainty about output quality can lead to conflicting interpretations of a high cost per student. By one interpretation high unit cost (say a high staff–student ratio) may be taken as an indicator of a high quality educational process. If there were a direct relationship between the amount of time allocated to students and the quality of degree obtained, then higher staff–student ratios would be associated with higher quality output. However, we have no information on the quality of degrees of the same class or grade from different institutions and hence we are unable to investigate the relationship between teaching time and student quality. In this sense, the existence of a high staff–student ratio is not sufficient to indicate high quality.

The second interpretation leads to opposite conclusions. If degrees of the same grade are of the same quality, irrespective of the awarding institution, and if the value-added to an individual of obtaining a degree of the same class is the same for all institutions, then average cost may, in certain conditions, be used as an index of efficiency. However, the conditions required for such a conclusion to be valid for inter-institution comparisons are fairly restrictive.

In order to draw straightforward inferences from comparisons of cost-effectiveness it is desirable, first, that different institutions have, or at least have access to, the same 'production technologies' and, second, that they face identical prices.

By a production technology we mean the ability to turn inputs into outputs, or, in other words, the ability to transform an individual without a degree into an individual with a degree. This also requires each department to have access to the technology and not be locked into a particular production process which may not be optimal; we must suppose that it can alter teaching intensity, equipment levels, and the like to the optimal level.

The latter condition requires that the cost of the same production process must be the same for different institutions, so that institutions are not disadvantaged by such factors as the inherited age structure of their staff, their location or differences in research potential. There are a number of reasons why these conditions are unlikely to hold.

First, universities have inherited various 'structural differences' which do not allow them to operate at the optimum level. 'Structure' here means the nature of the technology available to the university. This will include the staff (which may be tenured) as well as buildings and teaching equipment – for example, computers. The availability of these resources is also intimately affected by funding policies. If the allocation is not correct some institutions may not be able to achieve their optimal output because they have insufficient resources to do so; i.e. they may be constrained to an output level which is below that at which they would achieve maximum efficiency.

Using average cost as a measure of comparative efficiency now becomes problematical. An institution with higher than average costs may find itself in this position for two reasons (here we assume that outputs of all institutions are of equivalent quality). Either it may be inefficient in using its resources, or it may be forced by circumstances outside its control to incur higher than average costs. If the funding body is concerned only with minimising unit costs, it may adopt the same policy in either case – of concentrating resources on low unit cost institutions. If it is concerned with other objectives as well – for example, ensuring a regional balance in higher education institutions or providing incentives for efficient use of given resources – it will be more inclined to concern itself with the explanation of higher unit costs.

Data on costs incurred will not be adequate for such purposes, although some progress might be made by identifying subsets of comparable institutions and using those as benchmarks to evaluate performance. Secondly, as we have noted, the cost-effectiveness of a cost centre or department is also going to depend directly upon the quality of the inputs to the production of degrees, i.e. student quality. If different universities have varying qualities of student demand then average cost may vary for reasons unrelated to the cost-effectiveness of the cost centres.

The relationship here is again unclear. First of all, we need to ask whether students of higher quality benefit more or less from a given level of teaching than students of a lower quality. If there is no difference, variations in the quality of student demand for places do not affect average cost. This is because, other things being equal, the optimal amount of teaching input is uniform across departments, regardless of variations in student quality. In this case, average cost may well be a useful indicator of cost-effectiveness. However, if the quality of students directly affects the productivity of teaching resources this is no longer the case.

It was argued earlier that, because we are unable to measure the quality of degrees, the best we can hope to obtain from using average teaching costs is some measure of comparative efficiency. Departments with lower average teaching costs are producing degrees (of a uniform quality) more cost-effectively. However, a fair comparison requires not only that the quality of output is uniform, but also that each department has available, or at least access to, the same production technology and faces the same prices. This may not be the case; differences among cost centres in structure, in the opportunity cost of lost research, and in the quality of student input mean that average teaching cost may vary between departments without implying anything about relative cost effectiveness. Unless the effects of these differences can be removed from average teaching costs, differences in average teaching costs may simply indicate that departments are doing the best they can subject to their available resources. This may still leave a role for more disaggregated cost per student data as triggers of questions to be asked. For instance, if materials cost per student in one chemistry department are twice as high as the national average, it is reasonable to wonder why that state of affairs has arisen. Even at the level of total cost per student, the same sort of issues are raised.

In their second (1987) statement, the CVCP/UGC working group, as we saw in Chapter 2, note the criticism that their 1986 list of proposed PIs gave too much attention to inputs and too little to outputs. They also note the concern 'that due consideration and weight should be given to local or regional factors, be they geographical, structural or economic, especially in inter-university comparisons' (CVCP/UGC 1987a, p.2). Nevertheless, shortage of data meant that the *University Management Statistics and Performance Indicators* published from 1987 were overwhelmingly related in one way or another to costs.

Clearly what is lacking is an adequate data set which would enable us to unravel the interrelations between properly measured inputs into and properly measured outputs of the teaching process. If such a data set were available, it would be possible to estimate the same kind of statistical cost functions as have been estimated in other contexts. This approach would also have the considerable advantage of yielding estimates not only of average cost but also of marginal cost. One or two attempts of this kind have been made (see, for instance, Osborne 1989). But even with available data, there is clearly scope for more analysis of this kind. A good example is provided by Jill Johnes' (1990b) study of differences in unit cost among UK universities, which shows that two-thirds of the variation is accounted for by different disciplinary mixes, and a further one-seventh by the staff–student ratio and the student composition. But the remainder is unexplained and the author draws attention to the need for better output measures before conclusions about efficiency can be drawn.

More recently, unit costs have received an endorsement from the Joint Performance Indicators Working Group (CVCP 1995a). The working group recommended that a unit cost model should be developed to assist institutional self-assessment and inter-institutional comparisons, noting that unit costs are a more relevant and robust measure than, for example, staff–student ratios. Limited unit cost data are also included in the list of management statistics proposed by the Higher Education Management Statistics Group for publication from 1996 (see Table 2.3 above). Work is currently being undertaken in this area by the UK Higher Education Funding Councils but it has not yet borne fruit.

3.6 Measuring output: value-added

In this section we move from considering the relationships between inputs and outputs in terms of efficiency to a focus on effectiveness, educational and social value. The concept of value-added is deceptively simple. We consider two individuals identical in every respect until the decision to enter higher education is taken. One goes on to take a degree of a given quality; the other does not. The value added by the degree is the difference in the contributions made to the welfare of society by the two individuals. This definition of value-added in terms of social worth is necessarily broad. Education is of value to the individual in terms of the consumption benefits of undergoing it, the pecuniary advantages of increased earnings potential, and other benefits in terms of personal development. The benefits to society derive from having one more highly educated individual, which may be desirable in itself if society values education *per se*, and from any positive externality effects. An example of a positive externality of education often cited is that a well-educated person may increase the productivity of a less well-educated person, either by adopting more efficient methods of work, or by the less well-educated person learning from the highly educated employee (see Le Grand and Robinson 1979).

As we have already noted, the importance of the ability to measure value-added lies in the information which it could provide in respect of the relationship between inputs and outputs, i.e. the efficiency of the education process. The more efficient institutions produce more value-added at the same or a lower cost. In this sense the efficiency of one institution relative to any other can be crudely measured by the ratio of average value-added to average cost. The higher the ratio the more efficient the institution. Measuring value-added is also important because it should allow the nature of the returns to scale in teaching to be explored more fully. In order to be able to allocate resources efficiently information is required on how outputs change in response to marginal changes in inputs. At present we do not have a measure of the output of the teaching process and this might, in principle, be provided by the value-added measure. Egan (1986) even claims that a value-added testing programme can 'help determine if increments to undergraduate teaching budgets can generate increments to learning achievement of students, other things equal' and he suggests it could help with marginal funding decisions (p.35).

In practice, of course, it is impossible to realise the conception of value-added set out above. We lack the ability to perform a controlled experiment with two individuals, and the capacity to measure the benefits described above. Most attempts to implement the value-added approach do so by comparing the academic attainment of students entering the institution with their attainment on graduation; the assumption is that either all or a given proportion of the increase is associated with the educational process rather than due, say, to the passage of time. Compared with the simple output measure, this basic value-added method does try to 'correct' for differences in quality of student input.

Another ideal measure of value added by higher education would establish a relationship between all the benefits of the educational process, and all the relevant costs. Outputs include increases in the earnings potential of graduates associated with possession of a degree, other benefits to graduates which are not reflected in earnings potential, and the worth of the educational experience itself. Each of these outputs should be measured as the difference between an individual's experience as a graduate and the experience of an identical non-graduate. The outputs should then be related to inputs specific to the institution's teaching functions.

We discussed in Chapter 1.3 one method of attempting this procedure, that is, by computing the private or social rate of return to investment in higher education. As noted there, the technique captures only some of the benefits, and it adopts special assumptions about the allocation of costs between teaching and research. It is also applicable only at a high level of aggregation, and is thus incapable of discriminating between different institutions.

The attempt to find some ways of measuring the value added by higher education has, however, been a significant preoccupation of those concerned with the development of PIs in this field during the last two decades. It can be linked with a shift from the traditional absolute or exceptional concept of quality, the aim to maximise academic excellence, towards relative and transformative notions (Harvey 1995, p.9; see also Yorke 1991). 'The basic argument underlying the value-added approach is that true quality resides in the institution's ability to affect its students favourably, to make a positive difference in their intellectual and personal development' (Astin 1982, p.11). The emphasis is on the contribution of higher education to change in students, although indicators might be applied at a number of different levels: the institution, the department, the programme or the entire sector.

This is a far cry from the long-standing tendency in the UK to regard student entry qualifications, high A level scores, as an indicator of institutional quality. Here, as elsewhere, there is now substantial doubt as to whether they are usable as such. Entry qualifications were excluded, then included in the CVCP/UGC suite of PIs, and then excluded once more. In particular, this indicator fails badly on the ambiguity test. High entry scores are a measure of student demand and therefore of reputation. But the relationship between reputation and performance is an issue in its own right (Tan 1992; Elsworth 1994). There is also the question of what an institution's reputation is for: it might be the success of its students in the labour market or the quality of its teaching or its social status. As we have noted, it is most likely to be the research records of its faculty

(Tan 1992; Schmitz 1993), the relationship of which with teaching performance remains a matter of contention (Whiston and Geiger 1992; Brew and Boud 1995; Terenzini and Pascarella 1994; Gibbs 1995). Moreover, if widening the access to higher education and increasing the age participation rate are important objectives, low entry scores might be a better PI, though perhaps only if related to outputs (Fulton and Ellwood 1989).

If overall, interest has been centred on output rather than input indicators, there is growing scepticism of measuring the quality of education or teaching offered by institutions simply by reference to student achievements in the form of degree classifications and the like. Such a procedure ignores the different starting points of individuals and may be a function of 'what happens in the admissions office rather than... what happens in the classroom' (Egan 1986, p.10).

Developing value-added in the UK

There is a wide variety of evidence concerning the relationship between students' entry standard scores and final degree performance. In view of the debate about PIs the literature was reviewed by Barnett (1988) and Johnes and Taylor (1987). Some of it suggests that there is a weak or non-existent relationship. This can be interpreted as meaning that A level entry scores are a poor measure of students' actual level of attainment in areas relevant to their studies, though other interpretations are possible too.

However, Johnes and Taylor's work (1987 and 1990a) points in a different direction. Somewhat at odds with previous research based upon detailed surveys of individual graduates, they found that the mean A level score of a university's students is highly significantly related to degree results. 'Using regression analysis, it was found that over 80 per cent of the variation between universities in degree results can be explained (statistically) by a set of plausible explanatory variables, the main one being the mean A level score of each university's student entrants' (Johnes and Taylor 1990a, p.117).

The others were the percentage of students living at home during the term, Scottish universities, percentage graduating in arts subjects, percentage graduating in medical sciences, and library expenditure as a percentage of total expenditure. Their thesis is that in the case of all four measures of university output they examine 'with less than 20 per cent of the variation remaining unexplained after differences in input have been taken into account, this raises the question whether the unexplained variation is itself a useful indicator of performance' (Jones and Taylor 1990a, p.183). It might, in other words, serve as a quantitative indicator of comparative institutional value-added. They had warned in 1987 that 'it would be extremely rash and cavalier to assume that the unexplained variation in degree results could be attributed to teaching quality.' (Johnes and Taylor 1987, p.599).

Their work apart, the main effort in the UK towards devising methods of calculating value-added have concentrated on finding a way to measure the difference between entry and exit qualifications.

The most significant was the jointly funded PCFC/CNAA project commissioned by the Morris Committee to 'test different approaches to the measurement of value added, and determine a methodology for the calculation of value added, based on a comparison of entry and exit qualifications' (PCFC/CNAA 1990, para.1.2). This was acknowledged to be 'a narrow conception' of value-added, but it was seen as the only practicable one in the short term.

Six types of 'index' methods and a comparative method for calculating value-added were tested in the project against actual data sets. The 'index' methods all arbitrarily attribute scores to the measures of input (entry qualification) and output (degree class) and calculate value-added by relating the two scores. They attempt to relate separate measures of entry and exit qualifications by making arbitrary assumptions about how hard it is for students to achieve a given exit qualification. The research claimed to show that 'all of the index methods, through the weightings they assign to entry and exit qualifications, are wrong about the nature of the relationship between the two. They all assume that it is more difficult to get a good degree with low entry qualifications than is in practice the case' (para.7.1). As a result, the value-added scores they produce are biased in favour of courses with low A level and non-A level recruitment. By contrast, the report claims, the comparative value-added (CVA) method maintains the distinction between measures of entry and exit by comparing degree results expected for students with particular entry qualifications with the actual degree results achieved. The expected degree class is derived from the national relationship between degree results and entry qualifications, therefore it is the expectation of a student with a particular qualification gaining a particular degree. The value-added score of a course, a programme area, an institution or a sector, is a function of the difference between the degree results achieved and the results predicted from entry qualifications. The report claims there are two advantages of the CVA method:

> Firstly, it is not an arbitrary score, but is based on an empirically derived expected value. Therefore the claim that a particular course did better or worse than expected when compared to national data is likely to have a robust acceptability. Secondly, because the playing field has been levelled all institutions have an incentive to improve their value added scores whatever their current recruitment profile. (para.3.7)

This claim overstates what the CVA method can achieve. Any estimate of the value-added in a course, programme area, institution or sector involves aggregation of the value-added of many individuals. It is thus sensitive to the weights used to measure exit attainments. Although the CVA approach eliminates the need for explicit weighting of input qualifications, by adopting national performance as a yardstick, it still requires an explicit set of weights for exit qualifications. Thus it assumes that the difference in value between a first and upper second is the same as that between an unclassified degree and a fail. Clearly this is contestable, and it demonstrates the impossibility of devising any system of value-added which is wholly free of arbitrary weights.

An alternative attempt to implement the value-added measure is set out in Mallier and Rodgers (1995). Their aim is the rather different one of establishing the incremental value (compared with the earnings of an employee with A levels) of different classes of degrees. It relies upon the observation that income data show that the earnings of graduates vary directly with degree class: it is thus possible to estimate a monetary value of the better qualifications. Thus they estimate that the annual pay differential of a graduate employee over an A level educated employee over the period 1986 to 1992 varied from approximately £3000 for a graduate with a pass degree to £4200 for a graduate with first-class honours.

The results, though interesting, raise a number of questions. In particular, the income differences may be based upon differences in aptitude rather than the value-added of higher education. It is also quite clear that an analysis conducted on such an aggregate scale cannot provide insights into the performance of individual institutions in dealing with particular cohorts of varied entry qualifications.

The Morris Committee had high hopes for value-added measures. First, they suggested they could provide a macro PI to show at an inter-sectoral level that 'relatively high performance in terms of "value-added" is a distinctive characteristic of the PCFC sector, and of individual institutions within it' (Morris 1990, para.5.11). Further uses recommended by the PCFC/CNAA Report included informing the resource allocation process which they were attempting to link to quality monitoring of national trends in subject and sector differences in value-added; an aid to monitoring. At the institutional level it could be useful as part of quality assurance because the CVA method could calculate value-added for different kinds of entrant, even on the same course. Institutions were already routinely examining data on entry qualifications and student performance as part of course monitoring and validation procedures. It was claimed that the value of these data to these procedures would be enhanced by use of the CVA method because:

> (i) the CVA method can produce summary statistics of student performance that will be meaningful at academic board/ governors levels;
>
> (ii) it can also provide a very detailed breakdown of performance and the factors which have influenced it for use at the course committee level. (PCFC/CNAA 1990, para.7.5.3).

There are, however, several possible criticisms of the value-added approach as described. First, some would argue (Morrison, Magennis and Carey 1995) that the problems of measurement are insuperable, particularly in the British context where 'A level and degree scores are not even measured in the same test metric' (p.132) and where few disciplines use objective measures in their assessments. Second, one of the basic assumptions made is questionable, namely that degree classifications are comparable between institutions and between sectors. Furthermore, if CVA was to be used when assessing quality bids, the danger of manipulation might increase despite the existence of external examiners. The project also showed how value-added was greater on some courses for females and for mature students. However, it was not suggested that such factors could be allowed for when calculating the expected value-added and then the CVA for one course when compared with another, and yet, the differences between courses at different institutions might be entirely accounted for by such factors, and thus reveal nothing about the relative quality of the courses. As we noted earlier, Johnes and Taylor (1987) developed their predicted degree results for each university by standardising for inter-university variations in a range of explanatory variables.

A second fundamental objection is that the conception of value-added is too narrow. A much wider interpretation of the concept of value-added is being encouraged in UK higher education by, for example, the Enterprise Initiative. It is useful to examine the whole nature of the debate about value-added from a much wider perspective, and most of the examples come from the USA.

Developing value-added in the USA

In the USA Egan (1986) suggested that the instruments usually used in value-added measures were the SAT or ACT scores conventionally used to measure the academic ability or quality of students entering a higher education institution and the Graduate Record Examination (GRE) or similar tests conventionally used as measures of educational accomplishment at or near the time of exit of undergraduates from an institution. Both sets of tests are expressed in percentiles and therefore to use them to show value-added poses a threat to the top HEIs which recruit their students from the top percentiles and therefore 'no display of net learning is possible in these cases because no dramatic percentile improvement is possible... the development of testing or assessment instruments, free of percentile ranking is essential if value-added testing and measurement is to become a dominant movement in higher education' (pp.15–16). In the UK although there is room for debate about the extent to which A levels and degrees are norm referenced, similar fears might exist in the top ranking universities if the simple value-added approach was adopted. Morrison *et al.* (1995) in their criticism of the use of CVA measures in league tables constructed by the media, note that 'it is instructive to compare the Cambridge (ranked 1) value-added score of 50 with Manchester Metropolitan's (ranked 53) score of 99' (p.133).

An attempt by an institution to measure value-added on a concurrent basis was made in the 1970s at the Northeast Missouri State University (NMSU). Taylor (1985) describes the purpose of the value-added assessment at NMSU as to 'measure the gains in knowledge, skills and personal development within each individual' (p.191). He identifies two driving forces behind its introduction already noted. First, where the funding of universities in the USA has been based upon measures of through-put of students, the incentive for universities to do well against these quantitative measures has detracted from what should be an emphasis on quality. Second, there has been growing dissatisfaction with the traditional methods of assessing student performance and a greater public desire to measure the extent to which education results in an improvement in individuals in broader terms.

The NMSU programme grew from the modest beginnings of comparing students' results on the ACT entrance examination and those in a subsequent test after the second year. This was later extended to final-year undergraduates, and then the NMSU attempted to measure a wide range of perspectives on value-added in a variety of different ways including 'Attitude surveys, interviews, objective standard tests, course taking patterns, subjective tests and extensive performance sampling' (Taylor 1985, p.193). In addition, students' assessment prior to attending and after leaving university was introduced.

The diagnostic potential of the programme was illustrated at NMSU in 1979. Tests applied to business majors revealed that inadequate improvements had been made in the area of mathematics. Similar results were also indicated by tests applied to business graduates, by faculty experience in the classroom and by questionnaires given to students, the results of which indicated student perceptions of unpreparedness in mathematics. McClain *et al.* (1986) argue that the fact that all of these tests indicated a weakness provides clear evidence of the existence of a problem.

As a result, curriculum committees met to discuss approaches which could be taken to improve the mathematical skills of their students and recommended that a stronger mathematics foundation be required for all four-year business majors. The recommendation became effective in 1979–80 with the result that in each of the subsequent years, test results showed improvement and questionnaire results indicated higher satisfaction amongst students with their mathematics preparedness. In addition, since the university internal budget allocation was closely tied to student outcomes, the improvements achieved translated into fiscal benefits. Thus McClain *et al.* maintain that the programme at NMSU makes it possible to diagnose a problem and offers incentives for its solution. In addition, the agency responsible for organising and implementing the changes was the faculty and not an external institution.

Taylor believes that there have been two important side effects of the introduction of the value-added programme. First, it has meant that the faculties within NMSU come to take the view that 'students come first'. The emphasis has moved from attention to quantity to attention to both quantity and quality. Second, it allowed NMSU to demonstrate to funding authorities and the general public that the education process was contributing value to individuals, thus allowing NMSU to demonstrate that resources spent on educating their students had been invested well.

One of the problems most often raised in connection with specific value-added assessment is that the procedure itself bestows no direct positive benefit on the student. The results of the test are used solely for the purpose of evaluating institutions or departments and, as such, the student has no particular incentive to do as well as possible. This may limit the extent to which such tests can elicit increases in skills.

Even if the tests do draw out accurate information on the particular aspect of personal development with which they are concerned, what weighting should be used to combine scores into a composite index? It has been noted that at NMSU various student characteristics are evaluated in several ways. Which components are most important? In order to compare scores across universities it is necessary for each university to agree to the same weighting system. If the purpose is to measure private benefits then the weights should be consistent with the valuation which students make of the differing components of private benefit.

Assuming that the value-added programme accurately reflects the private benefit derived from the education process, can we maintain that such measures accurately reflect social benefits from higher education? One of the problems of comparing the value of different degrees is that they have different social values. Different graduates are compensated by the market at varying rates and provide different social benefits. Does the same value-added score for different types of graduates imply the same social worth? If not we cannot infer relatively high social worth from a relatively high value-added score over different subjects.

There are also practical difficulties involved in measurement. In order validly to compare the scores from different institutions, it is necessary for tests to be standardised. As a result, rather than being a measure of quality, the value-added score becomes the definition of quality. Institutions, if they derive benefit from high value-added scores, have an incentive to reorganise their teaching practices to score well in value-added assessments. The familiar problem of a regression towards the mean may occur, and after some time it may become difficult to discriminate between institutions on the basis of value-added scores. In the USA value-added has not been applied across institutions and there are other forms of multi-institutional and comparative measures.

Although value-added appeared in the earlier list of items given by Brinkman and Teeter that could be used for inter-institutional comparison, McMillan (1988) argues: 'value-added education is tailored to the student characteristics and unique mission of each institution. This promotes the maintenance of diversity in higher education by encouraging varied assessments that avoid inappropriate inter-institutional comparisons' (p.19).

Egan (1986) showed that not only students but also policies, programmes and personnel would be evaluated using value-added. He therefore claimed that faculty members as well as institutional leaders would be expected to oppose externally imposed value-added programmes. The only way out of this problem 'would be if the faculty members themselves choose to use value-added measurements to advance the goals of under-graduate instruction which they have chosen as their primary goal' (p.23). If this could be done it would provide information for the consumers/students; re-establish and institutionalise undergraduate teaching as a primary institutional goal; and show the students the progress they were making. Furthermore publication of the results would maximise the 'internal incentives for effective undergraduate education by subjecting the HEI to external market and/or political rewards and punishments for effective and ineffective education' (p.26). For reasons already discussed Egan believed that lecturers inevitably tend to devote more attention to research and postgraduate education than to undergraduate teaching and that 'HEIs have few or no incentives to adopt value-added measures' (p.51). A further practical difficulty with the operation of a concurrent value-added assessment is that it would be both time-consuming and costly. Even if appropriate standard tests could be agreed, testing would have to be carried out at least twice in each institution for each student, or for a large random sample of students, for a before and after measurement to be made. Whether the cost exceeds the benefit depends in part on how well value-added measures reflect the output of the education process. Research into a number of large research universities shows limited involvement in activities commonly associated with the assessment movement such as measures of value-added. It is argued that 'the logistical problems of testing and retesting using standardised exams prohibit any value-added analyses' (Ory and Parker 1989, p.384).

Is value-added the way forward?

Some of the problems of measuring the wider interpretation of value-added have been mentioned here. However, research in this area is still in its infancy and by no means at a stage where we can say whether value-added measures can or cannot be made operational at some level.

If we were able to measure value-added, the efficiency of institutions could be explored and the usefulness or otherwise of investment in higher education demonstrated. Additionally, we could examine the relationship between inputs and outputs at the margin and go some way towards estimating the optimal size of the institutions assessed. Yet, as we have seen, the measurement of value-added is not without difficulty. Even if reliable information can be derived from such tests, what relative weights should we apply to the aspects of personal development measured? Do measurements reflect social benefits? There are also practical difficulties. Once relevant and universal measures have been achieved the concurrent measurement of value-added would be expensive and time-consuming. Finally, the introduction of universal value-added measurement may, if institutions derive benefit from higher value-added scores, result in teaching practices being altered to prepare students to do well in such tests. Value-added measures may no longer measure what they were intended to measure.

Despite these difficulties, some authors feel that further studies in this area would be money well spent. However, as already noted, Astin (1982) points out 'such studies frequently take a long time to produce useful results, and the results are often so general that they are difficult for individual institutions to apply to their particular problems' (p.13). The result is that funds for such research, which would allow the usefulness of higher education to be tested, are not readily available.

The JPIWG in their report published in 1995 recognised some of the complexities of achieving worthwhile measures of value-added. And having declared firmly that the primary customers for their work were higher education institutions themselves, they concentrated not on devising a watertight measure of value-added but rather on enabling individual institutions to make comparisons between what their particular students were achieving in terms of progression, exit qualifications and employment destinations and what broadly comparable student populations at other institutions were managing. Hence their proposals for the calculation of standardised comparators or benchmarks for each institution. These issues will be discussed further in Section 3.7.

3.7 Student progression rates and exit qualifications

We have seen that the initial range of PIs proposed under the heading of teaching and research by the CVCP/UGC working group included undergraduate wastage rates. The Report by the JPIWG in 1995 (CVCP 1995a) suggests that in this area, perhaps more than in any other, they had made significant changes in the conceptualisation and the analysis of the issues.

The shift from the notion of wastage to those of student progression and student achievement in the 1995 report argu- ably represents the adoption of a more student-centred ap- proach, as well as a shift towards developing measures of input and process. The JPIWG stated that its work had been strongly influenced by a profile approach based on a comprehensive analysis of student progression from preparation for higher education through to first postgraduation destinations (Wil- liams 1994). This approach incorporated input, process and output measures for institutions establishing systems of self- evaluation that would examine their capacities to meet their responsibilities to students. The JPIWG did not adopt the pro- file, on the grounds that it went beyond its terms of reference and might overlap with the quality assessment methods being developed by the funding councils (CVCP 1995a, para.2.4). However, the quantitative indicators it proposed under the heading of student progression, exit qualifications and employ- ment destinations 'had been developed within the profile framework' (para.2.5).

The influence of this framework of student progression is even more evident in the new indicators proposed by the HEMS Group (1995) under the heading of teaching. They include indi- cators for application rates, participation rates, student popula- tion statistics, student progression, length of higher education experience, leavers' and exit qualifications and first destina- tions.

The CVCP/UGC working group had itself recognised that the problems of linking PIs with the policy context or objectives of higher education and ensuring that they are used properly by management are particularly acute in the case of wastage rates. In their 1986 report they pointed out that whilst the undergraduate wastage rate could be useful as a means of monitoring the success of an institution in the output of graduates and as a reflection of the quality of teaching, the maintenance of academic standards might mean that a certain level of wastage was unavoidable. At the level of postgraduate and research degrees, the problems are rather different.

The issue became more evident when the Secretary of State indicated that he wished to see an increase in access to higher education (Baker 1986 and 1987). The chairman of the UGC made it clear to universities that they would not be putting themselves at a disadvantage by 'lowering their admission standards for mathematics and physics courses in order to admit more students who are considering eventually becoming school teachers' (Swinnerton-Dyer 1986, para.1). The policies of widening access to higher education would be put in jeopardy if, as a result of taking more 'higher risk' students, institutions had a higher wastage rate for which they are penalised.

This links with the central problem we have identified before – that of quality control. Any institution has the theoretical capacity to influence its own wastage or completion rate by the standards it imposes. Departments are constrained from doing so both by a sense of academic and professional responsibility and by the system of accreditation and the external examining of undergraduate and postgraduate degrees and research theses. None the less, the adoption of wastage rates as a major PI means that the pressures to distort academic judgement become more severe.

There are further methodological problems with this superficially straightforward PI. In the ancient Scottish universities and some of the colleges of the University of Wales, transfer between courses is relatively common and therefore 'wastage' at departmental level does not have the same meaning as elsewhere. This would militate against their application at the departmental level in such circumstances. There are also problems with ascribing wastage to a department in the case of multidisciplinary courses. The issues have become more complex with the growing importance of modularisation in undergraduate curricula across the UK.

Despite the difficulties, the working group suggested in 1986 that this PI could be adopted in the near future. The 1987 White Paper (DES 1987e) also supported the use of non-completion rates as an indicator of the quality of teaching. Its value in revealing possible problems within the institution could be great provided it were used sensitively and in conjunction with other indicators such as entry standards, cost per student and research output. For example, an institution which combined high wastage rates with high entry standards, high costs and a low publication rate could be deemed to have problems. At the very least a high wastage rate suggests the need for an investigation into its causes. Some people would argue that even if the high level is a result of the high standards on the course, the institution could still be criticised for poor initial selection.

As the student population grows and becomes more varied, the issue of non-completion rates becomes more complicated. We suggested in our first edition that it would be useful to distinguish between voluntary and compulsory wastage. The JPIWG has taken the matter forward by recommending two indicators for student progression: the proportion of students assessed as being unable to progress at key stages in their student career and the proportion assessed as being able to progress but who do not do so. And the HEMS Group (1995) has suggested that the category of leavers from HEIs should be divided into three: those who leave with a qualification; those who leave in bad standing or because of academic failure and those who leave for non-academic reasons.

On the assumption that the function of these indicators is primarily that of enabling institutions or indeed government to diagnose problems and to analyse their nature, they open up a number of possible lines of enquiry. In a context where anxiety is growing about non-completion rates, reported to have risen in the UK by 25 per cent in the year 1992–1993 (*Times Higher Education Supplement* 29 December 1995), they raise questions about what is and what is not in the control of institutions. Could an improvement in their quality assurance systems for selection, induction, student housing, student counselling, contact with staff and other students, and assessment reduce the numbers of both academic failures and non-academic drop-outs? What stages of student progression are most risky and for whom?

However, as indicators of performance either of the quality of teaching or of the institutional provision as a whole, they have substantial weaknesses. Some are conceptual, to do with definitions of leaving or courses or even what constitutes a student. The problems of drawing a clear line between external or individual reasons for students leaving without a qualification that are beyond the control of the institutions and reasons to do with the educational opportunities provided are also partly conceptual. Other problems are to do with the relationship between input variables and outputs.

The JPIWG consultation exercise in 1994 produced more criticisms of the statistical indicators of teaching and learning than of any other category. One set of critiques drew attention to the huge variety in patterns of enrolment for study and options for progression that now exist in higher education. This makes it increasingly difficult to decide whether or not students can be said to have left a programme or succeeded in a qualification aim. The growth in numbers and types of off-campus learners also makes it more difficult to define what is meant by a student. Most telling was the complaint that the JPIWG indicators were declared to be only for full-time students and that the implications of part-time study and modular courses had not been confronted.

The importance of careful handling of non-completion rates was further underlined by the regression analysis undertaken by Johnes and Taylor (1989a). They show that a large proportion of the inter-university variation in the non-completion rate can be explained by three factors: the ability of each university's entrants (as reflected by A level score); the subject mix; and the proportion of each university's students accommodated in a hall of residence. This raises serious doubts about the validity of using non-completion rates as a PI of teaching. Johnes and Taylor suggest that for such comparisons to be much use 'each university's non-completion rate would first need to be "corrected" for at least some of the factors responsible for causing inter-university disparities' (p.224). Johnes and Taylor (1991) also show that many non-completers went on to get degrees elsewhere, though as a group, non-completers earned less than graduates.

The Morris Report recommended that an Index of Output Costs should be developed as one of the macro PIs to be used by the PCFC. It should be constructed by multiplying the Index of Revenue Resource by the reciprocal of the Course Completion Index. If there were then a fall in the Index of Revenue Resource, accompanied by a fall in course completion rates, there might be no improvement in the Index of Output Costs.

The recommendations of the JPIWG in 1995 suggest that they had been influenced by research such as that of Johnes and Taylor (a member of the group) on the impacts of input variables on outputs. They recognised the potential implications for student progression and achievement rates not only of subject mix but also of the gender and age balances in a student population and the pattern of the student entry qualifications. Hence their proposals for standardised comparators for use by institutions which would 'show the level of performance that would be achieved if progression and achievement rates were at the national average levels for the particular mix of student entry qualifications, subject mix and gender mix at the institution concerned' (CVCP 1995a, para.2.9).

The HEMS Group (1995) accepted the principle of bench-marking but decided that more research was needed before making a firm decision on what input variables to take into account. Responses to the consultative document had included suggestions for other variables, including students' ethnicity and socio-economic background. The HEMS Group decided that benchmarking would only be developed immediately for subject mix. That they opted for this was perhaps surprising in view of the major changes and greatly increased variety in study patterns already discussed. Subject mix might turn out to be a hugely complicated category.

The focus on student populations is salient for a number of reasons. The JPIWG mentions its importance for fairness to the institutions, that their achievements are not misrepresented. But perhaps more important is institutions' responsibility to exam-ine how far they are catering for new groups and new mixes of students and to decide whether the concept of quality on which they are working is appropriate and whether the education they are providing matches it.

The work of the JPIWG on student progression nicely illustrates how the concept of PIs becomes increasingly squeezed between sharpening technical and conceptual analysis, increasing attention to systemic rather than behavioural conceptions of quality (further discussed in Section 3.9), the growing diversity of higher education and the political interests of institutions as they seek to negotiate the twin pressures of state and market control.

3.8 Employment and first destinations

The extent to which higher education makes students more employable in the labour market is obviously and legitimately a matter of great concern to governments, institutions, employers and the students themselves. It is not surprising, therefore, that the destinations to which higher education leads have been used as an indicator of the effectiveness of institutions of undergraduate education by a number of organisations. The Department of Employment and the DES were keen to publicise first destination statistics (FDS) in order better to inform intending graduates about their career prospects (DES and DE 1985). For many decades the Careers Advisory Service has been collecting information annually on the first destinations of graduates. We have seen in Chapter 2 that the performance of students after graduation is regarded as an important component of the shift from input and process to output and outcome measures, particularly in the development at state level of PIs (see e.g. Ewell 1991).

Graduate destinations were among the first list of indicators produced by the CVCP/UGC (1986). However, their original intention to publish figures at two stages, 12 months and five years post-graduation, was modified by the following year to that of providing only figures for graduate employment after six months. The issue of timing for this type of measure has been a persistent feature in the literature on this subject and we will return to it later in the section.

In 1988 the CVCP/UGC refined the first destination indicators to take account of research showing that about 70 per cent of inter-university variations in the first destinations of graduates is explained by corresponding variations in subject mix

(Johnes and Taylor 1990a). Since then predicted numbers of graduates unemployed or in short-term employment have been calculated for each university in each subject by working out the number in these categories there would have been if the national rate for that subject had applied. The excess or deficit of the expected over the predicted number is expressed as a percentage of the total known numbers of short-term employed or unemployed so that negative figures indicate more than the predicted figures and vice versa.

The JPIWG suggested broadly that the categories of first destination used by the Association of Graduate Careers Advisory Service (AGCAS) should be adopted. These include, in addition to those entering permanent employment, those in short-term employment, and those unemployed, those proceeding to further education or training, those not available for employment and those whose destination is unknown. The JPIWG proposed that the category further education and training should be subdivided into further academic study and other types of further education and training so that the total number of categories under employment destinations would be seven. Aggregate institutional results would be given for each category, in addition to primary subject group results, and there would be separate figures for the main types of qualification aim. These did not include sandwich degrees, which they thought were preferably treated as separate qualifications but this would create data collection problems (CVCP 1995a, para.2.22).

The HEMS Group accepted these proposals, except for the subdivision of the category further education and training which it would not be possible to identify from the national statistics.

However, the use of first destination statistics as PIs is by no means uncontroversial. Johnes and Taylor (1990a), two of the leading early researchers into this issue in the UK, were unequivocal in their rejection of the idea (see also Brennan and McGeevor 1988). Boys and Kirkland (1988) were rather more optimistic about first destination statistics, finding them to be modest predictors of success in the labour market over the longer term.

Johnes and Taylor's research had suggested that not only was subject mix overwhelmingly important in explaining inter-university variations, but that in total about 90 per cent of such variations could be statistically explained. Relevant factors included recruiting practices of employers and the effects of geographical location on the labour market in which students of different institutions would be competing.

Brennan *et al*. (1993) found in their study of university and polytechnic graduates that after five years the key variables affecting graduates' financial rewards from employment were the subject studied and the institution. But while 'the differences between the lowest paid group of graduates, polytechnic humanities, and the highest, university accountants, was almost £12,000,... although type of institution matters, it is nothing like as significant as subject studied in determining future earnings' (Brennan *et al*. 1994, p.280). They conclude that whether success in employment is measured by income, job status or more subjective appreciations of the relevance of higher education to employment the subject studied remains the key variable (p.285).

AGCAS in criticising the approach to first destination statistics adopted by the Department of Employment had claimed that insufficient attention has been drawn to variations between occupations in career paths towards permanent employment. Some careers require further periods of full-time study after graduation; others, such as social work and graphic design, are typified by periods of short-term employment in the early stages (Porrer 1984).

A particular concern has been the relationship between the time at which employment data are collected and the robustness of any derivative indicators. The JPIWG itself proposed that the feasibility of undertaking graduate employment follow-up surveys two years after the completion of programmes should be carefully explored, an idea given some support in the consultation exercise (CVCP 1995a, para.2.26).

Brennan and McGeevor (1988) in their survey of CNAA graduates at work concluded that, because of the high volume of job changes during the three years after graduation, the use of first destination statistics to imply anything more than first destinations could be misleading. The year immediately after graduation has an important but very different role to play for different kinds of graduates in making the transition into employment. During the first three years of employment 58 per cent of CNAA graduates had two jobs or more. Of the 1982 graduates in the study 43 per cent changed their employment status between 1983 and 1985. In autumn 1985, 18 per cent were actively looking for a different kind of job.

Brennan *et al.* (1994), drawing on their wealth of experience of studying graduate employment, conclude that two years after graduation is probably the best time to study major aspects of the links between higher education and employment.

However, they also raise wider questions about the range and types of indicators that might be collected in order to get a more robust set of measures. They suggest that information of three main kinds should be collected: objective indicators of income, proportions of unemployed; subjective indicators such as graduates' perceptions of their career paths and aspirations; the 'match' between work tasks and content of higher education, for which both objective and subjective information would be needed.

No reference is made in the JPIWG report of the dramatic changes now taking place in the labour market and the implications such changes in career patterns and demands might have for the selection of measures of performance. The decline in 'traditional' graduate jobs and lifelong careers has, however, led in some cases to a shift of emphasis towards graduates' employability rather than their employment. A recent Australian report (Higher Education Council 1993) argued for attention to 'the attributes that graduates should acquire if exposed to a high quality higher education system' (p.19). The Association of Graduate Recruiters (1995) focuses on the types of skills required by graduates to enable them to survive in the 21st century, 'to manage a lifetime's progression in learning and work... They are process skills rather than functional skills' (p.21). However, they go on to argue for a combination of specialist and generalist and of self-reliance (planning and managing their own careers) and interactive or 'connected' skills (networking and negotiating).

This connects with the argument that PIs if they are to be useful must aid future planning rather than simply reflect past performance (Banta and Borden 1994).

3.9 Student and Peer Evaluation

Peer evaluation

Peer evaluation may be internal or external. As well as its importance in the evaluation of research, it has long been established as a mechanism for reviewing the educational function of higher education institutions. In the UK its best-known forms before the establishment of quality audit and the quality assessment functions of the funding councils were the external examiner system and the accreditation and validation systems of the CNAA. We have seen how its use in the funding council assessments of teaching quality has been converted into quantitative measurement that is effectively, if informally, being used as a PI.

As forms of summative judgement, peer reviews of the teaching performance of institutions and of individual colleagues have been the subject of severe criticism. At the institutional level, again, they are frequently indicators of reputation rather than of performance. Conrad and Blackburn (1985) identify the problems as rater bias, limited rater perspective and the frequent use of academic staff quality as the single evaluative criterion; Skolnick (1989) commented on the potential of peer review for stifling diversity and innovation (see also Elsworth 1994). At the level of the individual, 'academics typically have scanty and biased knowledge of their colleagues' teaching abilities; their judgements correlate poorly with other measures' (Ramsden 1991, p.130; see also Marsh 1987; Solmon and Astin 1981).

However, some writers have identified questions about teachers' performance that academic peers are in a good position to answer: the teacher's mastery of content; selection of content; relevance of content to the continuity of the course sequence; and the relevance and quality of the course syllabus and related materials (Miller 1986).

As far as formative evaluation is concerned, there is considerably more support for peer review of, in particular, programmes and individual teaching practice, in the latter case sometimes on a mutual or collaborative basis.

Student evaluation

Systematic student review of teaching, usually through the use of student questionnaires, is a long-standing and significant characteristic of higher education in the USA. Cook (1989) suggested that student ratings have provided the bulk of the data used in the USA in evaluating college teaching and, in their survey of large research institutions, Ory and Parker (1989) found that approximately 75 per cent 'collect student ratings of instruction which provide an indicator of instructional quality' (p.31).

Student evaluation is now widely valued and interest in its potential as a PI has sharpened in the 1990s, particularly in Australia and, to a lesser extent, the UK. One reason for this is that, apart from classroom observation by peers or inspectors, it is the most direct way in which teaching can be evaluated. But the developing interest also coincides with a perception of increasing consumer power and consumer rights, as the values of both public accountability and the market gain strength in higher education, and with the growing influence of theories of student learning on policy makers. Major influences on the development of systematic course evaluation by students in the UK have been the HEQC quality audit and the funding councils' teaching quality assessment exercises.

Those wishing to use student evaluations as indicators of educational quality have, however, to address a number of questions, not least those of acceptability to academics. Technical issues include their validity, their reliability and the feasibility of developing instruments and indicators that could be universally or even widely applied. Moreover, since the techniques for putting student evaluations into practice were first developed in the USA ideas have changed about what should be their focus (for example, teacher behaviour, course characteristics, institutional environment, student satisfaction). These link with more fundamental questions about the extent to which there is either theoretical or empirical justification for making connections between student evaluation and either good teaching practice or student outcomes. Can student evaluations indicate anything more than student satisfaction?

Such questions are clearly critical to issues of use: can they be used for summative as well as formative evaluation; for external as well as internal evaluation; for the awarding of rewards or the allocation of resources, as well as providing a basis for quality improvement? And what is the range of units of assessment from individual teachers, to courses or programmes, to institutions? Lastly there are administrative questions about at what stages in student careers and at what points in course programmes, student evaluations should be required.

According to Marsh (1987), who has probably conducted the most comprehensive reviews of the literature on students' evaluations of teaching effectiveness (see e.g. Ramsden 1991), it contains thousands of studies and extends back to the 1920s. Winter Hebron (1984) suggests that market research was a strong influence on the development of student questionnaires in the USA in the 1930s, and that this influence persists. But he also describes the move to develop 'behaviour referenced' systems, instruments inviting students to rate instructors either on what they did or how often they did it. An example is Instructional Development by Evaluation and Assessment (IDEA) developed at Kansas University and adapted by Winter Hebron for use in Britain before the advent of quality audit. His Assessment for Instructional Development (AID) scheme used a database drawn from six British universities and six (then) polytechnics. It was focused on the discipline area in which the users' teaching falls and different versions exist for different major groupings of subjects.

IDEA is concerned with student perceptions of teacher behaviour and of the progress made on a course towards agreed course objectives. The system is based on asking students to rate their teachers' behaviour on a five point scale and the results are assessed for consistency with the teachers' own objectives.

Winter Hebron (1984) claims that 'The system does not, in itself, suggest specific corrective action to change the scores to which it points: it leaves that final self-corrective task to the individual teacher or his educational development consultant. But it does produce data which are readily understood, and which can be easily used to propose self-corrective changes in teaching strategy' (p.148).

Two of the best-known student evaluation questionnaires developed in the USA are the Student Evaluation of Educational Quality (SEEQ) (Marsh 1987) and the Endeavor instrument (Frey, Leonard and Beatty 1975). Each of them is structured round a small list of similar components of effective teaching (nine in the case of SEEQ and seven in Endeavor).

Although the questionnaires appear course-oriented, their predominant use is for the evaluation of teachers. Marsh's nine dimensions of effective teaching include workload, teachers' explanations, empathy (interest in students), openness and the quality of assessment procedures (including quality of feedback). A number of these were similar to the categories developed by Feldman (1976), although Feldman also mentioned the stimulation of student interest and the encouragement of student independence.

Marsh (1987), Feldman (1978) and Roe and McDonald (1983) made a strong case 'for the usefulness and accuracy of student evaluation of instruction in comparison with other measures such as peer evaluations' (Ramsden 1991, p.131). Marsh argues that 'in spite of some academic myths that suggest otherwise' (Ramsden 1991, p.131), students are not prone to confusing 'good performance' with effectiveness. Marsh, Ramsden and Miller (1986) all emphasise that there are certain aspects of effectiveness on which students are the most authoritative judges. Miller cites the following examples: 'teaching methods (pedagogy); fairness, which primarily concerns testing; interest in me; interest in the subject; and global questions such as "How would you rate this teacher in comparison with all others you have had thus far?"' (p.165).

The substantial literature on bias in student evaluations has also been subjected to review and analysis (Centra 1979; Marsh 1984; Howard, Conway and Maxwell 1985) and the weight of opinion is that it is not extensive (Haladyna and Hess 1994). There are some dissenting voices. Their conclusions are based on experimental studies, in two cases using newly developed models. Nimmer and Stone (1991) concluded from two experimental studies that student ratings were affected by lecturers' grading practices (strict or lenient) and that the effect was a function of the time at which ratings were completed. This, however, seems to be contradicted by Pike (1991), who suggests that satisfaction exerts a stronger influence on grades than vice versa. Kishor (1995) developed a model of the processes through which students formed judgements and tested it on a sample of students, though not in relation to actual teachers. He argued that inference plays a strong role in the forming of judgement on teacher performance and that student raters' inferences were partly contaminated by their implicit theories of what constitutes a good instructor. From information about behaviour they deduced implied traits and went on to infer particular forms of behaviour for which there was no evidence in the information they had been given. Haladnya and Hess (1994) developed a model for detecting and also correcting bias. Through this they detected significant bias in an exploratory study using a sample of 724 students in the assessments of 34 faculty. It was attributable to gender and whether or not students were taking a course as a requirement or as an option. In this case it had led, they concluded, to over-lenient ratings.

Other concerns about the validity of student ratings are to do with the assumptions on which they are based. Overall there seem to be two types of question: first, how confidently characteristics of teacher behaviour or course characteristics can be said to result in desired forms of student learning. Linked with this is the continuing debate about whether a single global score for overall teaching performance can and should be used in student assessments, in order, for example, not to disadvantage maverick but effective performers when they are used for personnel decisions (see e.g. Abrami 1982; Abrami and d'Apollonia 1991; Hativa and Raviv 1993) or whether it is essential that they are multidimensional on the grounds that teaching itself is multi-faceted (see e.g. Marsh 1991a and 1991b). Much of this debate seems to be focused on teacher performance.

A second issue is the relationship between students' assessments of quality and their own achievements. Early studies by Frey (1973) and Murray (1984) suggest that there is at least a moderate correlation between student ratings and objective measures of student achievement. However, in 1995 Koon and Murray were arguing that studies should be designed 'to investigate the multiple correlation between student ratings of overall teaching effectiveness and a full range of instructional out-come measures (that is measures of student gains)' (p.65). 'Among outcomes that could be but typically are not evaluated in individual courses are abilities in critical-analytic thinking, problem posing and problem solving, synthesizing, aesthetic appreciation, speaking and (often) writing' (p.65).

Elsworth (1994) suggests that, for the most part, indicators or measures of educational quality have been developed in a theoretical vacuum. An important exception to this observation is the Course Experience Questionnaire (CEQ) designed by Ramsden (Ramsden 1991) and the subject of a national trial as part of the Australian Higher Education Performance Indicators Project (Linke 1991). It drew on earlier theoretical and empirical work, in particular the Course Perceptions Questionnaire designed by Ramsden and Entwistle (1981) to measure students' experiences in British higher education institutions. Analysis of the questionnaires showed that when departments and their staff were perceived to offer such things as clearly structured and helpful teaching, 'students were more likely to attempt to structure and understand the content of the syllabus'; conversely they were 'more likely to adopt minimalist approaches narrowly focused on assessment... when their workloads were high and their choices over methods and content of learning restricted' (Ramsden 1991, p.132). Moreover they claimed that interviews with students showed that there was a causal relation between teaching quality and student learning (p.132).

The Course Experience Questionnaire was specifically 'designed to measure differences between academic organisational units (departments and faculties)' (p.132) rather than simply teacher performance. It centred on aspects of good teaching on which students are particularly qualified to comment, such as enthusiasm, concern for and availability to students on the part of teachers, clear organisation and goals, appropriate workload and relevant assessment methods, and the provision of a suitably challenging environment. It aimed to produce 'quantitative data which permit ordinal ranking of units in different institutions, within comparable subject areas, in terms of perceived teaching quality' (132–133).

In this aim it was largely successful (Ramsden 1991). It demonstrated medium to very large, statistically significant, differences between institutions in perceived teaching quality within the four major fields of study represented in the trial and showed that it could give a clear picture of relative teaching quality at the level of major courses such as degree programmes provided by individual academic units. The CEQ was tested in one department of a British university and the results were broadly replicated at this level (J. Richardson 1994).

In Britain, evidence from the large interview-based study currently being conducted at Brunel University suggests that academic scepticism about the validity of student evaluations remains high. The development and use of student questionnaires, though extensive, have been largely institution-specific and not based on systematic or research-informed work. Probably the most significant exception is the work on student satisfaction by the Centre for Research into Quality (CRQ) at the University of Central England, Birmingham. It is being developed within a model of quality in higher education as a function of the perceptions and goals of multiple stakeholders and therefore potentially more multi-faceted than the definitions underpinning the CEQ. Early studies of the criteria of quality espoused by these groups (Harvey, Burrows and Green 1992) show a high level of agreement between students and staff on key criteria of good teaching and conditions for high quality student educational experiences. Criteria of good teaching tend to reflect those identified in the Australian and American instruments. A study by the Centre for Higher Education Studies reports similar findings and goes further to compare student and staff judgements on actual experiences. This shows strong agreement between staff and students about shortfalls on items such as lecturer characteristics, course aims and aspects of institutional culture contributing to effective teaching (CHES 1993). A longitudinal study of student expectations and experience has been undertaken at the CRQ (CRQ 1995).

The JPIWG (CVCP 1995a) expressed a general interest in student questionnaires and in particular the Course Experience Questionnaire. But they considered that further research and discussion were required on the value, effectiveness and potential costs of this approach before it would be possible to contemplate converting it into an indicator of comparative quality. Although they felt it was appropriate for internal institutional use, they were concerned that it might not be able to take sufficient account of institutional diversity. Others (e.g. Yorke 1995) warn about adopting it for cross-subject comparisons (and this was not an aim of the CEQ). This general problem for the use of student questionnaires was also recognised by Murray (1984). He suggested however that it might at least partly be overcome by devising a two-level instrument which includes core items used in all departments together with optional items developed by individual departments and/or faculty members.

This comes back to one of the principles which most writers on the subject of PIs see as essential, that they must be related to purpose and also to policy contexts (Yorke 1995 and see above, e.g. Nedwek and Neal 1994; Sizer, Spee and Bormans 1992). In America, student evaluations have been widely incorporated into mechanisms for the appraisal and promotion of faculty. This may to some extent account for the volume of writing there on issues of validity and bias. The CEQ was developed as part of a range of indicators that might assist government in the allocation of resources. Linkage to rewards and funding is likely to put a premium on validity and precision in PIs and to be more feasible in the context of relatively narrow definitions of effective teaching or good learning outcomes. Their development and use within a quality framework, particularly one focused on internal evaluation for the purposes of quality improvement, might favour a broader and more holistic approach and one where the emphasis was on qualitative rather than quantitative measures, although including both.

Some recent work opens up similar issues, including that of the CRQ whose framework, as we have seen, is that of a multiple stakeholder concept of quality. Yorke reports on a project in which questionnaires to students and staff have been used 'to generate performance data within a quality framework which might be (but does not need to be) built around the concept of Total Quality Management' (Yorke 1995, p.20). Its general purpose is, however, clear: quality enhancement.

Summary

Work on PIs of teaching and learning has been marked by advance and retreat. More rigorous conceptual analysis of what is being measured has been accompanied by more reflection about the theoretical and empirical underpinnings of selected indicators. One consequence is that the concern to produce output measures has been modified. There is more evidence of interest in the relationship between input, process and output, although as we have seen in Chapter 2, trends in the USA are more difficult to read (Ruppert 1994; Banta and Borden 1994).

The shift of interest towards process is partly because of the growing influence of theories that direct attention away from teachers to learners and from individual behavioural to interactive or systemic definitions of quality in education. It is probably also due to the growing importance of the quality movement and the complexities introduced by that. All these trends towards holistic and away from atomistic concepts reinforce questions about the value of individual indicators and perhaps even about the scope for clusters of indicators.

These developments have been enough in themselves to induce caution about selecting PIs. The JPIWG have registered interest in indicators of both value-added and student ratings but have not felt able to take this forward. But of perhaps more importance is the higher education policy environment in which work on PIs has been conducted. Diversity of aims and curricula, large increases and changes in the student population have also hugely increased the problems of finding universally applicable measures. At the same time, the growing importance of market forces for institutions has, if anything, increased the incentives for them to resist the external and summative application of indicators and to use them for their own purposes.

A more complex development has occurred in the quality assessment exercises. Certainly, it is noticeable that the role allowed to indicators in the largely peer-dominated processes of quality audit and quality assessment is at most ill-defined and apparently negligible. However, ironically, the judgement of the quality assessors are fast themselves coming to be used as PIs. Here, as in the research assessment exercises, to be discussed in the next chapter, there are emerging external and public comparative measures, potentially usable for the purposes of discriminatory resource allocation. For the most part, they appear to be advantaging the traditionally more powerful and well resourced. It will be interesting to see what balance of technical and political argument, and from whom, emerges on this issue.

Chapter 4

Performance
Indicators of Research

4.1 Introduction: assessing research performance

The development of PIs of research reflects a complex mixture of technical advances and policy changes. In particular, the place of evaluation of research performance in the UK should be viewed against changes in the funding of universities in recent years. In addition to the more general pressure for the development of PIs, and the increasing importance attached to assessing quality, the period since 1985 has seen four Research Assessment (or selectivity) Exercises (RAEs) which have had a profound effect on the funding of university research and its assessment. The relationship between quality and quantitative indicators of research performance has been the source of considerable and fluctuating debate. It is argued that the importance of quantitative PIs has not developed in the way that seemed likely by the end of the 1980s (Cave, Hanney and Henkel 1995).

In Chapter 2 it was noted that in many countries there was a move towards a more selective funding of research, and that, during a period of declining, or even level, funding, emphasis is placed on the search for more objective aids to use when making more selective funding decisions. Referring to the purposes of PIs, the Sub-Committee on Research Indicators (SCRI) claimed, in its consultative document *Issues in Quantitative Assessment of Departmental Research* (1989), that 'relatively objective data can be used both to assist the forming of judgements and to strengthen their public acceptability' (para.1). The claim was also made that the UK was the first to experience these pressures.

The pressure to evaluate research was felt across the board in the UK in the 1980s and led to an interest in the technical developments in bibliometrics which might permit policy-relevant use of measurement of publications and citations. At that time, the work of Martin and Irvine in analysing the convergence of partial indicators for comparing similar 'big science' facilities attracted wide attention in the UK (Phillips and Turney 1988). As a result of these factors, the ABRC and the Economic and Social Research Council (ESRC) commissioned a series of studies of bibliometric techniques. Each is described in detail in a special edition of the journal *Scientometrics* devoted to developments in the UK (Volume 14, No. 3–4 1988; see Carpenter 1988). The third study produced bibliometric profiles of all publicly financed civil laboratories in the UK including those in universities and polytechnics. The researchers claimed that 'the underlying objective was to test whether reliable research output indicators could be produced which might help the Research Councils and other funding agencies in determining future policies' (Carpenter *et al.* 1988, p.217).

These technical developments were obviously of interest to these responsible for conducting selectivity exercises. At a Science Policy Support Group (SPSG) seminar held in 1987 to discuss university research PIs and the 1985–86 UGC RAE it was pointed out that 'a great deal of published work on research evaluation already exists and that many of the issues raised during the seminar have already been the subject of sophisticated discourse. It is important that the UGC/UFC should be more fully informed of these sources before the next evaluation exercise' (Smyth and Anderson 1987, p.21).

Some of the research councils took considerable interest in developing bibliometric indicators with National Environmental Research Council (NERC) and Agricultural and Food Research Council (AFRC) leading the field (Anderson 1989). There are various overlaps between the pressures on higher education and on the research councils to develop PIs (Cave and Hanney 1990) and PIs will be used by research councils when they evaluate the research centres they support within higher education institutions. The role of indicators was less important in subject reviews undertaken in the second half of the 1980s by the UGC than in the selectivity exercises. Nevertheless, there was still a role for them and although in the Oxburgh Review the earth scientists were asked to undertake citation analysis of their own work, the UGC felt it was important to validate and further analyse the material. The bibliometric study by the Science and Engineering Policy Studies Unit (SEPSU) on the whole supported the decisions which had been made and, according to Anderson (1989), the unpublished report drew some useful methodological conclusions for future bibliometric exercises. These included the need for comprehensive publications lists to be obtained directly from university departments because at least half the output of earth sciences departments was missed by the Science Citation Index (SCI).

There are two main, interweaving, threads in the UK development of PIs for research: the work of the various funding council/CVCP committees dealing with PIs in general; and the four RAEs in 1985–86, 1989, 1992 and 1996. The history and key features of both will be briefly outlined. As seen in Chapter 2.1 the first statement by the CVCP/UGC working group (CVCP/UGC 1986) contained a range of PIs of research but only two, research income and number of research students, were thought appropriate for implementation in 1986–87. These indeed were the two in the second statement (CVCP/UGC 1987a) (and remained the only ones through to the 1995 final edition of *University Management Statistics and Performance Indicators in the UK* (CVCP 1995b).)

The coming together of technical advances and policy requirements for the development of research PIs was especially strong in the creation by the CVCP/UGC PIs steering committee of SCRI. Its membership combined those who had been responsible for developing PIs on behalf of the CVCP/UGC with experts on bibliometrics. This is a good illustration of the development in the late 1980s of a network of groups with overlapping membership which examined the potential role of various research PIs. SCRI had a number of tasks including: encouraging each university to set up an appropriate publications database which could be called upon when necessary; exploring which data on research output might be included in the annual volume of management statistics and PIs; and studying ways in which bibliometric methods might be used to assist judgements about the quality of research. SCRI commissioned SEPSU to conduct a survey of academics' views on quantitative assessments of departmental research. It considered the indicators appropriate for both the annual publication of PIs and the more periodic assessments and concluded:

> For annually published quantitative data on departmental research, only bibliometric data on the volume of research output found much favour among the respondents to this survey. The degree of favour depended on the extent to which the data were collected in a form that recognised the particular circumstances of individual disciplines. For periodic assessments carried out by the relevant experts, as opposed to annually published data that might be misinterpreted by those lacking the necessary knowledge, respondents agreed that esteem indicators had a useful role to play. However, there was virtually no support for the inclusion of citations in the annual data series, and little support for their use in periodic assessment. Respondents sent a firm message that, at departmental level, citation analyses added nothing to peer review. (SEPSU 1991, p.v)

As mentioned in Chapter 2.1, the CVCP, under the auspices of SCRI, started an annual publications survey but only the first was published (CVCP 1993). Details of this are given in Section 4.2. The work of SCRI was subsumed by the Joint Performance Indicators Working Group (JPIWG). Whereas the PCFC's work on PIs influenced thinking in other aspects of the JPIWG's analysis very little attention had been given to PIs of research in the PCFC reports on research (Roith 1990) or PIs (Morris 1990).

The JPIWG's primary concern was stated as being 'to ensure that indicators of research are available to institutions that assist them in the management of their research output' (CVCP 1995a para.3.1). It considered two tasks related to research: '(i) how data from the 1992 Research Assessment Exercise might be converted into performance indicators, and (ii) the development of a series of indicators which could be produced independently of future RAEs' (para.3.2). The JPIWG stressed the desirability of PIs being derived from activities which had had some element of peer-review, for example, papers in peer-reviewed journals or conferences, research grants and research studentships. One of the greatest difficulties faced was in applying one of its general themes, value for money, to research PIs.

The full list of its proposed indicators is given in Table 4.1. The HEMS Group decided, however, that implementation of the PIs of research, which would involve extra data collection rather than relying on HESA, could not commence in 1996.

Table 4.1 Research indicators

R1	Books published per member of academic staff by research unit of assessment
R2	Books edited per member of academic staff by research unit of assessment
R3	Short works per member of academic staff by research unit of assessment
R4	Refereed conference papers per member of academic staff by research unit of assessment
R5	Articles in academic journals per member of academic staff by research unit of assessment
R6	Reviews of academic books per member of academic staff by research unit of assessment
R7	Other public output per member of academic staff by research unit of assessment
R8	Total publications per member of academic staff by research unit of assessment
R9	FTE postgraduate research students per member of academic staff by research unit of assessment
R10	Value of research council/British Academy grants per member of academic staff by research unit of assessment
R11	Value of research grants from charities per member of academic staff by research unit of assessment
R12	Total external research income per member of academic staff by research unit of assessment
R13	Ratio of total external research income to funding council research grants/funds allocated per member of academic staff by research unit of assessment
R14	Income earned from patents and licences (by institution)

Source: CVCP 1995a

The Research Assessment Exercises

The major cuts in recurrent grant announced in 1981 were followed in May 1985 by Circular Letter 12/85 (*Planning for the Late 1980s*, UGC 1985a) in which the UGC made clear that there was to be evaluation so as to facilitate selective funding, which was necessary to 'maintain the quality' of university research. Universities were asked to give details of their research plans and priorities, their planning machinery and research profiles of individual subject areas (by cost centre). This last section specifically requested details of: the numbers of research staff and research students; the titles of not more than five recent books or articles, or other comparable examples of research achievement, which the university would regard as typical of the best of its research in the subject area; any explanation or justification of priorities in terms of likely economic or social benefit, advancement of the discipline, or in any other terms; and any other relevant indicators of research performance. The judgement reached by the UGC panels were declared in 1986 and determined the new (JR) element of research funding for universities – previously funding had not been so explicitly identified. Most of the remaining research money was related to staff and student numbers (SR). The judgement factor appears to have been based on 'peer reviews', the universities' own submissions, 'new blood' posts awarded to departments and the advice of external advisers and 'a wide range of other indicators' (letter, chairman of UGC, 1 August 1986).

The report from the UFC on the 1989 RAE states that the 1985–86 exercise 'was probably the first attempt in any country to make a comprehensive assessment of the quality of university research. It is not surprising that it was imperfect and came in for criticism' (UFC 1989c, p.2).

Compilations of criticisms were reported by Smyth and Anderson (1987) and Phillimore (1989). The latter, having set out the full list of desirable characteristics for PIs contained in the 1986 CVCP/UGC working group report, comments: 'it is not unfair to say that the UGC exercise in 1985–6 singularly failed to meet any of these criteria with the indicators it purportedly used' (p.266). A former chairman of the UGC is reported as saying that, as usual, the UGC had got it 80 per cent correct. Chartres (1986) said of the 1986 exercise that 'while the basis of advice has been more open and perhaps less imprecise, assessment based on a combination of research income and "judgement" is essentially the same as in the past'. As in 1981 the exercise can be criticised on the grounds of lack of consistency in criteria, anonymity and incomplete data. The exercise in no way met the criteria for proper peer review; had it done so the costs involved would have been very high.

In 1986 the UGC ranking exercise was opposed by a majority of academics according to a poll conducted for the *Times Higher Education Supplement* (5 June 1987). Questions have been raised, however, about the extent to which even the inadequate procedures laid down were followed. Zander (1986) suggests that it would have been impossible, in the time available, for the members of the UGC subcommittees to have read the five publications submitted by each cost centre. There are also suggestions that some cost centres submitted more evidence than the UGC requested and so different centres were considered on different grounds. The names of the people who acted as assessors or who provided additional information to the UGC subcommittees were not known.

Each of the subsequent RAEs saw debate about, and changes in, the data it was thought appropriate to collect. A comprehensive review of the criticisms of the 1986 exercise was undertaken and included in a consultative document, Circular Letter 15/88 (UGC 1988a). Nearly 300 responses were received and taken into account in the planning of the 1989 RAE. Circular Letter 45/88 (UGC 1988b) stated:

The main criteria to be used in determining ratings are:
(i)   publications and other publicly identifiable output;
(ii) success in obtaining research grants and studentships;
(iii) success in obtaining research contracts;
(iv) professional knowledge and judgement of advisory group and panel members, supplemented where appropriate by advice from outside experts.

The general approach will therefore be that of an informed peer review. (para.9)

This statement is problematic because judgements of panel members are listed together with those other items which are not peer review as we understand the term. This issue will be discussed at more length in Section 4.7.

The ratings were given on a five point scale (with the lowest being 1) using a common standard of interpretation across all units of assessments. The purpose of the selectivity exercise was to produce new JR values to influence the distribution of the research element of UFC funding from 1990–91. The proportion of research funding to be allocated selectively was raised by increasing the ratio of JR to SR from approximately 1:1 to 2:1.

Certainly compared with 1986 it seems fair for the 1989 UFC report (UFC 1989c) to say of the 1989 exercise: 'the level of criticism of the exercise has been muted' (para.19). It discussed some of the criticisms that were made. For example, the composition of some of the advisory groups and panels caused concern: 'the extent to which work by, say, younger researchers in the smaller universities would be known to and properly understood by older senior staff from the larger, more prestigious universities is at least for consideration' (para.33).

Criticism of the cost of the 1989 exercise was anticipated and was therefore estimated by means of a survey of eight universities. The total cost was thought to be £4.1 million, most of which was 'opportunity cost'. Some of the report's other points included: the discrimination against applied research; the very limited extent to which the exercise was formative; the extent to which the exercise was retrospective and underplayed the opportunities to demonstrate attempts at future improvement; and the unreliable nature of some of the publications data. The report stated that the numerical totals of publications were not found to be helpful 'and featured very little in the assessment process...the data were considered to be too unreliable and, where reliable, said nothing about quality of output' (UFC 1989c, para.23). The assessment panels did rely heavily on the publications data, but on the qualitative rather than the quantitative aspects. It was admitted that there was insufficient time to read the two items nominated by each staff member, but at least the procedure was an improvement on the five publications per cost centre allowed in 1986. As Phillimore (1989) noted, critics of the 1986 exercise advocated greater use of publications data. Such critics might reasonably have anticipated more use of numerical data about publications. With respect to publications data, and to research income – especially research contracts – the impression was created by the criteria set out in Circular Letter 45/88 (UGC 1988b) that the peer review process would be informed by quantitative data to a greater extent than turned out to be the case.

The subjects where there has been most criticism of the 1989 exercise include those in the humanities and social sciences. Historians, for example, according to the *Times Higher Education Supplement* (1 December 1989), were critical of the use of bibliometrics. The analysis above suggests that, if anything, too little use was made of quantitative indicators. The other main point made by the History at the Universities Defence Group, and some other subject groups, is that the singling out of research for evaluation created an absurdly one-sided view of the work of academics. Their argument that teaching should also be assessed was shown in Chapter 3 to be an increasingly widely shared view.

For the 1992 RAE, in addition to each academic nominating two publications, information on all publications was requested under a range of headings. The exercise was brought forward a year to allow the results to inform the first funding allocations of the new funding councils. This meant the former polytechnics were included for the first time and virtually the entire research funding was determined according to the RAE with none of this research money being received by institutions for its units of assessment graded as 1.

Despite, and sometimes because of, the various changes in procedure intended to improve the RAEs the criticisms have continued. Historians continue to feel the processes are particularly inappropriate for them (O'Brien 1994). The criticisms, however, are more broadly based. In some cases introducing assessment in itself has an effect – by, for example, encouraging a transfer market amongst highly rated academic stars. In other cases, the criteria thought to be used are, in some fields, narrowing the type of research that is regarded most highly, penalising radical research, affecting publication patterns, and downgrading the importance attached to applied research. Many of the criticisms made by chemists were drawn together in a report published by the Royal Society of Chemistry – see Table 4.2. They find echoes in other disciplines, including economics (Harley and Lee 1995) and sociology (Warde 1996), and the whole policy of having RAEs is subject to strong attack: 'The fact that they are so widely criticised, distrusted and cynically manipulated, represents a grave challenge to the legitimacy of authority in our scientific community' (Ziman 1994, p.16).

**Table 4.2 The opinion of chemists
about research assessment**

What research assessment currently does	What research assessment should do
Hinders collaboration and multi-disciplinarity	Reward collaboration and multi-disciplinarity
Rewards work within one's specialism	Foster breakout into new activities
Leads to secrecy and competition	Reward communication and information sharing
Results in poaching and head-hunting to boost ratings	Encourage cross secondments between universities and with industry
Penalises industrial collaborations	Reward industrial collaborations
Distorts departmental strategies resulting in uniformity and covergence	Reward and promote diversity

Source: Royal Society of Chemistry 1995

The main changes for the 1996 RAE are that only four publications per academic are being requested and grades 3 and 5 have both been split into two. Furthermore, following a legal case brought by the Institute of Dental Surgery over the grade it received in 1992, each of the panels has produced a statement of criteria it will use in 1996. Pressure is beginning to increase for units graded 2 not to receive a share of the research funds (see for example a recent report from the learned societies – National Academies Policy Advisory Group 1996).

The nature of research performance

Before considering specific research PIs it is important to note some of the various debates that surround the notion of 'research performance'. Phillimore (1989) proposes four aspects of 'performance' and matches the relevant indicators to them: output (publications); impact (citations); quality (research council grants; research studentships; awards, prizes, honours, etc.; committee memberships; journal editorships; peer judgement; reputation); utility (external income; patents, licences; contract/external staff). Although some of these points are taken into account in the discussion of specific indicators, there is possibly more agreement about the validity of most research PIs than there is about those for teaching. There is some unease in the social sciences and arts and humanities that a system of indicators designed to show research performance in the natural sciences is being inappropriately applied to them (see, for example, Minogue 1986; O'Brien 1994). There is some overlap between this argument and that advanced by Elton (1988b) that scholarship forms a third strand in the activities of universities, and is a vital link between teaching and research. Scholarship, the new interpretation of what is already known, is least prevalent in applied sciences and most common in the humanities. The idea that scholarship should be treated separately was considered but explicitly rejected in the Kingman Report (1989) but powerful calls are still made for its role not to be overlooked (see, for example, Kogan 1994).

In the next four sections the main research PIs are examined in turn: publications, citations, research income and number of research students. Then a section reviews the more speculative interest that is currently focusing on the possibility of developing PIs for the non-academic impact of research. Finally, peer review of research is examined.

4.2 Output, measures: publications, licences and patents

The publications of a department have always been an important informal indication of research activity. This is shown in, for example, the lists of publications which often figured in many universities' annual reports in both the UK and the USA. The indicator of research output has been formulated in many ways, some of which represent attempts to improve its usefulness and overcome the perceived disadvantages of previous formulations. In order to calculate the indicator, decisions have to be made concerning: the types of publication to be included; the weightings to be given to the various types of publication; sources of information about the publications; whether to count the total publications for the department or for each academic member of staff; and the appropriate period over which to count. Each of these issues is examined in turn followed by a discussion of the possible policy uses of the PIs and the costs involved.

Technical issues and developments

These technical issues become particularly controversial when the PIs form a potential element in resource allocation or when they affect public reputations, rather than remaining a purely academic exercise. As an illustration of the consequences of their use, one study of British university publication rates was not published in the journal for which it was originally accepted for fear of possible litigation (Crewe 1987).

There are two broad approaches to the types of publication to include. Either a range of publications is examined or the study is limited to journals. If a range of publications is used then it could include: books, journal articles, conference papers, reviews (for example, Cartter 1966), contributions to edited books (for example, Gillett 1986; UFC 1989c). Crewe (1987) revised his paper to include contributions to books edited by British political scientists but found that it made little difference to his original rankings.

The CVCP/UGC working group originally suggested that 'publications should be categorised by type, for example, book, contribution in major/minor journal, broadcast talk, etc.' (CVCP/UGC 1986 Appendix 2, p.5). This approach continued in the two trial exercises conducted by SCRI. In autumn 1988, all university departments of chemistry, economics, history and physics were asked to provide comprehensive lists of their published output for the calendar year 1987. Universities were given 11 headings under which to put the number of publications of the department: papers in academic journals; letters in academic journals; articles in professional journals; articles in popular journals; books; edited books; published official re-ports; contributions to edited works; contributions to confer-ence proceedings; other publications; contributions in other media. The work of SCRI influenced both the long list of possi-ble publication categories used in the 1992 RAE and the 20 categories used in the CVCP's first annual survey listed below:

1. Authored books.
2. Edited books.
3. Short works.
4. Conference contributions, refereed.
5. Conference contributions, other.
6. Departmental Working Papers.
7. Edited works: contributions.
8. Editorships: journal.
9. Editorships: newsletter.
10. Journal letters, notes, etc.
11. Academic journal papers.
12. Professional journal papers.
13. Popular journal papers.
14. Official reports.
15. Review articles.
16. Reviews of single academic books.
17. Other publications: research.
18. Other publications: research equivalent.
19. Other media: research.
20. Other media: research equivalent.

Source: CVCP N/93/51 Annexe 1

Different subjects seem to favour different forms of publication, and these preferences are related to the varying nature of sub-jects – as discussed in Biglan's (1973) typology. The JPIWG undertook a study of the statistical relationship between the research ratings awarded by panels in the 1992 RAE and the data provided to those panels. The results led JPIWG's 1994 consult-

Table 4.3 The indicators proposed for different subject groups

Indicators	Medical subjects	Sciences	Computing and engineering	Social sciences	Arts and humanities perform arts	Art, design media studies
Books	–	–	–	X	X	X
Edited books	–	–	–	X	X	X
Short works	–	–	X	X	X	X
Refereed conference papers	–	–	X	–	–	–
Articles in academic journals	X	X	X	X	X	X
Review of academic books	–	–	–	X	X	–
Other public output	–	–	–	–	–	X
Total publications	X	X	X	X	X	X
FTE postgraduate research students	X	X	X	X	X	X
Value of Research Council/ British Academy Grants	X	X	X	X	X	X
Value of research grants from charities	X	–	–	–	–	–
Total research income	X	X	X	X	X	X

Source: JPIWG 1994, para.3.44

ative document to suggest that different indicators should be collected for different subjects and this was presented in tabular form, reproduced in Table 4.3. Following the consultation, however, the JPIWG decided against advocating different indicators for different subjects.

Many assessments of publications, especially in science and engineering and in some social sciences, are compiled from journal articles alone: for example, Frame (1983) for sciences and mechanical engineering; Jones *et al.* (1982) for biological sciences; Drew and Karpf (1981) for physics, history, mathematics and chemistry; Laband (1985), Johnes (1986a), Liebowitz and Palmer (1984) and Bell and Seater (1978), Harris (1989), for economics; Cox and Catt (1977) for psychology; Rogers and Scratcherd (1986) for anatomy and physiology.

The analysis of journals can involve a variety of techniques irrespective of whether a range of publications or journals alone are considered. Crewe (1987) included all the journals in which British political scientists had published, which amounted to almost 200, whereas Knudsen and Vaughan (1969) used three leading journals and Cox and Catt used only the 13 published by the American Psychological Association. Glenn and Villemez (1970) included journals on the basis of their questionnaire described below. Drew and Karpf, and Liebowitz and Palmer included those journals with the highest average number of citations per article i.e. those with the greatest impact. Harris scored the journals according to the advice of several panels of economists. Some studies, for example, Frame, included all the journal articles appearing in various indexes. A PI could even be devised from the ratio of publications in Science Citation Index/Social Science Citation Index (SSCI) journals to publications in non-SCI/SSCI journals (Spaapen and Sylvain 1994).

There are many technical problems involved in devising a satisfactory method of assessing publications. A wide range of publications creates problems of scoring the various types of publications and implies that all journal articles are of equal worth. Including only a narrow range of 'top' journals may mean that books are ignored and that those who concentrate on specific fields are penalised. There is also the problem of favouritism in journal publishing practices, although Crewe (1987) could find very little evidence of this.

It is thus clear that many authors use an implicit quality weighting system (1 for recognised journals, zero for omitted ones). Some take quality adjustment further even when the count is limited to journals. Glenn and Villemez (1970) used six different scores for the various journals included. Others, for example, Drew and Karpf (1981) or Johnes (1986a), made no distinction among the leading journals (20 in each case) that they included. Some studies consider the number of pages (using a formula to take account of differing page sizes and, sometimes, differing average length of articles in the various journals) in addition to the number of articles produced. Bell and Seater suggested, however, that, 'it seems that the article and page methods are virtually identical' (1978, p.608). Crewe also found little difference between the rank ordering based on the aggregate page length of all publications and that based on the number of publications. Usually a scoring mechanism has to be devised to weight the various types of contributions (see, for example, Crewe 1987; Glenn and Villemez 1970; Harris 1989; Knudsen and Vaughan 1969; Rasmussen 1985). Some of these can be fairly sophisticated; for example, Glenn and Villemez weighted the score given to a sociology department for its published books (if they were reviewed in the *American Sociological Review*) according to the average quality of the journal articles of the department. This was measured by asking sociologists to assess the importance of various journals in which the department's articles appeared and scoring accordingly.

The importance of the weighting issue is demonstrated in the study by G. Johnes (1990) of research output in UK Departments of Economics over the period 1984–1988. This study was commissioned by the Royal Economic Society and prepared in connection with the UFC's 1989 evaluation of research. Johnes identified four different measures of staff input and 30 measures of departmental research output, based upon alternative weighting schemes. This yielded a total of 120 measures of per capita research output. Examination of the rankings produced by each measure showed that the 40 departments concerned can be broken down into a group of 14 whose ranking was fairly insensitive to the weighting system used, and a larger group of 26 where the ranking fluctuated violently. For example, the Department of Economics at Brunel was ranked fourth in the weighting scheme most favourable to it and 39th in the least favourable. The study illustrates the importance of choice of weights and the potential dangers of manipulation of them.

The types of publications included influence (and, as Bell and Seater (1978) show, can be influenced by) the source of information used to count the number of publications produced by each department. Various methods are used to calculate productivity: abstracts, indexes, self-reporting, examination of the journals, books reviewed in leading journals, etc.

Most studies give greater attention to the score for each member of the department than to the departmental total, but some (for example, Jones *et al.* 1982 in a major American multidisciplinary study and Rogers and Scratcherd 1986) count only the latter.

Crewe and many of the American studies suggest that there is often quite a high correlation between rankings based on total departmental publications and reputational rankings (for example, Cartter 1966; Jones *et al.* 1982) but not such a good correlation when the publications per capita are considered. This suggests that the per capita method has an advantage in presenting a picture that is not distorted by size.

If the generally more satisfactory approach of counting publications per capita is to be used it raises the difficulty of who exactly should be classed as a member of the department. What, for example, is the position of research staff? Various authors (see, for example, Ziman 1989; Hare and Wyatt 1988) question the appropriateness of per capita figures when, according to Lotka's law a high proportion of output comes from a small number of researchers. Crewe (1987) showed however that this did not have a major impact on the ranking of government departments, and, anyway, could be discounted if necessary. Publications with more than one author can have their score divided, as for example by Laband (1985) and Crewe (1987), or, if the authors are in different institutions, each institution can gain the full score (see, for example, Glenn and Villemez 1970). In the SCRI trial exercise attempts were made to take account of the distortions introduced by multiple authorship of publications: universities were asked to count both on a whole and on a fractional basis. The latter is regarded as the most appropriate form of analysis but is time consuming and difficult logistically because of the volume of data. It was therefore thought unlikely 'that publications will be fractionated when the full publications database is established' (Anderson 1989, p.105).

Most studies credit the department of which the author was a member when the publication appeared but some, for example Bell and Seater, or Laband, credit the Department at which the author is currently based. However, when Bell and Seater compared their approach with that of Niemi (1975), who researched at much the same time with a similar coverage, but attributing articles to the department at which the author was based at the time of publication, they found the results were similar. In its 1989 research selectivity exercise the UFC was keen to check on any changes in staff compared with those for whom the production figures related. In its report on the exercise it recognised that attributing all the output to the department at which the author was based at the 'census date would have the added benefit of giving due weight to departmental endeavours to improve the level and quality of research activity' (UFC 1989a, para.40).

The period over which publications are counted also varies greatly, ranging from 13 years in Laband (1985) to only one year in the study by Gillett (1986). For the 1989 exercise the preceding five years were considered but in the 1996 RAE recognition was given to the fact that a longer period is more appropriate in some subjects than others.

Policy use

There is considerable debate over the appropriateness of using research outputs as a PI to influence funding or policy. According to Gillett (1986), with reference to the UK, publications provide 'the most valid, fair and direct way to compare the research performance of departments' (p.4). In a 1989 study of various PIs Gillett concluded that only those based on journal peer review, i.e. articles in journals, constitute PIs that are capable of yielding a reasonably valid measure of departmental performance. Yet the measurement of publications has only begun fairly recently. The ranking of doctoral programmes by the American Council on Education (ACE) carried out by Cartter (1966) and Roose and Andersen (1970) were primarily reputational rankings (although Cartter provided publication assessments in a few subjects). These rankings led to many attempts to develop objective rankings of departments based on publications and to compare with and improve on the subjective reputational rankings. Cox and Catt (1977) found that 'subjective measurements based upon "reputation" and "opinion" are intuitively unsatisfying, and our study showed that there can be large and dramatic differences [between them and] ratings based on objective measurement of productivity' (p.808).

Publication of the 1986 UGC research rankings also encouraged the preparation of research output measures, which were set alongside the UGC rankings. These exercises indicated considerable divergences, particularly in the humanities and social sciences – see for example, Sheppard *et al.* (1986) for German, or Gillett (1986) for psychology. Crewe (1987) also concluded that the correlation between the UGC rankings and departmental publications rates was 'at most, patchy'. Harris (1986) noted that the UGC rankings have proved to be more acceptable in the sciences and engineering but, even here, Rogers and Scratcherd (1986) produced objective rankings based on publications in anatomy and physiology that differ strongly from the UGC rankings. Frame, too, in America, suggested that quantitative evaluations, especially those based on publications and citations, had advantages over reputational rankings in science and engineering. The various attempts at producing research output measures in the UK in 1986 were described and discussed at the Science Policy Support Group (SPSG) seminar on the 1986 research selectivity exercise (Smyth and Anderson 1987) and were analysed by Phillimore (1989). He listed the characteristics of each study, which displayed considerable variations in the criteria used.

The UGC rankings were not entirely reputational but were also based on an assessment of five publications for each cost centre and many other factors. In so far as emphasis was placed on the five representative research publications, it has been strongly argued that the use of such a technique is faulty, and that total publications provide a better PI of research. According to Phillimore (1989), this was common ground amongst all the critics. Gillett (1986) shows how the system of providing five publications favoured larger departments and that the UGC attempted to hide this. In rebuttal of this proposition Sizer told the SPSG meeting that the demand for a list of five works was mainly intended to identify weaker centres, some of which could not even muster this many publications for scrutiny (*Times Higher Education Supplement*, 4 December 1987). Rankings based on total departmental publication output rather than per caput output are at least open about the impact of size. Rogers and Scratcherd (1986), for example, have argued that: 'The measurement of research activity by output is direct, open and fair. By introducing a heavy reliance on conspicuous expenditure and on personal judgements of the worth of particular types of research, the UGC has substituted a complicated, hidden process' (p.2).

The attention paid by the UGC to these various criticisms has been noted. A more sophisticated approach was adopted in asking for information about publications in Circular Letter 45/88 (UGC 1988b). Each relevant staff member was invited to nominate up to two books, book chapters or journal articles and publications considered to be of major significance in the field could be marked with an asterisk. Each department was also asked to submit totals for each of the three publications categories. Staff were also requested to list, if appropriate, not more than two other forms of public output. Possible examples of such output were given: computer software/languages; conference proceedings; engineering designs; musical compositions; paintings/sculptures; patents; copyrights; licence agreements; translations of published work from other languages.

In the count of total departmental publications in the three main categories no attempt was made to fractionate the publication counts according to the number of co-authors. Precautions were taken to ensure that publications were not 'double counted' (e.g. where staff in the same department were co-authors) and publication counts were expressed per staff member. As we have seen in the 1992 RAE an extensive amount of information about publications and other outputs was collected. However, HEFCE's 1993 report on the 1992 RAE explained that generally limited use was made of the lists of publications for various reasons including that 'it cannot be stressed too much that the Exercise was concerned with quality rather than quantity' (HEFC 1993d Report, para.23) and the 1996 RAE has moved away from collecting full lists of publications.

Whatever limitations exist on the use of publication lists within the RAEs, publications can provide useful information to policy makers. Frame (1983) argued that quantitative indicators could enable managers to make fine-tuned adjustments to research and development efforts. Crewe (1987) suggested that by discounting the most productive 20 per cent of a department's staff, a measure could be obtained of the collective strength of a department and that departments with the strongest collective strength should be given priority by the UGC, since individually strong members of other departments could be supported by individual grants. Johnes (1986a) claimed that the value of publications as a PI is that 'it points to those factors which enhance research productivity' (para.7). These factors, which will be of interest to policy makers, include optimal staffing levels, library stocks and staff–student ratios. Hare and Wyatt (1988) claimed that the factors determining departmental research output were not well known and it could be dangerous to pursue major restructuring policies without such knowledge. PIs could, as Johnes has shown, be useful in identifying such factors and Harris and Kaine (1994) measured the relationship between individual productivity of Australian economists, as measured by publications, and the preferences and perceptions of researchers on a range of issues. Their results imply that research performance 'is more a function of individual motivation than resource support' (p.191).

SEPSU produced the first detailed analysis of how university departments spend money on research. The author of the report, Peter Collins, insisted that the findings 'nail forever the idea of economies of scale in research – the notion, which has driven a succession of policies for rationalising science departments, that the large departments are more productive than small ones' (Ince, *Times Higher Education Supplement*, 12 October 1990). Although there is a threshold below which a department cannot be viable, being in a bigger department does nothing to provide researchers with more support staff, capital spending or other inputs which size is meant to ensure. Furthermore, several projects at the Science Policy Research Unit (SPRU) used bibliometric methods to examine some of the factors influencing research productivity that are relevant to the current policy of concentrating resources. Hicks and Skea (1989) for example

investigated the research productivity of departments of physics in the wake of the restructuring of earth science departments
and the Edwards Report (1988) *The Future of University Physics*.
They concluded that: 'on the one hand there appears to be
evidence that, overall, larger departments are more productive,
on the other hand, this dependence is extremely weak and can
easily be explained by departmental characteristics not related
to size' (p.31). However, evidence from Johnes and Taylor
(1990b) suggests that a statistical analysis of the results of the
1989 research selectivity exercise demonstrates that economies
of scale exist in research. This finding is examined, and questioned, in Chapter 4.7.

In Australia the policy of concentrating research resources in
economics in research centres was examined by Harris (1989).
His study of research output revealed that, once allowance was
made for the greater research time available in research centres,
they were not any more productive. Similarly Ziman states, 'The
sheer visibility of a large unit or institution often gives an
impression of overall quality that does not survive detailed
examination. Expected economies of scale and scope are often
negated by human factors' (1994 para.44). Detailed research in
Norway does not in general support the view that faculty in
large departments will be more productive than their colleagues
in smaller ones, although there are exceptions including in
medicine (Kyvik 1995).

Blume and Sinclair (1973) showed that those engaged on
theoretical work were more likely to gain recognition. The inclusion of patents, licences and copyrights is particularly important as a way of ensuring that adequate recognition is given to
departments whose work is largely orientated towards practical
rather than theoretical work. However, there are many technical
difficulties with devising such indicators and the JPIWG suggested that patents did not form a satisfactory basis for PIs.
Nevertheless, it did recommend that a PI be based – at institutional level – on the income from patents and licences.

It is argued that even though some publication rankings take
some account of quality (for example, by counting articles only
in top journals; by using different weightings; by counting
books reviewed only in top journals; or by using the citations
impact of journals) they are not a real measure of the quality of

research carried out by a department. It is difficult to see how publication counts can ever give due weight to seminal articles. There is also a danger that a concentration on the number of publications produced will lead to an over-production of poor quality articles. Such a fact was highlighted by Collini (1989) in the article *Publish and Be Dimmed*. Interestingly, this does not seem to have happened in Norway even where money is linked to the publications produced. More fundamental questions are often raised about the extent to which publications are a valid reflection of scientific achievement (see, for example, Gibbons and Georghiou 1987; Phillips 1989). Furthermore, some of the results of rankings based on publications have been so unexpected (for example, Robey's (1979) study of American politics departments) that they have weakened the credibility of publications as a measure of activity.

With a few exceptions – for example, Rasmussen (1985) and Monash University (Baldwin 1995) – publications rankings have not been used much in providing intra-institutional comparisons. As many have shown (see Frame 1983; Drew and Karpf 1981, and Smith and Fiedler 1971), different subjects have different publication rates. This suggests the need for a concerted, system-wide approach to defining and calculating the PI. Furthermore, publication practices vary widely between different fields of the same subject.

Our discussion has left open the important practical question of the cost of preparation of comparative data. However it is clear that most institutions presently collect data on publications for their own records. There is therefore no reason why it could not be processed according to agreed procedures and collected centrally, although detailed instructions are needed to ensure consistency. This method has the disadvantage of involving self-reporting. An alternative approach is to use abstracting or equivalent services, though the cost of doing so would be greater.

In certain subjects, including political science (*Times Higher Education Supplement*, 10 November 1989), there was unease about the accuracy of the publications figures produced in the 1989 selectivity exercise using the self-reporting method. The UFC report stated: 'it has become apparent that the assumptions of honesty and veracity was not always justified and in one or two subject areas, at least, it would seem that deliberate "misre-porting" occurred' (UFC 1989c, para.24). The creation of an annual database of publications as part of the regular PIs would help overcome this problem, but as we have seen the technical difficulties involved in achieving this are considerable.

4.3 Measuring quality/impact

The case for using citations

Perhaps the most important objection to the use of a quantity index as a measure of research performance is that the number of articles published is only a measure of quantity and, as a result, the relative quality of articles is ignored. What is required therefore is a means of adjusting the number of articles publish-ed for their relative quality or impact.

One such method of impact adjustment is to count the num-ber of citations which are obtained by a department or individ-ual over a given time period. It has been argued by many authors that citations provide an objective way of assessing the relative quality or, more precisely, the impact or influence of research output (see, for example, Laband 1985 and Moed *et al.* 1985).

Citations data are collected by the Institute for Scientific Information (ISI) and published annually in the Science Cita-tions Index (SCI). Data are collected on citations of books and articles from over 5200 journals and information is provided on citation counts which include, for each author, the number and source of each citation and, for each journal, the number of times the journal is cited and the average number of citations an article published in a particular journal will receive (the journal's impact factor). This database has been the source of information for most of the citation studies carried out. However, as Field *et al.* (1992) discovered when analysing citation counts in two fields of applied professional knowledge, continuous education and management education, the ISI indices are heavily weighted towards North American sources and need supple-menting for use in the UK.

The economic basis of using a citation as an indicator of quality lies in the analogy with market signalling behaviour (Laband 1985). During the process of research, relevant literature is surveyed and articles selected for citation on the basis of their relative 'quality'. Quality may be taken as the degree to which the cited articles have made an impact on and improved understanding in the subject area. In this sense, the researcher has revealed a preference for the work cited and this may be taken as an indicator of its quality relative to other publications in the subject area. This procedure entails a presumption that quality depends on the extent to which research is used. As we shall see later such an interpretation has been criticised and Cozzens (1989, p.437) asked whether citations 'measure quality, importance, impact, influence, utility, visibility, all of the above, or something else?'

A number of studies have been carried out to establish empirical evidence on the relationship between citation counts and various measures of quality (Clark 1954; Bayer and Folger 1966; Sher and Garfield 1966; Garfield 1970 and 1977).

This evidence led Garfield to conclude that of all the variables that can influence citation rates, the scientific quality of the work published is the dominant one (Garfield 1979). More recently Narin (1987), another leading proponent of citations analysis, claimed that 'the results of bibliometric studies are seldom counter-intuitive: they usually agree with expert expectations'. Such agreement, however, might still leave room for differing interpretations of the meanings of citations. Nederhof and Van Raan (1989) review the points made by critics such as Mac-Roberts and MacRoberts (1986) that citations are often either rhetoric instruments 'used not to convince others by the strength of arguments but to persuade them by non-logical means' or they are 'ceremonial citations' which are 'references made to individuals whose work has not actually been influential, but to whom the citer feels obliged' (1989, p.427). A comparison was made between bibliometric indicators of productivity and impact and the results of peer review process – the awarding of a *cum laude* degree to graduates in chemistry. Highly significant differences in impact and productivity were obtained between the *cum laudes* and the non-*cum laudes*. It is unlikely there would be differential ceremonial or persuasive value in a citation towards the work of a graduate student. Therefore Nederhof and Van Raan conclude 'even though a percentage of the citations may have been given for perfunctory or negative reasons, these results support the contention that when sufficiently large numbers of papers are examined, citations counts may provide a useful partial indicator of quality, and can be used fruitfully to monitor scientific research' (1989, p.435). More recently Nederhof and Van Raan (1993) were funded by the ESRC to conduct an evaluation of six economics research groups participating in a large national programme. Simultaneous evaluation by peer and by bibliometricians (using both productivity and impact counts) produced complementary and mutually supportive results. 'The participants of the bibliometrics – peer review "confrontation" meeting regarded the exercise as most valuable, with lessons for the Research Council both for the future of research programmes and the form of evaluation used for large awards' (p.353).

The use of citations analysis at Leiden University was referred to in Chapter 2.3. It is described in some detail here to illustrate various points. Moed *et al.* (1985) used the SCI to compile citations data for the faculties of Medicine and Mathematics/Natural Sciences of the University of Leiden in Holland for the period 1970 to 1980. The data handled included 5700 publications and 42,000 citations. The procedure used to count citations was in essence to compile a list of publications and search the SCI for citations.

Moed *et al.* encountered several problems in compiling the data. First, they found that missing data accounted for about ten per cent of the sample, but that, more importantly, these omissions affected several individual departments more seriously than others. An example provided by Moed *et al.* was that a programming error had resulted in all citations to a number of journals being omitted. These accounted for only three per cent of the total sample, yet for the departments which published in these journals up to 50 per cent of the citations were omitted because of this error. This problem is exacerbated when a highly cited article is missed from the publications list.

The second problem encountered by Moed *et al.* was that the research units studied were often small, of the order of two to ten researchers. As a result, relatively few publications were produced and, as a consequence, only a small number of citations recorded. In these circumstances, small errors or omissions can lead to misleading conclusions. Moed *et al.* argued that this problem can be overcome to a large extent by aggregating research groups, but at a high cost of loss of information.

Moed *et al.* finally obtained 99 per cent completeness of citations of articles published from Leiden, and maintain that in order properly to evaluate small university research groups this level of completeness is required. However, much effort was expended to achieve this degree of accuracy; if citation indexes are to be calculated as a matter of course in order to evaluate research performance, they would prove expensive. This is an important consideration when evaluating the usefulness of a PI for the purpose of resource allocation or simply for continuous assessment. Citation studies may however, play a role in major reviews of particular subject areas and in the development of strategies for subject area rationalisation.

The problem of how to allocate citations has been highlighted by Laband (1985). It has been the practice when constructing citation counts to examine the articles published from a source, as in the Leiden study quoted above. Laband maintains that this may not be a good indicator of how well a department is likely to perform in the future, since some of the members of the department who published in previous years may no longer be there, and may have been replaced by new researchers with altogether different levels of research output. He therefore argues that in order to evaluate a department's future performance we need to allocate the citations record of the current members of that department. Future research performance will be related to the present composition of research staff, not to an average over some previous time period.

Numerous schemes for weighting quantity of output have been applied in the literature. One example related to citation indexing is provided by Jones *et al.* (1982) in their assessment of biology research doctorate programmes in the USA, and the method proposed also provides a convenient and computationally less difficult method of calculating citation indices. It has been noted that the SCI provides data on the 'impact factor' of each journal. The impact factor is based on the average number of citations which an article in a particular journal is likely to receive. For each journal the average influence per paper is calculated by working out the average number of times papers in the journal are cited, each citation having first been weighed by the influence weight of the citing journal, i.e. a citation from an influential journal is scored more highly than one from an obscure journal. The influence weight of a journal is in turn defined as 'the weighted number of citations it receives from other journals, normalised by the numbers of references it gives' (Carpenter *et al.* 1988, p.216). High profile journals are likely to have higher impact factors and this can be taken as an indication that articles selected for publication in these journals are of a higher quality.

A citations index can be calculated by multiplying the number of articles published in a particular journal by the associated impact factor. This procedure is computationally much easier than compiling citation indexes by author, since it requires only the number of articles published in each journal. Thus impact factors provide a very convenient method of adjusting research outputs for quality and it may be argued that impact factors are a more objective measure of a journal's quality than the various subjective methods of assessment which have been applied. Anderson found, however, that the complexity of the journal influence weights system often lost the meaning of the citations to many researchers and sometimes produced suspicious results. Phillips and Turney (1988) reported that in relation to the study by Carpenter *et al.* (1988) 'the lack of transparency of the method has made getting to grips with the results take longer than expected, thus partially negating the time advantage of by-passing citations' (p.196).

Analysis of the arguments against using citations

There has been a very considerable and highly technical debate about the use and value of citations analysis. Many of the issues debated are included in Cozzens' (1989) list of factors that might inflate or reduce citations. They include: the effects of timing; journal of publication; self-citation; negative citations; whole, fractional or first name counting; in-group citations; language of publication; obliteration by incorporation; field differences and cross-disciplinary citation patterns. Only some of the major points will be considered below using evidence drawn from, amongst others, Aaronson (1975) and Garfield (1979).

In the SCI, citations are listed by senior or primary authors. The citations of junior authors can be counted, but this requires knowledge of the senior author and a search for citations under the senior author's name. Counting junior citations is again likely to be a time-consuming operation. Further, there is the question of the weighting which should be applied to citations of junior authors.

There are number of reasons why a citations count is 'measured with error'. The presumption underlying citations as an indicator of research performance is that a citation indicates a positive quality in the article cited. This need not always be the case. Some citations are negative or derogatory. In an article somewhat modifying his earlier enthusiasm for citations as a robust measure of quality, Lindsey (1989) referred to the fact that Jensen's controversial paper on racial superiority was one of the most highly cited social science papers. Many of the citations, however, were critical of, or outraged by, the paper primarily because of its political and ethical characteristics. Some citations may be 'sloppy' in the sense that the citing author may not have carried out an exhaustive literature search, or may simply have misunderstood the arguments in the cited article. As part of his rejection of the concept that citations are an indication of quality Woolgar (1991) claims that few of the papers since 1976 criticising citation analysis have cited Gilbert and Woolgar's 1974 refutation of the use of citations as indicators: 'It is as if they themselves have independently discovered the faults of citation analysis for the first time' (p.320).

One particular potential source of measurement error is self-citation. The analogy made above between citations and market signalling behaviour essentially describes a process of peer review. A citation by a peer indicates recognition of quality. Can self-citations be regarded in this light? In general one might say that self-citations should not be included since they do not, in principle, follow the process of peer review. However, the exclusion of self-citations may introduce a potentially serious bias into the construction of an index for scientists who are researching new or innovative areas, since there may be little or no work, other than their own, to be cited. As Porter (1977) points out, 'self-citations could be used to note the most relevant earlier work, or work with which one is most familiar; they could then reflect real influences and contributions' (p.263). Incorrect citations are sometimes given by authors and there can be programming errors made in the SCI. For example in the 1988 Social Science Citation Index the first author of the first edition of this book is incorrectly cited as Cave, S., although the author of the book review in which the citation appears gave the correct name.

Some of these possible sources of error could be eradicated by careful analysis of the data, but, again, the cost of removing even those sources of error which can be identified is likely to be high. However, if these sources of error are not removed, then any index of citations must be treated as random to some degree.

Many writers have maintained that citation indices can be used providing there is no systematic bias involved in the measurement of the index. Garfield (1979) argues that 'sloppy, biased bibliographic practice is a random variable that tends to get cancelled out' (p.70). There are other biasing influences but, in general, these measurement errors do not affect one department more than another and as a result a high citation score indicates high quality.

However, whilst it is correct to say that if such influences are random (and more citations indicate higher quality) then citations scores are unbiased, the point estimate obtained for the citation score tells us little about the possible range of values which the citation score may take allowing for the stochastic nature of the variable. In principle, therefore, in order to be able to imply anything about quality of research on the basis of citations scores we need to know the variance associated with citation indices. We could then say with some degree of confidence that a score from a particular department is statistically different from a score obtained from a different department.

Seminal or primordial research may not receive the number of citations which the quality of the research would imply that it should (see Johnes 1986a; MacRoberts and MacRoberts 1986; Cole and Cole 1972). There are two reasons why this may be the case. First, it is argued that when an idea becomes accepted universally it requires no formal citation. An example provided by Johnes is that of the concept of 'rational expectations' in economics, first proposed by Muth (1961). When referring to 'rational expectations' few writers refer to Muth; they are more likely to refer to later applications of Muth's original idea. This is an example of obliteration by incorporation.

Second, the primordial paper may be difficult to understand, since by definition the research is not known to anybody. Subsequent papers which refine the concept may be quoted more freely. In particular, in the area of natural sciences, the primordial paper may be the discovery of a chemical reaction. Subsequent papers may provide easier methods of carrying out an experiment to demonstrate the reaction and as such may be more likely to be cited.

Cole and Cole (1972) argue that the same may be true for radical work which is again by definition contrary to the main trend of thought in any subject area. As a result radical work may not be quoted often or, alternatively, may receive negative citations.

There are two issues related to the weighting of citations: first, the relative contributions of co-authors and second, the relative weighting of citations from different articles. These points have been mentioned above and therefore only brief comments will be made here.

In case of co-authorship the issue is what weighting should be applied to each author. Should they have equal weighting, implying that both authors contributed equally to the work? Or should the work of one author be weighted more heavily and, if so, on what basis? Additionally what weight should be applied to a co-authored citation relative to a single-authored citation? With respect to journal quality, what weighting do we apply to citations in different journals?

The answers to these questions depend upon the purpose for which the citation index is being derived, and the suitability of any particular weighting scheme must be judged on the basis of prevailing circumstances. What seems certain is that at present we do not have enough information to weight citations in an objective way, and as a result citation counts must be interpreted carefully. The possibility of serious error may be reduced by calculating indices based on various weighting schemes to see how sensitive the outcomes are to changes in the weights.

Thus a number of important theoretical and practical difficulties still exist, and as overcoming these is likely to prove costly and time-consuming, the economic viability of citations indices for concurrent evaluation becomes suspect. Field *et al.* (1992) conclude: 'Our evidence broadly confirms the pessimistic view

of citation counting as a proxy indicator for research quality'
(p.39).

It is also obvious that any bibliometric research involves
considerable cost. Work by SPRU at Sussex University contains
an indication of what is involved (Martin, Irvine and Crouch
1985). The SPRU team was requested by the Advisory Board for
the Research Councils to conduct detailed bibliometric case
studies of two fairly small scientific fields – ocean currents and
protein crystallography. The studies involved a survey of publications and citations in the relevant fields over a period of
years, using the 'manual' method of inspecting selected journals. The results showed how the quantity and 'quality' of UK
research output had fared over time, compared with those of
other countries. It was also possible to compare institutions
within the UK, although in such small fields there are comparatively few research centres. The SPRU team estimate that the
cost of such a study for special fields involving 50 to 100 UK
researchers is of the order of £3000–£4000. Laband's 1985 major
study of 50 US economics departments, which involved collection of citation data for each faculty member, absorbed the time
of two individuals on a virtually full-time basis for three
months. Data collection and preparation for Crewe's 1987 study
of British political science departments, which did not involve
citation data, were comparatively inexpensive – costing less
than £2000. It would be simple to adjust Crewe's study by using
journal 'impact factors' as quality weights. This suggests that
the 'impact factor' approach may be an inexpensive short cut
but the difficulties referred to earlier mean that the method is
unlikely to be widely used.

According to Sizer (1989 p.5–6), SCRI recognised that publication counts provide relatively little information about the
quality of publications and that citation analysis may be undertaken in three distinct contexts:

1. When reviewing the provision of individual disciplines.
2. When undertaking periodic assessments of departmental
    performance, either externally by the UFC and research
    councils, or internally by an institution's planning and
    resources committee and/or research committee.
3. As part of an annual series of management statistics and
    PIs.

SCRI's 1989 consultative document *Issues in Quantitative Assessment of Departmental Research* suggested that citations analysis is 'a partial indicator of the impact of the published output of research, and is capable of generating a variety of useful measures such as citations per paper, numbers of highly cited papers, numbers of uncited papers' (para.4). However, various difficulties were stressed including the delay before the citations record of a paper becomes apparent and the reduced relevance to those disciplines where the typical form of published output is not a paper in a refereed journal. It was there 'open to discussion whether the insights generated by citations analyses are worth the effort and cost of collecting and analysing data' (para.4). The responses to the consultative exercise revealed much scepticism about citations analysis. The JPIWG also emphatically ruled out the use of citations.

In its report of the 1989 research selectivity exercise (UFC 1989a) the UFC was also dismissive of citations analysis and they have not been used in either 1992 or 1996. Despite the lack of enthusiasm for citations analysis it was noted earlier that it was used effectively in the Oxburgh Report on earth sciences (1987). More use of citation analysis as a PI is made outside the UK, including in the USA and Germany.

There have been some studies (for example Collins and Wyatt 1988) showing how citations to patents could form a PI for more applied research.

4.4 Research income

The data needed to compute research income were readily available from USR returns and so it came as no surprise that the 1987 CVCP/UGC statement on PIs (CVCP/UGC 1987a) listed research income per full-time equivalent staff member as one of the indicators to be included in the 1987 list and, as Table 2.2 shows, it remained in the CVCP list of indicators through to the final edition in 1995. However, the use of research income in this way raises a number of difficult issues. Some kinds of research in all disciplines depend less on research income than others. In many cases, more abstract and theoretical work, which often is accorded the greatest prestige, is not so dependent on research income as work requiring experiments or the collection and analysis of large amounts of data.

Second, the process of getting and implementing research contracts diverts academics from what might be more rewarding research activities. There is thus a risk that maximisation of research contract income may promote pedestrian or even routine activity. Success in gaining research contracts, especially in attracting 'repeat purchases', is a sign of relevance or success in the market-place.

One may view the allocation of funds as the outcome which results from departments competing in the market for research income. Viewed in this light the allocation of research income may tell us something about the relative efficiency of the competing products, i.e. the research from different departments. At the same time, research income is an input into the research production process, and should be taken into account in evaluating research productivity.

Using research income as a measure of relative product competitiveness exploits the economic concept of market share. The relative competitiveness of research may be indicated by the willingness of the awarding body to provide funds. The best products therefore obtain the most research income, and as a result the level of research income allocated to a department may be taken as a measure of its relative competitiveness. There are, however, three important qualifications to this line of argument.

Large departments can produce a great deal of research and as such are likely to take a larger share of total research income. When judging performance on the basis of research income obtained it is necessary to make some adjustment for the amount of resources available for obtaining the research income. However any adjustment must avoid ambiguities. For example, departments which are successful in gaining research contracts use the revenue to engage research staff. Standardising for department size by dividing research income by total staff (including those supported by research grants) would be a false measure of the energy and success with which research contracts are sought, because as fast as research funds are added to the numerator, the denominator is increased by the employment of more staff. A more satisfactory approach is required which relates research income to the number of centrally-funded full-time equivalent staff in a department, thus measuring their success per capita in attracting research grants. An alternative approach proposed in the JPIWG's list of research PIs (see Table 4.1) is ratio of external research income to funding council research funding per academic staff member (CVCP 1995a).

The second and related point is the nature of economies of scale in the production of research. Unit costs may vary with department size. If there are economies of scale in the production of research – i.e. if output increased more than proportionately for every increase in resources – this would imply that large departments have a relative cost advantage over smaller departments. Large departments may therefore appear to be performing more efficiently than smaller departments by taking a larger share of total research income than their size might otherwise dictate. Naturally this situation is reversed if there are diseconomies of scale.

This presents a problem in interpreting market share since some departments may be constrained in size in the short run. In the long run, one might expect the forces of competition to generate an equilibrium in the research income market allowing departments to adjust to their optimum size. Once this has occurred market share becomes a more appropriate measure of product competitiveness. If there are no economies or diseconomies of scale then market share will not be distorted by relative cost advantages. Furthermore, identifying those departments who take the largest market share as being the best does not identify those departments who would produce the most from increased resources. Diseconomies of scale would imply that giving greater research income to smaller departments would produce a larger increase in research output than applying the same increase to a larger research department.

Third, the degree of 'competition' differs in each of these markets. Many view grants from research councils as the most prestigious, and they always have the potential of generating publishable research results which will be picked up in research output indicators, whereas research contracts often lead to 'closed' reports. It is thus important to distinguish between sources of income as well as the aggregate amount.

There is, however, an alternative interpretation to the idea that in essence research income is a measure of market share and that relative market share may provide information about the competitiveness of the 'firms' in the market. In this second view, research grant and contract income is seen as an additional input into an institution or department. This extra input should be reflected in higher output. On this view, high research and contract income creates the expectation of more output and the evaluation should be reduced for those producers who fail to achieve better results.

Therefore the use of research income as an indicator of research performance, as was the case in the 1986 and subsequent UGC research selectivity exercises, has attracted criticism (see, for example, Gillett 1989; Hare and Wyatt 1988). Gillett (1989) listed 15 defects in indices based on research income, 'the cumulative effect of which is that the predictive validity of grant-giver peer review is likely to be extremely low' (p.26). Some of the main criticisms include that it is an input measure that provides no information about the quality and quantity of research produced; there are a number of structural factors in the grant allocation scheme which create the 'illusion of validity' of funding decisions; there is an unmerited twofold advantage to grant holders who, with research assistants, ought to be able to produce more papers; departments which concentrate their research effort in areas where grants are in short supply, or the research is comparatively inexpensive, are discriminated against; and inefficient departments might be rewarded and cost-effective ones penalised.

At the SPSG seminar Sizer defended the use of research income in the 1986 UGC exercise and claimed, for example, that information was provided by research councils on research which was funded but considered unsatisfactory and research proposals which were alpha rated but remained unfunded.

Concern was also expressed that in the 1986 exercise subcommittee assessors gave more weight to grants from research councils and charities than to contracts from industry as measures of performance. This operated against more technologically orientated departments with close links with industry. Based on the information (quoted in Chapter 4.1) from the Circular Letter 45/88 (UGC 1988b) Anderson concluded, the

'UGC now make it clear that no distinction is expected' (Anderson 1989, p.148).

The 1989 UFC report on the selectivity exercise (UFC 1989a) shows that the way research income was taken into account was not entirely in line with the impression created in Circular 45/88. The report states that the research income data were

> of considerable importance to the Science, Technology and Medical Panels but of no real significance, even where it existed, for the Arts/Humanities, and of only very limited significance in the Social Sciences. In the main greater weight was given to grant income especially from the Research Councils, and less weight to industrial and commercial contracts. (para.25)

The report later justifies the greater emphasis given to research council grants on the grounds that the focus of the UFC's

> science research funding is towards basic and strategic work; for more applied research, universities are expected to seek funding from other sources, both public and private... Given that the assessment process concentrated very much on the academic quality of published work, it naturally followed that departments with high outputs of good quality pure science scored more highly than departments with a largely applied science bias. (para.38)

It is not surprising, therefore, that there was some initial criticism of the 1989 research selectivity exercise from the technological universities (*Times Higher Education Supplement*, 8 September 1989) with Professor Ashworth, then vice-chancellor of Salford University, suggesting the results reflected the criteria used as much as performance. If it was the original intention of the UFC to give greater attention to grants than contracts, it would have been better had this been made clear in Circular Letter 45/88, rather than the impression created that the bias against applied research in the 1986 exercise was going to be corrected. Furthermore, the bias against applied research to some extent runs contrary to the PIs being developed for the research councils which stress the importance of collaboration with industry and contracts being gained by research centres from the private sector (Cave and Hanney 1990). The 'very limited significance' given to research income in the social sciences is also a matter for concern to those who share with the former chairman of the ESRC, Professor Howard Newby, a belief in the importance of field work and data collection in the social sciences.

Internationally this is seen as an important research PI and was the third most commonly occurring of all PIs at state level in the ten states examined in the USA (R. Richardson 1994). Increasingly success in gaining external research income is being used as a PI to determine government funding of university research in various countries. We have seen this in Australia and it was recently proposed by the Danish Government (Hansen and Jorgensen 1995).

In our first edition we calculated an index of performance based on research and contract income for a natural science cost centre, physics, and human science cost centre, psychology. The aim was to show that the ranking of departments by research income is highly sensitive to whether research income is measured absolutely or on a per capita basis. We also showed that there existed a fairly weak relationship between research income adjusted for department size and the 1986 UGC ranking.

We adopted a similar general approach to analyse the relationship between research and contract income and the UFC evaluations of 1989. A simple regression of the UFC research grading on research income per full-time staff member was carried out for the 14 cost centres at Brunel University. It showed that the relationship is significant (as measured by standard statistical tests) in 10 of the 14 cases, the exceptions being 'other biological sciences', materials technology, education and 'other social sciences'. However, only in four of the ten cases where a statistically significant relationship exists is the relationship strong in the sense that research income per capita contributes substantially to the research grading. These four cases were: general engineering, physics, electrical engineering and chemistry. When staff numbers were introduced as an additional independent variable, the same general pattern was maintained, although not surprisingly the explanatory power of the equation increased.

Thus in general the relationship between the research rankings and research income adjusted for department size did not appear to be strong. One might have expected income from research contracts and grants to have provided a stronger positive relationship with the rankings since one would expect research grants to be allocated to those departments which the UGC/UFC considers best. There is evidence that some UGC subcommittees adopted the approach of viewing research income as an extra input which creates the expectation of higher output and this may contribute to the explanation of the weak relationship between research rankings and research grant and contract income in many cost centres. However, in the statistical analysis of the 1992 RAE conducted by JPIWG quite strong correlations were found although there were variations between subjects as shown on Table 4.3 and discussed in detail by Jim Taylor (1995). In the criteria set out for the 1996 RAE the panels for many units of assessment, for example those in medicine, stress the importance of research income, particularly where based on a peer-review process, as evidence of esteem (HEFCE *et al.* 1995).

4.5 Research students

The number of research students is a measure of the attractiveness of a department or institution to potential research students. Numbers will however depend on availability of grants (and thus on research council policy), and there will be wide variations across disciplines. In the 1989 research selectivity exercise numbers of research students and of successful doctoral thesis submissions were, according to the UFC report, 'thought by many panels to be significant indicators of research quality' (UFC 1989c, para.25). In the statistical analysis of the 1992 RAE undertaken by the JPIWG the following were significantly related to research ratings across the entire subject range although not in all subjects: doctoral students; FTE postgraduate research students; Research Council/British Academy studentships and total research studentships.

In only 11 of the approximately 50 units of assessment included in the analysis was 'none of these four variables significantly related to research rating' (CVCP 1995a, para.3.39). Taylor claims 'the number of full-time equivalent postgraduate research students and research council studentships are together significantly related to research rating in around half the units of assessment. Research students and studentships are particularly important in language-based subjects' (Taylor 1995, p.258). In the criteria for assessment for the 1996 RAE the French panel stated: 'Appropriate credit *will* be given to submissions showing evidence of the recruitment of postgraduate students and the development of postgraduate studies. Credit *may* also be given where there is evidence that research income has been generated' (HEFCE et al. 1995, Annex 51, para.4). This was also seen to be an important PI in countries such as Australia and Norway.

The number of research students is also linked, as a measure of input, with completion rates of research degrees. There is an overlap here with some of the issues of student progression discussed in Chapter 3 and we saw in Chapter 2.2 that this is used as a PI in some of the rankings of graduate schools conducted in the USA.

In 1986 the CVCP/UGC working group had proposed a (non) submission rate for doctorates and other research degrees as the graduate equivalent of the undergraduate wastage rate. This was not adopted into their suite of indicators. Submission rates have been used for many years by the research councils to help determine their allocation of studentships. The Science and Engineering Research Council (SERC) and the Economic and Social Research Council (ESRC) set an optimum length of four years full-time, sponsored, research for a PhD; students who have not submitted their thesis within that period do not receive further financial support. The ESRC developed its use of this PI further, putting a greater onus on the institution training the student to exact submission of a thesis within the four-year period. Amidst strong protests, institutions with ESRC-sponsored students which achieved a four-year submission rate of less than 25 per cent over a three-year period were blacklisted: students were not permitted to take their studentship awards to those institutions. The ratio was raised in steps and is going to be 60 per cent by 1998. Refinements were introduced to allow institutions to put forward selected departments for recognition and so overcome the problem that some institutional blacklistings resulted from a single department with very low completion rates. It has now been recognised that the submission rate measures not only student input but also the institution's admission policy, the quality of its supervisory practices and the level of research activity within its departments.

The outcry over the ESRC's code of practice confirms that the use of the PI is not without problems. The criticisms of the policy have continued; in a letter to the *THES* Skoyles claimed in relation to 'the ESRC's unseen unvalidated measure of depart- mental performance... [that]... if reasoning of the type justifying blacklisting was found in one's PhD... we would be immedi- ately failed' (23 February 1990). Amongst the social sciences departments blacklisted under the 25 per cent rule were those at established, well-regarded research centres such as Univer- sity College, London; Bath; Bristol; Sussex; and, under the 40 per cent rule, Cambridge and Manchester.

Some have argued more generally against the use of wastage rates as a PI on the grounds that success in training postgradu- ates leads to wastage: students are attracted to highly paid jobs in industry before they can complete their degrees. This is a particular problem in areas such as electrical engineering and computer science and it is not clear how it can be satisfactorily incorporated in a PI. SERC, however, have used the PI as a 'tin-opener', in the terminology of Klein and Carter (1988), to raise questions about the appropriateness of the current nature of PhDs in engineering.

The ESRC attempted to minimise the distortions caused by small samples by using a rolling three-year average on which to calculate submission rates. But this, too, is open to problems and several institutions have appealed against blacklisting on this historic basis.

The use of submission rates as a PI may have long-term consequences for the nature of postgraduate student research in this country. If the PI becomes a definition of success rather than one of several measures, it could lead to distortion of the doc- toral system; students would be admitted to undertake narrow, superficial or barely original research assured of completion within four years. There seems to be consensus that the majority of full-time students should submit a PhD within four years, but it is not proven whether past submission rates in all areas would justify this – some of the most highly regarded, for example those submitting doctorates in history at Oxbridge, are encour- aged to take longer by the award of college research fellowships. The emphasis on submission rather than completion or award must also be noted, as this criterion could be open to abuse.

The sanctions policy, and use of the PI as a 'dial' in the terminology of Klein and Carter, are important to the ESRC. The policy has dramatically increased the submissions rate of social science PhDs. Furthermore, the then Chairman of the ESRC expressed the fear that the number of research studentships would not be sufficient to produce a sustainable social science community in the 1990s. To gain more money to increase the number of studentships, particularly in the light of critical comments from the House of Commons Public Accounts Committee, it was thought necessary to increase the PhD submissions rate still further to convince people that the ESRC was serious about improving training: 'the ESRC cannot make a credible case for additional resources unless this crucial "performance indicator" improves' (Newby 1990) (*Times Higher Education Supplement* 30 March 1990). It is clear that PhD submission rate is used as a PI for research councils as well as for universities. Further impacts of this policy have been reviewed by Ayers (1994), Becher, Henkel and Kogan (1994) and Collinson and Hockey (1995).

4.6 The non-academic impact of research

The utility or non-academic impact of research is suggested as being important in various lists of items to include in the performance measurement of research (see, for example, Gibbons and Georghiou 1987 and the list from Phillimore 1989 given earlier in this chapter). This issue covers a range of approaches with different ones being more important for different subjects and various methods being suggested as ways of assessing the impact.

We noted in Chapter 4.2 that the JPIWG considered, under the heading 'Technology Transfer', the development of PIs from patents and licences and concluded the most satisfactory one would be based on the income from patents and licences. There has long been interest in the possibility of developing ways of valuing the non-academic impact of university research. Byatt and Cohen (1969, p.vii) attempted 'to suggest one method by which a major and hitherto unquantified benefit, namely the long-term economic benefit of curiosity oriented research, might be measured'. The Council for Scientific Policy considered how to take this work forward, but its intended report disappeared with the disbanding of the whole body (Johnson 1975). There have been more recent attempts in the USA to measure the economic impact of industry-funded university R&D (see, for example, Berman 1990), and analysis such as Chrisman's (1994) assessment of the economic development, as measured partly by the number of jobs created, by research at the University of Calgary. There had also been much earlier attempts in the USA through projects such as Hindsight and TRACES to 'trace out historically the development from research to application or vice versa and to try and identify the major events which link the former with the latter' (Gibbons and Georghiou 1987, p.41). Various criticisms were made of the tracing attempts but more recent developments of the approach include the concept of techno-economic networks (TENS) (see, for example, Callon *et al.* 1992).

In the UK on various occasions there have been ministerial expressions of concern that research selectivity should give greater credit to research of use to industry and commerce. This was seen in the 1987 White Paper (DES 1987e), and the 1995 Competitiveness White Paper states that measures to develop the links between industry and universities include 'taking greater account of industrially-relevant work' in the 1996 RAE (DTI 1995, para.11.33). Much health and medical research is conducted in conjunction with higher education institutions and there have been various recent moves to assess the benefits of such research. The DHSS incorporated both policy relevance and the quality of research in its evaluation of research units (Kogan and Henkel 1983). The review of the research of the London postgraduate Special Health Authorities used peer review to assess not only the quality of the research, but also its importance to the NHS (Department of Health 1993).

Medical and health research have also seen various attempts to combine a range of perspectives in the assessment of impacts. For example, in relation to basic biomedical research in the USA a case study approach was adopted which integrated cost-benefit analysis with historical tracing of important scientific developments leading up to a specific research discovery: 'The tracing also provides further evidence of the inextricable and unpredictable role of non-directed, investigator-initiated fundamental research in the subsequent evolution of new technology' (Raiten and Berman 1993, p.v). Paybacks from health research can be categorised and a series of possible measures identified (Buxton and Hanney 1994 and 1996). An input-output model suggests various points at which these benefits might occur and measurement could be attempted. This model informed the development of Figure 1.2 in Chapter 1. It is possible the measurements could be used to develop PIs but there have been other, more specific, attempts to develop PIs for the non-academic impact of research.

A Dutch team suggested eight indicators could be used to form a societal quality profile of the research conducted by research teams (Spaapen and Sylvain 1994). These include the ratio of conference presentations to total output (written and non-written). A high value would indicate 'active participation in meetings is a sign that effort is put into dissemination' (p.47). Further indicators of research impact have been suggested by another part of the Dutch project (Van der Meulen and Rip 1995). Various analyses of suitable performance measurements for use by research councils have examined possible PIs of the non-academic impact of the research they fund. Particularly for social science research these include policy usefulness (Cave and Hanney 1990; Whiston 1990). The pressure to fund research that makes non-academic impacts has been experienced much more strongly by the research councils than the funding councils (see, for example, the 1993 Office of Science and Technology White Paper *Realising our Potential*). Correspondingly, it is the research councils that are under pressure to develop indicators to demonstrate that at least some of the research they fund does produce benefits. Where university research is funded by contracts from bodies such as government departments, there is likely to be even greater pressure for the research to make a non-academic impact (see, for example, Buxton and Hanney 1994 for health research; Fulton 1992 and Valimaa and Westerheijden 1995 for research on higher education policy; and Kogan and Tuijnman (1995) for educational research in general).

Before considering how specific PIs could be developed it is important to note that even within the field of social science research many different meanings of research utilisation have been identified and many models developed (see, for example,

Caplan, Morrison and Stambaugh 1975; Weiss 1977 and 1979; Kogan and Henkel 1983; Thomas 1985; Bulmer 1987; Booth 1988; Richardson, Jackson and Sykes 1990). Lessons from these can be drawn upon in developing PIs, and the distinction made by Yin and Gwaltney (1981) between knowledge utilisation as an outcome and as a process seems useful.

A number of methods have been proposed for the measurement of policy impact. One approach involves convening panels of users of research, possibly on a regular basis, and asking panel members, who might be business executives or policy makers, to indicate what research they have been aware of and have utilised in decision taking. It might be possible by this means to infer what are the characteristics of potentially policy-relevant research and what methods of dissemination are capable of getting the information to users. When questioning such panels it would be very important to have identified what definition of research utilisation was intended. On reanalysing the taped interviews with policy makers in the USA, Caplan *et al.* (1975) changed their findings because it was clear the original analysis had used too narrow a concept of research utilisation.

Another possible approach involves tracking the transmission of information through a range of possible networks to see how it influences policy makers and practitioners. These networks are overlapping and have been conceptualised in various ways including Yin and Gwaltney's (1981) idea of social networking as a process; academic networks; socio-intellectual networks (Platt 1987); epistemic communities (Haas 1992); and policy networks (see, for example, Rhodes and Marsh 1992; Dowding 1995). The identification of such policy networks and analysis of their operation may shed light on how research results are spread amongst users. An illustration of an exercise of this kind can be found in Henkel (1994).

Work in developing specific PIs in this area is still in its infancy, but we anticipate that it will grow as research funders become more concerned with measuring the effects of their activities. Knowledge of research results on the part of potential users is a pre-requisite for research results to have an extra-academic effect, and for this reason attention is likely increasingly to be focused on indicators of impact building on work such as that described in Bozeman and Melkers (1993).

4.7 Peer review of research

As Chapter 1 explains, peer judgements made on a reputational basis were traditionally the major form of evaluation used by the UGC. The move towards PIs can be seen as implicitly representing a weakening of trust in peer review – a move towards displacing evaluation by peers with evaluation by methods that managers rather than academics can master and control. However, the use of PIs can also be seen as a way of informing, and thus strengthening, peer review: 'peer review and performance indicators should, and must, complement each other' (Sizer 1990, p.25). Similarly Anderson (1989) shows how several visiting committees involved in peer review of AFRC establishments generated their own bibliometric indicators to assist them. He describes the role of indicators in 'democratising' research funding in several research councils by improving the transparency of the resource allocation process by making it more open and visible to both the donors and recipients of funds.

Peer review of research is difficult to define precisely and can be considered to include a variety of activities. Gillett (1989) suggests that 'peer review' is a generic term which includes impressionistic peer review (which provides an overall judgement), grant giver peer review, and journal peer review. In this section, however, we are concentrating on the first of these categories which is what is most commonly understood by peer review. The decision to include peer review in a list of PIs is controversial. It is not a PI inasmuch as it describes a judgemental process, which may nevertheless both be informed by PIs and lead to PIs. As we shall see, how far the judgement can be used as the basis for a PI depends upon the context in which it is used. As in other sections consideration is given here to: the nature of the indicator (including esteem indicators and reputational rankings); UK usage; and criticisms.

Paradoxically, whilst the move towards PIs could be seen as reducing the significance of peer review, the financial and reputational impacts of the peer judgements made in 1986, 1989, 1992 and 1996 have been more severe and controversial than many previous ones. At the same time the current moves towards more systematic evaluation have had an impact on the nature of peer review. The more peer judgements become systematic and based on general criteria, the nearer they are to being a PI, but the less appropriate it might be to describe the process as being peer review as it has been traditionally understood.

The 1986 statement of the CVCP/UGC working group suggested that peer review was a PI but, in making that observation, it did not distinguish between PIs for research and for teaching. The working group defined peer review as being 'assessments of departments by individuals or groups who are acknowledged experts in the field of study' (CVCP/UGC 1986, Appendix 2, p.9). Some of the other PIs listed by the working group, for example being an officer of a learned society or a member of a research council, can be seen as being based on peer review of the overall work of individuals. This illustrates the point made by the working group that 'various aspects of peer review are hidden in others of the proposed PIs' (Appendix 2, p.9). Although the working group did not mention them, the number of departmental staff with prizes, honours, and/or membership of bodies such as the Royal Society or the British Academy, can also be regarded as a PI based on peer review of the research of individuals. A list of esteem indicators along the above lines was developed by SCRI but as we saw in Table 4.1 none of them were included in the list of research indicators developed by the JPIWG. In the USA this is regarded as important in a number of multidimensional lists and provides a quantifiable indicator that can be used to compare departments.

Peer review of departments, it can be argued, should involve the following: those being reviewed knowing who are the reviewers; the reviewers getting to know the full range of the work of those being reviewed; those reviewed having the opportunity of being interrogated on their work so that misunderstandings can be adjusted and the reviewers become more knowledgeable about that which they are judging. It can also be argued that peer review ought to mean review by 'genuine' peers who are not too different in status from those being reviewed and yet are experts in the field being reviewed. The CVCP/UGC working group cited UGC subcommittees as an example of bodies which practised peer review; these disappeared, however, with their parent body.

Prior to the mid-1980s, the relationships between the UGC visiting committees and the allocation of resources by the UGC was not made clear. The distinction between peer review of teaching and of research was not made. Perhaps this distinction was not relevant at a time when the funding decisions were taken by the UGC subcommittees on the basis of what has been described as 'informed prejudice' (Moore 1987), and there was no attempt to develop a formula under which the contributions of the varying elements could be considered.

By 1986 the decisions of the UGC subcommittees had become more systematic and authoritative. The process was referred to as 'peer assessment' by Harris, a member of the UGC, and as 'informal peer review' in the 1989 UFC report (UFC 1989c). Criticisms of it have, however, been raised. The 1986 RAE process did not meet the definition of peer review offered in the previous paragraphs and Zander (1986), indeed, referred to it as a 'spurious peer review'. Critics also suggested that the 1986 process was unsystematic and 'riddled with flaws, with prejudice and with circularity of argument' (Chartres 1986).

The lack of clarity about the position of peer review emerged again in the list of criteria to be used in the 1989 exercise. In this list in Circular Letter 45/88 (UGC 1988b, quoted in Section 4.1) professional knowledge and judgement were itemised as one of the four main criteria to be used in the whole process which was again described as informed peer review.

Gillett (1989) suggested that impressionistic peer review did not provide a true PI because there was currently no meaningful way to link impressionistic peer review with any input measure. He went on to suggest that if each of the PIs employed in the 1989 research selectivity exercise were to be combined into a single rating, then a mechanical weighting scheme would be preferable over a judgemental one. He cited psychological research to support the view that 'the predictive validity of a mechanical formula is almost always superior to that of a judgemental approach' (p.37). Whilst most academics would be likely to reject this, there is perhaps a growing interest in exploring ways in which quantitative and qualitative evaluation can be combined. There were several discussions on this at the 1988 CIBA Foundation Conference on the Evaluation of Scientific Research (Evered and Harnett 1989) and the work of Nederhof and Van Raan was described in Chapter 4.3. It is an issue of growing interest across the board in evaluation studies.

A major example of the use of peer review alongside that of bibliometric indicators has been the techniques of 'converging partial indicators' developed by Martin and Irvine at SPRU and referred to earlier (see, for example, Martin and Irvine 1983). They believed that traditional peer review was subject to limitations. A complex procedure was devised in which the research output and impact of a centre were compared with those of matched equivalents in other countries, with input figures being used to construct productivity and performance measures. Structured interviews were used to produce peer-rankings and in many cases showed 'a strong association exists between bibliometric data and expert judgement' (Irvine 1989, p.143).

More formal reputational rankings than those traditionally used by the UGC have sometimes been considered to be a category of peer review. Such rankings are based neither on visits nor discussion by a small group. Instead, a large number of experts, for example heads of department, are asked to rank the departments in a particular subject across the nation. Some of the major American examples of reputational rankings were discussed in Chapter 2.2 and an example in the UK was the rankings organised by the *Times Higher Education Supplement*. These have been criticised as being limited in coverage and crudely interpreted by the journalists who published them. Such rankings are not always limited to a consideration of research, although this is the field for which they are probably most suited. It is easier and more appropriate to convert reputational rankings into a quantifiable PI than it is to convert the other forms of peer review but there are various problems with them. Complaints have been made that reputational rankings lack objectivity and are over-influenced by tradition and the size of a department. Thus Crewe (1987) found that reputational rankings on political science were more closely correlated with departments' total output than with output per capita. Reputational rankings may do less than justice to departments straddling disciplines, or with many specialist subdivisions, unless care is taken to include explicit judgements on them all. There is also a danger of a halo effect (Jones *et al*. 1982; Fairweather 1988) whereby departments may benefit unduly from the reputation of the whole institution.

In 1986 the CVCP/UGC working group appeared to anticipate that peer review of research would involve a visit by external reviewers because it suggested that it would probably only be used as a 'selective mechanism to probe more deeply into a particular department when other performance indicators suggest that there may be problems or causes for concern' (CVCP/UGC 1986, Appendix 2, p.9). Several departments which were dissatisfied with the 1986 assessment of their research asked for a peer review exercise to be conducted on their research. The 1989 UFC report (UFC 1989c) made clear, however, that this was considered to be prohibitively expensive and time-consuming.

If some of the difficulties can be overcome, and appropriate ways found for developing PIs, evaluation by peer review offers considerable attractions to academics, as being the PI most in keeping with traditional academic norms. However, as an overall judgement of research it is not really sensible to view it as a PI. It only really becomes one when the judgement about research is combined with PIs of other aspects of the university.

The use of peer review as a PI of research is, we have seen, criticised from several angles. At a theoretical level it is argued that peer review, if conducted in the full sense of an interactive review by visiting peers, can never be sufficiently systematic to be regarded as a PI. However, even when full visits are carried out they can be criticised for failing to capture the unique qualities of the research being assessed. Kogan and Henkel's (1983) analysis of the peer review of DHSS-funded research units carried out by the Office of the Chief Scientist reveals several potential problems with peer review. Many of the points raised by Kogan and Henkel are likely to apply widely to peer review conducted by means of visits. The 1986 UGC assessments of research did not directly involve visits, although previous visits could have had some impact on the peer judgements made. As we have seen an attempt was made to make the process more systematic than it had been in 1981 and earlier years.

The 1986 RAE led to the development of some bibliometric PIs in the UK. The more specific collection of quantified information in 1989, and in particular for the 1992 RAE, has enabled statistical analyses to be undertaken.

Uncertainty about how far the 1989 research selectivity reflected the quantitative data received makes it difficult to assess the statistical analysis conducted by Johnes and Taylor (1990b) on the results of the exercise. Their main findings were, first, that large departments appear to have a better chance of obtaining a high research rating than small departments, and, second, for half the cost centres included in their analysis, the research ratings were significantly related to the mean research ratings of other cost centres within the same institution. They propose alternative explanations of the latter finding. It does suggest that the halo effect was at work, but it is also consistent with a competitiveness effect, whereby the competition for resources within institutions is a powerful inducement for individual cost centres to improve their research performance. The interpretation of the first finding is more problematic. Johnes and Taylor suggest that 'there is substantial evidence that research performance benefits from scale economies, particularly (but not exclusively) in the sciences'. Although they admitted their results were preliminary and should treated with caution, it can be seen that this conclusion disagrees with evidence referred to in Chapter 4.2 which questioned the existence of economies of scale in research. Furthermore, the general discussion in this section and in 4.2 demonstrates the possibility that unless peer review or reputational ranking is strongly informed by quantitative data, there is an inevitable tendency for there to be a bias in favour of larger, and therefore usually better known, departments. It could be argued that it would only be appropriate to draw the conclusion that the findings demonstrate the existence of economies of scale, if it were known that quantitative data about research inputs and output had strongly influenced the 1989 exercise.

Following the 1992 RAE, however, Jim Taylor undertook a major exercise on behalf of the JPIWG to show the statistical (but not causal) relationship between grade and size of unit, outputs in the form of publications and inputs in the form of research income and students. This analysis, which formed the basis of Table 4.3, was much more extensive than that based on the 1989 RAE and enables statistical links to be shown between the various PIs described in previous sections and the informed peer review. He showed that in all the units of assessment bar one – mineral and mining engineering – the unweighted rating achieved was lower than the weighted rating which means that on average the larger the number of research active staff in a unit, the higher the grade it received. The possible reasons for this correlation discussed by Taylor (J. Taylor 1995) show some acceptance of our analysis above that whilst it might be because of genuine links between size and quality, it could also be that the larger the unit, the more likely it is that its good work is known by one of the small number of peers on the assessment panel.

Others have also examined the correlation between size and grading. Some large institutions, including Leeds and Liverpool Universities, performed less well than might have been expected, so much so that in one classification they were put in as teaching rather than research universities (Hoare 1995). He goes on to claim that evidence from his paper shows that departmental size 'is *not* the major control upon the research ratings achieved by different university departments' (p.256). Some small institutions with comparatively few departments, which are nevertheless quite large, did well (Johnston, Jones and Gould 1995) and this could have policy implications.

Taylor's analysis of the correlations with inputs and outputs showed that a small number of quantitative indicators could explain, in a statistical sense, most of the variation in grades. This led him to suggest that a small number of PIs should be collected and used for the next RAE.

According to the report on the 1992 RAE the electrical and electronic engineering panel 'decided at the outset that the first sift could only be done using a formula approach based on performance indices' (HEFCE 1993d, Report Annex A, para.1). The indices were generated from the information contained in each submission and therefore included publications, research students, research income and research plans. It is thought that some other panels also adopted a formulaic approach for the first sift but lack of information about the extent and nature of such approaches makes thorough analysis of the relationship between the peer judgements and the various items of information supplied extremely difficult.

Summary

By contrast with the assessment of teaching, the evaluation of performance and research is widely seen as providing a more acceptable focus for the use of PIs.

This chapter has described the methods adopted by the successive funding bodies in their adjudications on research status. These constitute a gradual introduction of PIs into resource allocation. The use of output measures such as publications, licences and patents were then reviewed. Until recently, such work was mainly based on US experience, but partly by way of reaction to the UGC research rankings alternative British research output measures have now been published. We then discussed the problem of identifying quality or impact through an adjustment of quantitative measures, noting the use of citations indices and the difficulties associated with them. Research and contract income and numbers of research students have the advantage of readily available data but, again, there are problems associated with their use. There is some interest in the possibility of developing PIs for the non-academic impact of research, but the problems here are formidable.

Finally, we discussed the relationship between peer review and PIs. We reported criticisms of the use of peer review and identified possible ways in which it can be developed. In the late 1980s subjects such as physics and chemistry faced successively subject reviews, selectivity ratings and the SCRI publications pilot study. As was reported with regard to assessment of teaching in the USA, there is an air of evaluation fatigue within the university community. Although the various exercises were conducted for different objectives, there is as strong a case in research as there is in teaching for the development of an authoritative set of PIs which could then be used for a number of purposes. Always providing, that is, that the objectives of the evaluation are compatible with those of institutions to which they are being applied. As the JPIWG and the HEMS Group have discovered, however, there are still considerable obstacles facing the development of such a set of PIs. Furthermore, information collected for the 1996 RAE shows that current thinking is emphasising qualitative assessments rather than quantitative indicators.

Chapter 5

Types and Models and Modes of Application

5.1 Introduction: the importance of frameworks

As performance indicators and the arguments about their use proliferate, it is increasingly suggested that if purposeful and sound decisions about them are to be made, that needs to happen within conceptual frameworks that can structure evaluation, choice and application. We now draw on a range of frameworks developed in the literature, some of which were described in Chapter 1.4, to propose our own. We suggest that there are three different levels of analysis that ought to be applied.

First, we propose a classificatory schema within which individual PIs can be interrogated for their usefulness. Second, we focus on some key conceptual and structural issues that must be addressed by those whose task is to develop and use systems of PIs. Finally, we show how the selection and use of PIs are significantly affected by the broader policy context, the nature of the state and the resource allocation mechanisms embedded within that.

Throughout the book we have noted how the development and use of PIs have been influenced by the interplay between political decisions to establish structures, policy goals, technical advances and the interests of key actors. But it has also become clear that the larger contexts in which the various forms of interplay take place are in transition. PIs have been forged in higher education systems in which resource allocation is either centralised or market-based. Now a new allocative system is emerging in a changing political economy, characterised by multiple stakeholders, of which government is one. Section 5.4

of this chapter analyses the three systems and the implications of the change for the deployment of PIs, and the final section draws on themes from throughout the book.

5.2 Classifying PIs

A selection of the indicators on teaching and research which we have identified from the literature as applicable are listed below. None of the possible indicators for the non-academic impact of research were sufficiently well developed to be included.

1. Relating to teaching:
   (a) Entry qualifications.
   (b) Exit qualifications.
   (c) Cost per student or staff–student ratio.
   (d) Value-added.
   (e) Rate of return.
   (f) Student progression rates.
   (g) Employment on graduation.
   (h) Student and peer review.
2. Relating to research:
   (a) Number of research students.
   (b) Output of research.
   (c) Quality or impact indices.
   (d) Research incomes.
   (e) Peer review.
   (f) Reputational rankings.

It is useful to classify and evaluate these PIs according to a number of criteria (see also Sizer 1979 and Ewell and Jones 1994). We propose to adopt the following:

1. Type of indicator

Is the indicator a measure of input, output, productivity or final outcome? Is it a simple quantity index, or is it adjusted for quality?

2. Relevance

How accurately does the PI measure true underlying performance, relative to the organisation's given objectives?

3. Ambiguity

Is it possible to identify a high or a low value of the indicator as
unambiguously favourable or unfavourable? This may seem a
minimum requirement, but it is not hard to cite instances where
it is not met. For instance, a high cost per student can be
interpreted either as a sign of wasteful extravagance or of the
giving of more individual attention.

4. Manipulability

If a PI can be manipulated by the individual or body which it is
intended to assess, its value is reduced. For example, numbers
of research students can be inflated if selection is undiscriminat-
ing.

5. Cost of collection

Some PIs can be calculated readily from data already available
to institutions or the higher education system. Others require
costly and perhaps infeasible data collection. For many purposes, comparative data are required, because the department's
performance compared with others in the same field is a better
guide than its absolute level. In cases where data are already
collected, the marginal cost of preparing them for use as PIs is
small. This consideration virtually dictated the coverage of the
CVCP/UGC list of indicators published in 1987 although the
1989 gradings exercise cost about £4 million. For other indicators, only occasional estimates of cost of collection are available.
Some writers have properly maintained that an indicator should
be used only when the benefits from its use exceed the costs. But
there are problems in making a cost-benefit appraisal indicator
by indicator. These arise in part because of jointness of costs –
for instance publication and citation data are often conveniently
collected together. More fundamentally, the return to developing PIs in higher education is not simply the summation of
returns to individual indicators, but rather the overall effect of

the total process. A single indicator may be subject to strategic manipulation which can be prevented by use of another related indicator. Equally the use of indicators across the board may trigger a change in attitudes to resource management not realisable by small-scale experiments.

6. Level of aggregation

Each PI has its own natural level or levels of aggregation – individual, department, discipline, institution or the higher education system as a whole. They may thus be correspondingly difficult to bring together or weight.

7. Relation to other indicators

Often several indicators are used to measure the same or a similar aspect of performance. In such circumstances, the existence of multiple indicators is a useful consistency check, but these variables should not be regarded as independent in an overall evaluation. In other cases a single indicator, for example number of research students, measures several dimensions of activity.

Table 5.1, at the end of this chapter, gives a preliminary evaluation of the characteristics of the 14 indicators listed above, based upon the more detailed discussion in Chapters 3 and 4. Thus, indicator 1, 'entry scores', is a measure of input quality, recording the strength of demand for places. Yet a high entry score does not of itself unambiguously denote good performance because, taken in conjunction with some levels of final degree results, it may indicate low added-value. The indicator can also be manipulated. On the other hand, it is cheap to collect and process on a comparative basis.

5.3 Using PIs

The frameworks we propose for structuring and enhancing the value of using PIs focus, first, on the importance of clarity about the levels and purposes of their use and the functions of those who use them. Second, they address issues of authority, linking these with the conceptual coherence of PIs and the structures and strategies developed for their co-ordination and acceptance.

Finally, the relationship between PIs and the use of judgement is discussed.

PIs have a potential role at several levels of the higher education system. The focus of concern may be on the performance of the system as a whole, the comparative or complementary performance of various parts of the system (such as sectors or institutions) or the work of individual institutions, departments, programmes, disciplines or individuals. A key set of questions is, therefore, at what levels are PIs to be used, by whom and with what purpose. Are the indicators primarily used by actors or bodies external or internal to the unit concerned or both? If external, do these actors or bodies represent a higher level in the system, with authority to affect the unit in a decisive way? Or are they stakeholders who may or may not be conceived of as belonging to the system but have a particular set of interests and potential influences? Or are they peers or competitors?

We have seen in the course of the book how attention may shift between levels from the performance of individuals to the performance of the institution as a whole; and from state policy making and policy implementation to institutional planning. In the UK a prime concern with the potential of PIs to aid funding bodies or government to allocate resources in accordance with overarching goals or to call institutions to account for the economic and efficient use of resources seems to have given way to concern that individual institutions can effectively assess their own performance and act upon that assessment. In the USA, it seems that in some states the prime usage of PIs has recently shifted from institutions to states and then possibly back again to institutions.

Institutions certainly vary in the degree to which there has been systematic development of PIs and in the importance they attach to them. Davies (1993) argues that 'they are a prime characteristic of a self-evaluating organisation' with a 'self-evaluating ethic' (p.122).

But organisations using PIs need a framework in which they can make connections between levels, actors and the purposes and modes of use. A number of authors (e.g. Sizer, Spee and Bormans 1992; Nedwek and Neal 1994) have identified categories of use. Drawing on their work, we can identify four modes of use and link them with four kinds of purpose: indicators might be used summatively with a view to determining or informing decisions or judgements and perhaps making them more robust, transparent, rational or just; formatively with a view to challenge, interrogation, dialogue, reflection or diagnosis; as monitoring instruments with a view to maintaining a system or assuring an agreed level of quality; as instruments of presentation with a view to marketing or attracting investment or support or recruitment.

Some commentators (for example Banta and Borden 1994; Ewell 1994) make the point that PIs should overwhelmingly be used with reference to future action rather than past performance. In this context, it can be noted that indicators may be used to measure trends. For this reason it is often useful to have data covering a series of years, and to look at changes over that period. As well as reducing the effect of measurement error or of anomalous results in particular years, this procedure makes it possible, when used with caution, to discern deterioration or improvement. It not only identifies future problem areas but also enables resources to be allocated on the basis of forecast as well as recorded performance.

The confidence or authority with which PIs are used would depend on another set of issues: conceptual and structural. It is important to ensure that PIs are valid, that they are theoretically and/or empirically sound, and developed within a conceptual framework coherent with the ideas and purposes for which they are used. We have seen that the dominant model for the development of PIs is a production model linking input, process and output. Within this, emphasis may be laid primarily on input or output or the relationship between these two. It has a strong conceptual link with the objectives of economy (reduction or control of resources) and efficiency (the productive use of resources). It may encourage thinking of institutions as production systems, whose prime task is to convert inputs into desired outputs or add maximum value to specified inputs. It might therefore be consistent with promoting relative concepts of quality but at the same time, used in the context of teaching, suggest the assignment of passive or inert roles to students in higher education institutions. We have seen that the JPIWG has consciously located its most recent suite of indicators (albeit statistical rather than performance indicators) in a framework of student progression, which might suggest stronger emphasis on students as agents and their interaction with the people and the environments that go to make up their institutions.

As more attention has been paid, at least in some countries, to defining what is expected of both higher education institutions and their students, together with how that is to be achieved, so more concern has been expressed that PIs are consistent with those definitions and what underpins them rather than taking it for granted that existing measures such as attainment tests or degree classes reflect stated objectives. Banta and Borden's statement (1994, p.95) that 'performance indicators (PIs) derive their significance from their ability to link outcomes both with purpose and with processes' represents a growing trend towards ensuring that indicators derive from a grounded understanding of how processes are linked to outcomes (see, for example, Ramsden 1991; Elsworth 1994; Dill 1995a).

The authority of PIs will be easiest to achieve when the values in the systems where they are applied are stable and coherent. The degree of integration between values at key, distinctive levels of the system and between the significant actors in it will facilitate the choice of robust indicators. Yorke (1991 and 1995), for example, posits a highly integrated heuristic model of higher education 'construed as a nested set of levels ranging progressively inwards from that of government to that of the student experience' (1995, p.15). While this is a useful tool for defining the extent to which measures need to be shared between levels, it may overstate the coherence of actual systems.

In practice, values are unlikely to be either stable or coherent across higher educational systems. We develop this point later in the chapter. Using PIs might be more straightforward if a dominant set of values were imposed through a centralised and relatively uniform system. But in practice the challenge will be the management of PIs when values are in conflict or tension with one another. This is partly a function of the contemporary political environment. But it is also that higher education institutions are widely assumed to require a level of independence, self-determination, reflection and value criticism if they are to fulfil the demands laid on them. At most one can ask, 'How far are values shared between different levels and different stake-holders in the system?' 'How and how easily are different values (for example, public accountability and quality improvement (Ewell 1994; Banta and Borden 1994) or efficiency and quality or accessibility and rigorous standards) reconciled?' And do different modes of reconciliation emphasise the role of different levels or actors in the development and use of PIs?

Up to a point, the multiplicity of values required of higher education may be accommodated through a differentiated system, in which institutions can carve out their own distinctive missions and devise PIs to match them. But this is unlikely to provide more than part of the answer where higher education is conceived as fulfilling important functions on behalf of the state and is part of a general funding system. It is important to think about what degree of consistency between indicators it is essential to establish through the system and how this is to be achieved.

The importance of self-activation and motivation in higher education suggests that a premium needs to be placed on establishing structures for maximising consent and co-ordination in the selection and use of PIs. However, the balance required between public accountability and quality improvement functions of PIs may need to be aligned with that between consent and coercion in their application. Experience of research selectivity in the UK would support Ewell's arguments that 'budget-bargain strategies' which 'trade additional accountability measures for more resources or for increased budget flexibility' (Ewell 1994, p.160) are accepted by institutions, even if they also require vigilance as to the manipulability of evaluative systems and PIs. Also incorporating institutional autonomy into national development of PIs does not necessarily mean an over emphasis on consent and independence. Institutions need internal coherence and compliance and are likely themselves to establish structures that make these possible, alongside the recognition of diversity in, for example, disciplines.

The relationship between PIs and the use of judgement is complex but it is important for thinking about the use of PIs. We observed in Chapter 2.3 how in the Netherlands PIs can be seen as a way of providing an incentive to make the qualitative reasoning more precise. PIs play a role in increasing the transparency and accountability of decision taking. But using PIs as an aid to judgement raises a weighting problem: how much weight should be given to the numbers and how much to the judgements, especially in cases where the two diverge? In practice, the weighting problem is often resolved in favour of judgement, but the additional data made available can influence and sometimes justify the judgement. Collecting and presenting PIs need not always strengthen the hands of managers and information collators: the effect is sometimes, paradoxically, to strengthen the role of professional judgement rather than to weaken it. For instance in the UFC's 1989 research selectivity exercise final judgements were made by expert subcommittees. These were to some degree protected from criticism by the data collection exercise which preceded them, despite problems with that exercise which the UFC itself acknowledges. The potentially complementary roles played in quality assessment by PIs and qualitative approaches, including peer review, are subject to considerable analysis (see, for example, Allsop and Findlay 1990; Goedegebuure, Maasen and Westerheijden 1990; Nederhof and Van Raan 1993). However, as we have seen, the importance of quantitative output information has been reduced in the 1996 RAE in the UK by the decision not to collect data on numbers of publications.

The weight to be given to expert judgement and the importance of errors and ambiguities in the measures vary with the level at which the data are used. Within the framework of managing higher education, at least five areas of use can be discerned: in dialogues between the Treasury and the Department for Education and Employment (DfEE), between the DfEE and the funding bodies, between the funding bodies and institutions, within the institutions, and within departments.

Having set out our views about how decisions about the use of PIs might be structured, we now go on to analyse some key characteristics of the institutional and policy environments in which they are being deployed. We note that they are in transition and examine the implications this has for the role of PIs in higher education, illustrating our analysis by reference to the British system.

5.4 PIs and resource allocation

Resource allocation models for higher education

Higher education funding is in transition all over the world. At a general level, the transition tends to be towards systems which are more reliant upon private funding, and less on government grants for both tuition and maintenance, and towards systems which are more akin to a market, in the sense that there is a degree of competition among suppliers to meet the need for teaching places. This may be direct competition for students' purchasing power (in the form of their own money or in the form of vouchers or equivalent supplied by the state) or teaching services may be purchased on their behalf by an intermediary, such as the funding councils in the UK. This arrangement is often known as a quasi-market.

For the purposes of our initial analysis of the role of PIs, it is useful to present the polar resource allocation models – the 'administered' system and the market – in a stylised way. A pure market-based higher education system will involve students choosing which institutions to enrol in. With exclusively private finance, higher education institutions would be either commercial organisations or, more plausibly, non-profit-making organisations with some kind of charitable status. As noted above the broad contours of this arrangement would still operate if some, or even all, institutions were in the public sector. However, for a market system to operate, there would have to be some arrangements for failing institutions to exit the market or to be taken over. The broad arrangement would not be affected either if some or all of the student body were financed by the government, provided that they still went on to make their choices directly and individually in the market-place.

It is clear that a system like this of an unregulated kind would have quite serious information problems. Higher education is an example of what is sometimes called an 'experience good' – one where the consumer finds it hard to estimate the quality in advance of enjoying it. The process of study would thus disclose the value of the consumption benefits of higher education. The 'return to investment' in the form of a better job or a higher salary will never be fully appreciated by the student, because his or her subsequent career will be affected by many other considerations as well.

While it is probably impossible for a student to get a complete picture of the quality of education offered by an institution, the situation is not hopeless. For example, information could be collected on the qualifications of those entering the institution, the nature of the syllabus, the assessment system, results in the form of degrees and diplomas and subsequent careers of graduates. In any system, we would expect information of this kind to be provided as a service to potential students. The proliferation of guides and handbooks suggests that such information is indeed available. However, the market system itself may not generate adequate information and – as we discuss below – some further form of regulatory intervention may be necessary.

We can contrast a market-based system with one characterised by central planning (or in its UK less extreme form, administrative guidance) and predominantly or entirely public funding, at least for tuition. Under a regime of this kind, a funding body would allocate and subsidise the provision of student places in particular subjects to a chosen set of institutions. The latter would then typically choose for such places the applicants whom they considered most suitable. There might be a limited and indirect feedback from the pattern of application to the availability of places (with the funders expanding popular institutions and contracting unpopular ones) but – compared with the market system – this aspect would be weak and secondary.

The role of PIs

How do PIs fit in with the two stylised 'models' of resource allocation in higher education set out above? Broadly, PIs can play a role both in support of a market system and in support of a system of allocation.

In the former case, the collection and publication of comparative information can be seen as a form of consumer protection. As noted above, it is costly or even impossible for students to acquire detailed information about a range of higher education institutions. Without some form of disclosure provision it would be particularly difficult for them to acquire such information in comparable form. The poorer institutions would thus be able to disguise their deficiencies through failure to disclose (although a failure to disclose might be evidence of poor quality), or by a decision to disclose in an unfamiliar metric which would make comparison difficult or impossible. Performance comparisons undertaken by the private sector thus have a market and social value. In addition, there is a 'consumer protection' case for requiring some form of disclosure.

The importance of this role is borne out in the USA, which has a framework for higher education which is probably the closest to the market model. However, it has been suggested that disaggregated and detailed information is of more value to students than overall quality ratings. Such valuations are in any case contestable. Thus Dill (1995b, p.14) argues that 'This logic [of information disclosure] rests upon a long and complicated causal chain which assumes that reliable and valid measures of academic quality readily exist, and that students will base their choices on this type of information'.

He suggests that quality ratings do not decisively influence undergraduate college choices. More useful than quality ratings, he argues, is the provision of information which will be useful to particular students in evaluating whether a programme or institution is best for them. These data might include: characteristics of the student body; typical educational experiences the student will encounter; student and graduate satisfaction; and first destination information.

In a centrally planned or administered system, by contrast, the role of student choice is limited. Typically, public subsidies create excess demand on the part of students who gain a high private rate of return to investment in higher education. The resulting disequilibrium gives the providers greater power of choice than the consumers. They are thus subject to the moral hazard of diminishing their teaching effort in favour of alternative activities, such as research, consultancy or leisure. In this framework the role of PIs is essentially a regulatory one. Its purpose is to identify inadequate performance. How the funders use evidence of poor performance is a separate question. They might either have an incentive system which rewards good performance, or use the stick of a threat to withdraw funds from inadequate programmes or institutions. The information provided may also be of benefit to students, but in the system of central planning, their role is largely a passive one.

The use of PIs in such a context is open to well-known difficulties. Those interpreting the data and making funding decisions will lack access to the fine-grained information which is available to and processed by large numbers of consumers in a market-based system. If, however, an activity is left out of the measurement process, there is a risk that it will be ignored.

As in many other countries, the higher education system of the UK is currently undergoing a rather chaotic transition from the relatively liberally administered system which characterised the post-war period until the 1980s, towards a system in which elements of a more market-based system coexist with increased government control. The characteristics of this transition are:

- the introduction of competition among institutions for additional funding

- the central implementation or discussion of policies to remunerate institutions in accordance with the quality of their research or teaching outputs

- increasing reliance on private funding, often through a loan scheme, of tuition and maintenance.

Chapter 2 has noted the development of this process in a number of countries, and the role in it of PIs. It tends to be a process of fits and starts and embodying movements in different directions. General trends are that governments are spurred on towards market methods by a desire to increase productivity and reduce public spending at a time when they perceive the need to expand and improve higher education in pursuit of economic competitiveness. It is important for them to increase the potential sources of income for higher education. In doing so they often face significant hostility, both from students and from higher education institutions themselves. But they need to encourage more, rather than less, commitment to and investment in it on the part of the whole population and key interest groups. What might be emerging from this is not so much a purely market-based system as a multiple stakeholder system, in which governments remain substantial investors with incentives to retain significant degrees of control.

At present, however, what we perceive is that the higher education systems of various countries are currently experiencing an unstable period of transition from the regime in which central planning predominated to one with an increasing reliance on market forces and private finance. Despite its political sensitivity, it is now fairly clear that, within a relatively short period, students will be expected to make a contribution to their tuition costs. Already, a quasi-market in higher education places has been tried or proposed.

In the 1980s the two UK funding councils tried to establish tendering systems in which institutions would bid for additional places. In the case of the Polytechnics and Colleges Funding Council (PCFC), the system operated for a number of years with the interesting element that institutional bids were adjusted for quality: those programmes which were deemed excellent received preferential treatment in the allocation process. Although the end of the era of rapid expansion in UK higher education has limited the resources for which institutions can compete at the margin, it is likely that the trend towards a more competitive funding environment will later be resumed.

Nor is this trend confined to teaching activities. The UK government's increasing emphasis on research as an adjunct to the competitiveness of the economy has the general effect of placing greater power in the hands of the customers for research, at the cost of institutions' own preferences. The extension of decentralised market-type procedures into research funding is in tension with the fact that the RAEs have certainly entailed more planning of research activities within institutions.

This suggests that PIs are making a transition from essentially a regulatory role to one of providing information as an adjunct to market-type processes. This has a number of probable consequences. First, performance measurement will cease to be a centralised monolithic system, and become a joint product of the principal public sector funding organisations and a variety of more specialised, possibly private sector, organisations. The development of consumer guides such as *The Times Good University Guide* is an example of this tendency.

It is also highly likely that the new purchasers of information about higher education institutions will want it in a variety of different forms. We have already cited Dill's observations about the information needs of prospective American students. Equally, research funders will be interested in much more micro information about the capacities of individual research groups rather than departments or faculties.

There will remain, however, a substantial or more probably predominant element of public spending in higher education. There will thus be continued interest in aggregate performance relating to such measures as the overall number of students, average costs, the UK's overall performance in different areas of scientific performance, overall destination data, etc.

5.5 Changing policy environments and their implications for the development and use of PIs by funding councils and institutions

Our history of PIs in higher education has shown how they were an essential part of the initiatives from governments that have come to be known as the 'rise of the Evaluative State' (Neave 1988). In this process governments have used a range of evaluative mechanisms and institutions to reinforce the accountability of public institutions for the economic, efficient and effective use of resources. At the centre of the strategy was a commitment to neo-Taylorian concepts of management (Henkel 1991; Pollitt 1993) and the drive to ensure that clear objectives were set against which performance could be easily measured and resource allocation policies linked with that performance. PIs, reducing complexities of judgement to simple measures, were part of that.

However, at various points in the 1980s different governments were moving towards more complex concepts of the State, in which the market would assume a more central role and the structures and mechanisms of the public sector would be modelled on those of the private sector. Management continued to be seen as a key part of the strategy but in the form of 'new public management', with its emphasis on decentralisation, organisational missions, contracting, income generation and the management of multiple objectives. Paradox and ambiguity, for example 'centralised decentralisation', became part of the language of management (Hoggett 1991). Public as well as private organisations were persuaded that their survival depended on maximising not only economy and efficiency but also quality.

Evaluative institutions and managements themselves began to place more emphasis on self-evaluation and quality assurance.

The trends are reflected in higher education policies and can be illustrated by reference to Britain. The determination to harness higher education more closely to the needs of the economy has entailed emphasis on both accountability and autonomy, on control by the state and the market, and on a combination of size, economy and quality. The unification and enlargement of the higher education system have brought with them policy commitments to diversity. Absolute and taken for granted concepts of quality in the form of academic excellence have been, at least in theory, superseded by relative concepts such as fitness for purpose and value-added in national policies.

However, government as well as universities themselves have expressed anxiety about the standards of British higher education and the need to ensure at least common threshold standards. The Higher Education Quality Council's graduate standards programme is attempting to define core criteria across an increasingly wide range of undergraduate curricula. Governments, increasingly conscious of the global economy, know that they need to ensure that the highest intellectual capacities must be developed, stretched and exploited, at the same time as the multiple talents of the whole population are maximised. They need research which will advance the frontiers of discipline-based knowledge, innovative (mode two – Gibbons *et al.* 1994) collaborative forms of knowledge production and more routine applied research and development.

These developments have placed the higher education system under increasing strain, partly through the creation of policies and institutional frameworks that impose demands that are difficult to reconcile. They also make the tasks of performance measurement and evaluation potentially far more complex. The funding councils have instituted evaluative mechanisms to ensure public accountability and to enable them to allocate reduced resources on the basis of normative quality judgements. At the same time, and in part through the same mechanisms, institutions are propelled towards greater autonomy by generating private income through contracts with organisations that will have a range of requirements and a variety of quality criteria.

As yet, the evidence is that new measures incorporating more diverse criteria have not been institutionalised and that the dominant forms of evaluation are those of the state rather than those of the market. As we have seen, the main influence on the funding councils' research and teaching quality assessments is that of peer review. The role of PIs in the processes is either negligible, as in the case of teaching quality, or unclear, as in the case of research assessment. In each case the criteria adopted appear overwhelmingly to have been those of high academic excellence and reputation, despite policy commitments in the areas of research and teaching to more diverse concepts of quality.

As far as research is concerned, high rankings appear, as we have seen, to be more likely to be associated with theoretical and uni-disciplinary research, the securing of research council grants, the numbers of research students and research council studentships and the size of departments. Thus success is highly associated with resource inputs. New universities who were given access to the research selectivity exercise for the first time in 1992 found that either they were bound to be disadvantaged in a system working on this basis (even if they actually gained resources) or they would be obliged to reorientate their research agendas and invest a high level of resources in doing so. Such strategies entail considerable risk and, at least in some cases, diversion from a teaching commitment to adding value to students with relatively low academic achievements on admission to the university. It is argued that theoretical and fundamental research must be given priority by government, since other sources of funding are unlikely to be willing to invest in it, at least at the level required. There is some evidence to suggest that the universities strongest in fundamental research are also in the strongest position to secure contracts, patents and licences. Institutions at the bottom of the funding council rankings argue that research selectivity and the publication of research ratings have made it harder for them to secure local and applied research contracts.

As far as the assessment of the quality of education is concerned, we have seen that traditional academic criteria seem to have increased rather than reduced in influence since 1993, at least in the HEFCE system, although it is possible that the new profile system may change this.

It is also noticeable that the combination of technical advances and academic political interest and power seems to have made the reaching of consensus on PIs for the quality of teaching particularly difficult. The dual status of PIs as managerial tools designed for institutions' use and as public expressions of relative performance, readily convertible into league tables, makes the design of measures a highly political process in which compromises have to be reached. The latest PIs for teaching and learning produced by the JPIWG attracted far more criticism than other categories. And those indicators which embody consumer criteria or commitment to transformative or value-added concepts of quality have been shelved on the grounds of the need for more research. (Employer views are, of course, implicated in the graduate destinations indicators but it is not clear that employers are any more wedded to these alternative concepts of quality than are the majority of academics). Ironically one of the grounds for the decision to shelve in the case of the Course Experience Questionnaire was that it might not be able to accommodate institutional diversity. All the while the task of producing PIs is becoming more daunting as the range of factors recognised as affecting student learning multiply and the balance among them tips away from internal, and towards external, factors. It is this type of conclusion that helps explain the observation from Spee and Bormans (1992), noted in Chapter 2.4, that PIs had played a relatively minor role.

At one level, therefore, it seems that traditional values and mechanisms of control are proving resistant to change or dilution. State mechanisms and peer review seem to be holding their own against the grosser intrusions of the market, consumerism and externally imposed quantitative measurement. At the same time, the difficulties of objective measurement and of fair allocative systems based on them have been exposed.

One of the effects of the developments just described has been to make higher education institutions a key site of development for PIs. Institutional leaders recognise that despite the various forms of resistance, the world in which they and their institutions have to survive is one in which market forces and the demands of policy makers are growing more powerful. It is increasingly important for them to establish their own strategies to meet the changes. They need to know how they are performing in relation to their own objectives and their closest rivals. Technical advances in the development of PIs, combined with understanding of the variety of demands on higher education, have focused attention on their value in more narrowly defined contexts than that of national comparisons. Recognition of the economic imperatives of higher education policies towards enhanced efficiency and quality has impelled institutions towards more rigorous self-evaluation. Indicators which can enable institutional leaders to identify, or at least raise questions about, strengths and weaknesses of comparable departments and programmes are welcomed. They want to ensure that they are optimising their performance. Within the confines of one institution, it is more feasible to take account of key variables in measuring it. At the same time, institutional leaders may calculate that league tables of various kinds are probably here to stay, together with the use of simple measures to highlight different forms of achievement. The incentives to develop indicators which emphasise their achievements are likely to increase.

These ideas are supported by comments from Kells in the Foreword to the 1993 *Compendium* that although interest in PIs has been instigated largely by governments in the OECD countries, 'the trend towards quality assurance and control systems will probably continue for some time and these processes will probably be increasingly self-(institutionally) regulatory as institutions discover that it is beneficial to design and control their own evaluation system' (Kells 1993, p.8). The pressures noted above will tend to encourage greater managerialism and use of PIs within institutions whatever model of funding is adopted by the state. There has been a move away from collegialism and professional bureaucracy and towards both managerialism and entrepreneurialism and these fuse at many points (Davies 1993). The information revealed by PIs will often be open to various interpretations by institutional leaders as to the most effective way of using it. For incentive reasons extra funds should be directed to high achievers, although such resources may be most productive at the margin in low-performing departments with, for example, tired and discouraged staff.

However, the developments of quality assurance, the continuing importance of peer review and the emphasis on comprehensive and holistic evaluative frameworks have posed some questions about the continuing role of PIs. They draw attention to the importance of process in education and the variety of influences upon student learning. They tend to support arguments for caution in ascribing value to measures of quality that may not have any foundation in evidence or theory. But it may be easier to work at these issues at the level of the institution and of the programme and the working out of what constitutes quality in detail may eventually lead to the definition of some more reliable PIs. In the meantime, the emphasis might be on the wide range of functions that indicators can fulfil in, for example, raising questions, creating dialogue, monitoring the progress of specific and perhaps quite narrow or short-lived objectives, and identifying as yet unrecognised trends.

In other words, at least at the lower levels of aggregation, the development of the quality movement might make it possible for PIs to be used more precisely and more beneficially.

Table 5.1 Characteristics of 14 selected Performance Indicators

Indicator	Type	Relevance	Ambiguity
Teaching			
1 Entry qualifications	Quality of input	Measures strength of demand	High entry scores may imply low value-added
2 Degree results	Quality-adjusted measure of output	Measures central teaching function of higher education	Good degree results may reflect high entry scores of other inputs
3 Cost per student or staff–student ratio	Productivity measure (no quality adjustment)	Involves difficult problems of cost allocation	High cost per student may reflect higher qualit of teaching and better output, staff–student ratio ignores complementary inputs
4 Value added	Input-adjusted and quality-adjusted output measure	Measures of net output can be combined with input data to generate 'productivity' indicator	Typically measured through differences in qualifications Monetary value of such increases not available
5 Rate of return	Quality-adjusted productivity measure	Assumes optimal valuations of output, ignores consumption benefits	Both private and social returns can be computed, levels will normally differ
6 Wastage and non-completion rates	Measure of 'wasted inputs'	Identifies problems with process of selection or teaching	Ignores quality of students on entry, use discourages wider access
7 Employment on graduating or after five years	Measure of output 'quality'	Does not capture long-term employment prospects or market value of employment	High employment rates on graduation may result from too short a period of search, and leads to poor 'job matching'
8 Student and peer review	Measure of output and process quality	Contains major elements of subjectivity	Difficulty of defining good teaching (e g avoidance of 'spoon feeding')
Research			
1 Number of research students	Input quality	Measures student demand	Corrections for department size and discipline necessary
2 Publications patents, etc	Measure of quantity of research output	Problem of making research outputs commensurable, differences in practices across disciplines of sub-disciplines	Difficultly of weighting teaching and research staff in establishing per capita measure, ignores complementary inputs – should work be attributed to current location of research or institution where work was completed?
3 Research quality based on a) citation of publication or b) impact factors of place of publication	Quality adjusted output measures	Difficult to produce complete sample	a) Citing of mistakes or summary rather than original work, b) based on 'average' values
4 Research income	Measure of input and 'competitiveness'	Can be broken down by type of contract, e g research council commercial organisations, etc	Problem of choosing appropriate standardisation for department size
5 Peer review	Quality-adjusted output measure	Contains major element of subjectivity	
6 Reputational ranking	quality-adjusted output measure	Contains major elements of subjectivity	Problem of low response rate, may reflect historic performance

Manipulability	Cost of collection	Level of aggregation	Relation to other PIs	
Manipulable by, for example, concentration on entrants with non-standard qualifications	Already available on a comparative basis	Department, institution	Input into calculation of value-added	1
Number and degree class of graduates partly at the discretion of department or institution	Already available	Department, institution (corrected for subject mix)	Gross output measure forvalue-added indicator	2
Should be corrected by wastage rate to prevent excessive 'low quality admissions'	Already available	Department, institutions (corrected for subject mix)		3
Form of test may distort teachingand marking patterns	Often involves resolution of major measurement and conceptual problems and longitundinal study	Department, institution	Related to rate of return difference between degree result and 'entry scores'	4
	Substantial, arising from need for longitudinal study	Discipline	Related to 'value-added' (as production measures)	5
Subject to institutions own examinations procedure	Already collected	Department, institution	Links with 'number of research students'	6
Relies on institutional (unaudited reporting)	First destination currently collected, subsequent employment monitoring involves major expense	Department, institution	Element of 'rate of return' calculation	7
Manipulable through form of assessment given to students	Already done in some institutions, varies according to the method adopted	Individual teacher, department (?)		8
Admission policy at department's discretion	Already collected	Department	Related to non-completion rates	1
Encourages publication of 'low grade' research	Already collected in most institutions but practices differ (e g are non-referred articles included?)	Department or individual	Related to 'research income'	2
Encourages 'citation circles'	a) Substantial, involving lag b) Impact factors available from citation sources	Individual, department	Quality adjusted for 'research output'	3
May encourage performance of academically 'valueless' research	Already available	Department	Input into research output	4
	Cost depends on frequency	Department, individual	Builds on or complements other PIs	5
Risk of collusion in anonymous questionnaires		Department		

Bibliography

Aarre, M. (1994) 'Akademia eller management.' In *Hovedoppgave i administrasjon og organisasjonsvitenskap*. Bergen: Institutt for administrasjon og organisasjonsvitneskap.

Aaronson, S. (1975) 'The footnotes of science.' *Mosaic 6*, 23–27.

Abrami, P. (1982) 'Students SEEQing truth about student ratings of instruction.' *Educational Researcher 18*, 43–45.

Abrami, P. (1989) 'How should we use student ratings to evaluate teaching.' *Research in Higher Education 30*, 2, 221–227.

Abrami, P. and d'Apollonia, S. (1991) 'Multidimensional students' evaluations of teaching effectiveness: the generalizability of N=1 research.' *Journal of Educational Psychology 83*, 411–415.

Adams, A. and Krislov, J. (1978) 'Evaluating the quality of American universities: a new approach.' *Research in Higher Education 8*, 97–109.

Adelman, C. (ed) (1986) *Assessment in American Higher Education*. Washington: Office of Educational Research and Improvement.

Advisory Board for the Research Councils (1987) *A Strategy for the Science Base*. London: HMSO.

Ahn, T., Charnes, A. and Cooper, W.W. (1988) 'Some statistical and DEA evaluations of relative efficiencies of public and private institutions of higher learning.' *Socio-Economic Planning Sciences 22*, 6, 259–269.

Aitken, A. (1991) 'The subtle links between teaching and research.' Symposium on the Quality of Teaching in Higher Education Institutions, Canberra.

Alewell, K. and Göbbels-Dreyling, B. (1993) 'Germany.' In H.R. Kells (ed) *The Development of Performance Indicators for Higher Education: A Compendium for Twelve Countries*, (second edition). Paris: Programme on Institutional Management in Higher Education, OECD.

Alkin, M. and Solmon, L.C. (eds) (1983) *The Costs of Evaluation*. London: Sage Publications.

Allen, D., Harley, M. and Makinson, G. (1987) 'Performance indicators in the national health service.' *Social Policy and Administration 21*, 1, 70–84.

Allsop, P. and Findlay, P. (1990) 'Performance indicators as an agent of curriculum change: broadening the base of HE.' In M. McVicar (ed) *Performance Indicators and Quality Control in Higher Education.* Portsmouth: Portsmouth Polytechnic.

Anderson, J. (1989) *New Approaches to Evaluation in UK Research Funding Agencies.* London: Science Policy Support Group.

Ashworth, T. and Thomas, B. (1987) *The Influence of School Performance on University Performance in Economics.* Durham: Department of Economics, University of Durham.

Association of Graduate Recruiters (1995) *Skills for Graduates in the 21st Century.* Cambridge: Association of Graduate Recruiters.

Astin, A. (1982) 'Why not try some new ways of measuring quality?' *Educational Record 63*, Spring, 10–15.

Astin, A. and Solmon, L. (1981) 'Are reputational ratings needed to measure quality?' *Change 13*, October, 14–19.

Audit Commission (1985) *Obtaining Better Value from Further Education.* London: HMSO.

Audit Commission (1986) *Performance Review in Local Government: Education.* London: HMSO.

Australian Vice-Chancellors' Committee, Australian Committee of Directors and Principals (1988) *Report of the AVCC/ACDP Working Party on Performance Indicators.* Canberra: AVCC/ACDP.

Ayers, R. (1994) 'The restructuring of higher education in economics.' *Higher Education Quarterly 48*, 37–55.

Baker, K. (1986) Speech to CVCP Conference at Edinburgh, September.

Baker, K. (1987) Report in *Times Higher Education Supplement.* 6 February 1987, 1.

Baker, K. (1988) Speech reported in *The Times.* 5 October 1988.

Baldwin, G. (1995) *An Australian Approach to Quality in Education.* Institutional Responses to Quality Assessment Conference, Centre for Educational Research and Innovation (CERI)/IMHE, OECD, Paris, 4–6 December.

Banta, T. and Borden, V. (1994) 'Performance indicators for accountability and improvement.' In V. Borden and T. Banta (eds)

Using Performance Indicators to Guide Strategic Decision Making. New Directions for Institutional Research 82, Summer 95–106.

Barnett, R. (1988) 'Entry and exit performance indicators for higher education: some policy and research issues.' *Assessment and Evaluation in Higher Education* 13, 1, Spring, 16–30.

Barnett, R. (1993) *Scottish Higher Education Funding Council: an Evaluation.* London: Institute of Education, University of London.

Barnett, R. (1994a) *Assessment of the Quality of Higher Education: A Review and an Evaluation.* London: Centre for Higher Education Studies, Institute of Education, University of London.

Barnett, R. (1994b) *The Limits of Competence: Knowledge, Higher Education and Society.* Buckingham: SRHE and Open University Press.

Barrow, M. (1990) 'Techniques of efficiency measurement in the public sector.' In M. Cave, M. Kogan and R. Smith *Output and Performance Measurement in Government: The State of the Art.* London: Jessica Kingsley Publishers.

Bauer, M. (1990) 'Sweden.' In H.R. Kells (ed) *The Development of Performance Indicators for Higher Education: A Compendium for Eleven Countries.* Paris: OECD.

Bauer, M. (1993) 'Sweden.' In H.R. Kells (ed) *The Development of Performance Indicators for Higher Education: A Compendium for Twelve Countries,* (second edition). Paris: Programme on Institutional Management in Higher Education, OECD.

Bauer, M. (1995) *Demands on Quality in a National Reform of Higher Education and Quality as Viewed by University Teachers and Leadership.* Paper presented at the 17th EAIR Forum, Zurich, 27–30 August.

Bauer, M. and Kogan, M. (1995) *Evaluation Systems in the UK and Sweden: Successes and Difficulties.* Paper presented to the A.F. Forum, Conference on Evaluating Universities, Rome, September.

Bayer, M. and Folger, J. (1966) 'Some correlates of a citation measure of productivity in science.' *Sociology of Education* 39 Summer, 281–90.

Becher, T., Henkel, M. and Kogan, M. (1994) *Graduate Education in Britain.* London: Jessica Kingsley Publishers.

Becher, T. and Kogan, M. (1980) *Process and Structure in Higher Education.* London: Heinemann.

Becher, T. and Kogan, M. (1991) *Process and Structure in Higher Education,* (second edition). London: Routledge.

Beeton, D. (ed) (1988) *Performance Measurement: Getting the Concept Right.* London: Public Finance Foundation.

Bell, J. and Seater, J. (1978) 'Publishing performance: departmental and individual.' *Economic Inquiry 16*, October, 599–615.

Berman, E. (1990) 'The economic impact of industry-funded university R&D.' *Research Policy 19*, 349–355.

Beyer, J. and Snipper, R. (1974) 'Objective versus subjective indicators of quality in graduate education.' *Sociology of Education 47*, 511–557.

Biglan, A. (1973) 'Relationships between subject matter characteristics and the structure and output of university departments.' *Journal of Applied Psychology 57b*, 204–213.

Billing, D. (1980) 'Introduction.' In D. Billing (ed) *Indicators of Performance.* Guildford: The Society for Research into Higher Education.

Birch, D., Calvert, J. and Sizer, J. (1977) 'A case study of some performance indicators in higher education in the United Kingdom.' *International Journal of Institutional Management in Higher Education 1*, 2, October, 133–142.

Birnbaum, R. (1985) 'State colleges: an unsettled quality.' In A. Cohen *et al. Contexts for Learning: The Major Sectors of American Higher Education.* Washington D.C.: The National Institute of Education and the American Association for Higher Education.

Bleiklie, I. (1994) *The New Public Management and the Pursuit of Knowledge.* Bergen: LOS-senter Notat 9411.

Bligh, D., Caves, R. and Settle, G. (1980) 'A Level scores and degree classifications as functions of university type and subject.' In D. Billing (ed) *Indicators of Performance.* Guildford: The Society for Research into Higher Education.

Blume, S.S. and Sinclair, R. (1973) 'Chemists in British universities: a study of the reward system in science.' *American Sociological Review 38*, February, 126–138.

Bogue, G.E. (1982) 'Allocation of public funds on instructional performance/quality indicators.' *International Journal of Institutional Management in Higher Education 6*, 1, 37–43.

Booth, T. (1988) *Developing Policy Research.* Aldershot: Gower.

Borden, V. and Banta, T. (eds) (1994) *Using Performance Indicators to Guide Strategic Decision Making. New Directions for Institutional Research 82.*

Borden, V. and Bottrill, K. (1994) 'Performance indicators: history, definitions, and methods.' In V. Borden and T. Banta (eds) *Using Performance Indicators to Guide Strategic Decision Making. New Directions for Institutional Research 82*, 5–21.

Bormans, M. *et al.* (1987) 'The role of performance indicators in improving the dialogue between government and universities.' *International Journal of Institutional Management in Higher Education* 11, 2, 181–193.

Bottrill, K. and Borden, V. (1994) 'Appendix: examples from the literature.' In V. Borden and T. Banta (eds) *Using Performance Indicators to Guide Strategic Decision Making. New Directions for Institutional Research 82*, 107–119.

Bourke, P. (1986) *Quality Measures in Universities*. Belconnen ACT: The Commonwealth Tertiary Education Commission, Australia.

Bourner, T. and Hamed, M. (1987) *Entry Qualifications and Degree Performance*. London: CNAA Development Services Publications 10.

Boyer, E. (1985) 'Changing priorities in American higher education.' *International Journal of Institutional Management in Higher Education* 9, 2, July, 151–159.

Boyer, E. (1989) 'Olive branches out with five year tenure.' *Times Higher Education Supplement*, 9 February 1989, 17.

Boys, C.J. and Kirkland, J. (1988) *Degrees of Success: Career Aspirations and Destinations of College, University and Polytechnic Graduates*. London: Jessica Kingsley Publishers.

Bozeman, B. and Melkers, J. (1993) *Evaluating R&D Impacts: Methods and Practices*. Boston: Kluwer Academic Publishers.

Bradbury, D. and Ramsden, P. (1975) 'Student evaluations of teaching at north east London polytechnics.' In *Evaluating Teaching in Higher Education*. London: University of London, Teaching Methods Unit.

Brennan, J. and McGeevor, P. (1988) *Graduates at Work. Degree Courses and the Labour Market*. London: Jessica Kingsley Publishers.

Brennan, J. *et al.* (1993) *Students, Courses, and Jobs: The Relationship between Higher Education and the Labour Market*. London: Jessica Kingsley Publishers.

Brennan, J. *et al.* (1994) 'The experiences and views of graduates: messages from recent surveys.' *Higher Education Management* 6, 3, 275–304.

Brew, A. and Boud, D. (1995) 'Research and learning in higher education.' In B. Smith and S. Brown (eds) *Research, Teaching and Learning in Higher Education.* London: Kogan Page.

Brinkman, P. (ed) (1987) *Conducting Interinstitutional Comparisons. New Directions for Institutional Research 53.*

Brinkman, P. and Teeter, D. (1987) 'Methods for selecting comparison groups.' In P. Brinkman (ed) *Conducting Interinstitutional Comparisons. New Directions for Institutional Research 53,* 5–23.

Brown, S.J. and Sibley, D.S. (1986) *The Theory of Public Utility Pricing.* Cambridge: Cambridge University Press.

Bud, R. (1985) 'The case of the disappearing caveat: a critique of Irvine and Martin's methodology.' *Social Studies of Science 15,* 548–553.

Bulmer, M. (ed) (1987) *Social Science Research and Government.* Cambridge: Cambridge University Press.

Buxton, M. *et al.* (1994) *Assessing Payback from Department of Health Research and Development, Vol. 2: 8 Case Studies.* Uxbridge: Health Economics Research Group, Brunel University.

Buxton, M. and Hanney, S. (1994) *Assessing Payback from Department of Health Research and Development, Vol. 1: The Main Report.* Uxbridge: Health Economics Research Group, Brunel University.

Buxton, M. and Hanney, S. (1996) 'How can payback from health services research be assessed?' *Journal of Health Services Research and Policy 1,* 1, January, 35–43.

Byatt, I. and Cohen, A. (1969) *An Attempt to Quantify the Economic Benefits of Scientific Research.* London: Science Policy Studies, HMSO.

Cabinet Office (1989) *Research and Development Assessment: A Guide for Customers and Managers of R and D.* London: HMSO.

Callon, M. *et al.* (1992) 'The management and evaluation of technological programs and the dynamics of techno-economic networks: the case of the AFME.' *Research Policy 21,* 215–236.

Caplan, N., Morrison, A. and Stambaugh, R. (1975) *The Use of Social Science Knowledge in Policy Decisions at the National Level.* Michigan: University of Michigan Press.

Carnegie Council on Policy Studies in Higher Education (1986) *Classification of Institutions of Higher Education.* Berkeley, CA.

Carnegie Foundation for the Advancement of Teaching (1984) *Faculty Survey.*

Carpenter, M. *et al.* (1988) 'Bibliometric profiles for British academic institutions: an experiment to develop research output indicators.' *Scientometrics 14*, 213–233.

Carswell, D. (1988) Letter to *Times Higher Education Supplement*, 18 March 1888.

Carter, N. (1989) 'Performance indicators: backseat driving or hands off control?' *Policy and Politics 17*, 2, 131–138.

Cartter, A. (1966) *An Assessment of Quality in Graduate Education.* Washington D.C.: American Council on Education.

Cave, M. and Hanney, S. (1989) 'Performance Indicators in Higher Education: An International Survey.' Department of Economics Discussion Paper, Brunel University.

Cave, M. and Hanney, S. (1990) 'Performance indicators for higher education and research.' In M. Cave, M. Kogan and R. Smith. *Output and Performance Measurement in Government: The State of the Art.* London: Jessica Kingsley Publishers.

Cave, M. and Hanney, S. (1992) 'Performance indicators.' In B. Clark and G. Neave (eds) *The Encyclopedia of Higher Education.* Oxford: Pergamon Press.

Cave, M., Hanney, S. and Henkel, M. (1995) 'Performance measurement in higher education – revisited.' *Public Money and Management 15*, 4, 17–23.

Cave, M. and Mills, R. (1992) *Cost Allocation in Regulated Industries.* London: Centre for the Study of Regulated Industries.

Cave, M., Kogan, M. and Smith, R. (1990) *Output and Performance Measurement in Government: The State of the Art.* London: Jessica Kingsley Publishers.

Centra, J. (1979) *Determining Faculty Effectiveness: Assessing Teaching, Research and Service for Personnel Decisions and Improvements.* Jossey-Bass.

Centre for Higher Education Studies (1993) *Identifying and Developing a Quality Ethos for Teaching in Higher Education.* Newsletter 3, April. London: Institute of Education, University of London.

Centre for Research into Quality (1995) *The 1995 Report on the Student Experience at UCE.* Birmingham: University of Central England in Birmingham.

Chartres, J. (1986) 'Selectivity – the latest cuts.' *AUT Bulletin*, September.

Chen, H-T. (1990) *Theory-Driven Evaluations.* London: Sage Publications.

Chrisman, J. (1994) *Economic Benefits Provided to the Province of Alberta by the Faculty of Calgary.* Calgary: University of Calgary.

Christensen, T. (1992) *Virksomhetsplanlegging – Myteskaping eller intrumentell problemslosning.* Oslo: Tano.

CIPFA (1984) *Performance Indicators in the Education Service.* CIPFA Consultative Paper. London: CIPFA.

Clark, A. and Tarsh, J. (1987) 'How much is a degree worth?' In *Educational Training*, Policy Journals.

Clark, K. (1954) 'The APA study of psychologists.' *American Psychologist 9*, 117–120.

Clayton, K. (1987) *The Measurement of Research in Higher Education.* Norwich: University of East Anglia.

Clift, J., Hall, C. and Turner, I. (1989) 'Establishing the validity of a set of summative teaching performance scales.' *Assessment and Evaluation in Higher Education 14*, 3, Autumn, 193–206.

Cole, J. and Cole, S. (1972) 'The ortega hypothesis.' *Science 178*, 17, October, 368–375.

Collini, S. (1989) 'Publish and be dimmed.' *Times Higher Education Supplement*, 3 February 1989.

Collins, P. and Wyatt, S. (1988) 'Citations in patents to the basic research literature.' *Research Policy 17*, 2, April, 65–74.

Collinson, J. and Hockey, J. (1995) 'Sanctions and savings: some reflections on ESRC doctoral policy.' *Higher Education Review 27*, 3, 56–63.

Committee of Vice-Chancellors and Principals – Steering Committee for Efficiency Studies in Universities (1985) *National Data Study.* London: CVCP.

Committee of Vice-Chancellors and Principals and University Grants Committee (1986) *Performance Indicators in Universities: A First Statement by a Joint CVCP/UGC Working Group.* London: CVCP.

Committee of Vice-Chancellors and Principals (1986) *Reynolds Report. Academic Standards in the Universities.* London: CVCP.

Committee of Vice-Chancellors and Principals and University Grants Committee (1987a) *A Second Statement by the Joint CVCP/UGC Working Group.* London: CVCP.

Committee of Vice-Chancellors and Principals and University Grants Committee (1987b) *University Management Statistics and Performance Indicators.* London: CVCP.

Committee of Vice-Chancellors and Principals and University Grants Committee (1988) *University Management Statistics and Performance Indicators in the UK,* (second edition). London: CVCP.

Committee of Vice-Chancellors and Principals/Universities Funding Council – Performance Indicators Steering Committee (1989) *Issues in Quantitative Assessment of Departmental Research.* London: CVCP/UFC.

Committee of Vice-Chancellors and Principals/Universities Funding Council (1989) *University Management Statistics and Performance Indicators in the UK,* (third edition). London: CVCP/UFC.

Committee of Vice-Chancellors Principals/Universities Funding Council (1990) *University Management Statistics and Performance Indicators in the UK,* (fourth edition). London: CVCP/UFC.

Committee of Vice-Chancellors and Principals, Committee of Directors of Polytechinics, Standing Conference of Principals (1991) A New Quality Assurance Organisation for Higher Education. Report to the Minister of Higher Education. London: CVCP, CDP, SCOP.

Committe of Vice-Chancellors and Principals Academic Audit Unit (1991) *Notes for the Guidance of Auditors.* Birmingham: CVCP Academic Audit Unit.

Committe of Vice-Chancellors and Principals Academic Audit Unit (1992) *Annual Report of the Director 1990/91.* Birmingham: CVCP Academic Audit Unit.

Committee of Vice-Chancellors and Principals (1993) *Research Performance Indicators: Annual Publications Survey, First Annual Publications Survey: CalenderYear 1991, N/93/51.* London: CVCP.

Committee of Vice-Chancellors and Principals (1994) *CVCP 11 Point Plan.* London: CVCP.

Committee of Vice-Chancellors and Principals (1995a) *Higher Education Management Statistics: A Future Strategy.* London: CVCP.

Committee of Vice-Chancellors and Principals (1995b) *University Management Statistics and Performance Indicators in the UK*, (ninth edition). London: CVCP.

Committee of Vice-Chancellors and Principals (1995c) *Developing Quality Assurance in Partnership with the Institutions of Higher Education*. London: CVCP.

Conrad, C. and Blackburn R. (1985) 'Program quality in higher education.' In J. Smart (ed) *Higher Education: Handbook of Theory and Research 1*. New York: Agathon Press.

Cook, S. (1989) 'Improving the quality of student ratings of instruction: a look at two strategies.' *Research in Higher Education 30*, 1, 31–45.

Coulter, W. and Moore, A. (1987) 'Utilisation of performance indicators for financing higher education at state level in the United States. The Ohio case.' *International Journal of Institutional Management in Higher Education 11*, 2, 195–207.

Council for National Academic Awards (1989) 'Towards an educational audit.' Information Services Discussion Paper 3. London: CNAA.

Council for National Academic Awards (1990) *Performance Indicators and Quality Assurance*. Information Services Discussion Paper 4. Lodnon: CNAA.

Cox, W.M. and Catt, V. (1977) 'Productivity ratings of graduate programs in psychology.' *American Psychologist 32*, 793–813.

Cozzens, S. (1989) 'What do citations count? The rhetoric-first model.' *Scientometrics 15*, 437–447.

Crewe, I. (1987) *Reputation, Research and Reality: The Publication Records of UK Departments of Politics 1978–1984*. (Essex Papers in Politics and Government No.44.) Colchester: Department of Government, University of Essex.

Croham (1987) *Review of the University Grants Committee*, Cm.81. London: HMSO.

Cuenin, S. (1986) *International Study of the Development of Performance Indicators in Higher Education*. Paper given to OECD, IMHE Project, Special Topic Workshop.

Cullen, B. (1987) 'Performance indicators in UK higher education: progress and prospects.' *International Journal of Institutional Management in Higher Education 11*, 2.

Daffern, P. and Walshe, E. (1990) 'Evaluating performance in the department of the environment.' In M. Cave, M. Kogan and R. Smith (eds) *Output and Performance Measurement in Government: The State of the Art*. London: Jessica Kingsley Publishers.

Davies, J. (1993) 'The development and use of performance indicators within higher education institutions: a conceptualisation of the issues.' In H.R. Kells (ed) (1993) *The Development of Performance Indicators for Higher Education: A Compendium for Twelve Countries*, (Second Edition). Paris: Programme on Institutional Management in Higher Education, OECD.

Davis, D. (1996) *The Real World of Performance Indicators: A Review of Their Use in Selected Commonwealth Countries*. London: Commonwealth Higher Education Management Service.

DeHayes, D. and Lovrinic, J. (1994) 'Activity-based costing model for assessing economic performance.' In V. Borden and T. Banta (eds) *Using Performance Indicators to Guide Strategic Decision Making. New Directions for Institutional Research 82*, 81–93.

Department of Health (1993) *Special Health Authorities: Research Review*. London: HMSO.

Department of Trade and Industry (1995) White Paper *Competitiveness: Forging Ahead*, Cm.2867. London: HMSO.

Dersjant, N. (1993) 'The Netherlands.' In H.R. Kells (ed) *The Development of Performance Indicators for Higher Education: A Compendium for Twelve Countries*, (Second Edition). Paris: Programme on Institutional Management in Higher Education, OECD.

DES (1985) Green Paper *The Development of Higher Education into the 1990s Cmnd. 9524*. London: HMSO.

DES (1987a) *Accounting and Auditing in Higher Education*. London: DES.

DES (1987b) *Changes in Structure and National Planning for Higher Education, Universities Funding Council* (Consultative Document). London: DES.

DES (1987c) *Changes in Structure and National Planning for Higher Education. Contracts Between the Funding Bodies and Higher Education Institutions* (Consultative Document). London: DES.

DES (1987d) *Changes in Structure and National Planning for Higher Education. Polytechnics and Colleges Sector* (Consultative Document). London: DES.

DES (1987e) White Paper *Higher Education: Meeting the Challenge, Cm. 114*. London: HMSO.

DES (1991) White Paper *Higher Education: A New Framework*, Cm 1541. London: HMSO.

DES and Department of Employment (1985) *Graduates and Jobs: Some Guidance for Young People Considering a Degree*. London: HMSO.

Dill, D. (1995a) 'Through Deming's eyes: a cross-national analysis of quality assurance policies in higher education.' *Quality in Higher Education 1*, 2, 95–110.

Dill, D. (1995b) 'Accreditation, assessment, anarchy?: the evolution of academic quality assurance policies in the united states.' Institutional Responses to Quality Assessment Conference, CERI/IMHE, OECD, Paris, 4–6 December 1995.

Dochy, F., Segers, M. and Wijnen, W. (eds) (1987a) *Quality Assurance in Higher Education*. The Dogue: Dutch Ministry of Education.

Dochy, F., Segers, M. and Wijnen, W. (1987b) *Managerial Context of the Research Project, The Use of Performance Indicators as a Part of the New Steering Conception in the Netherlands*. Limburg: Limburg University (mimeo).

Dochy, F., Segers, M. and Wijnen, W. (eds) (1990) *Management Information and Performance Indicators in Higher Education: An International Issue*. Asen/Maastricht: Van Gorcum.

Dowding, K. (1995) 'Model or metaphor? A critical review of the policy network approach.' *Political Studies 43*, 136–158.

Dowell, D. and Neal, J. (1982) 'A selective review of the validity of student ratings of teaching.' *Journal of Higher Education 53*, 1, 51–62.

Drew, D. and Karpf, R. (1981) 'Ranking academic departments: empirical findings and a theoretical perspective.' *Research in Higher Education 14*, 4, 305–320.

Edwards Report (1988) *The Future of University Physics*. London: UGC, HMSO.

Egan, J. (1986) 'Value-added testing and measurement: will it save higher education from its critics?' Paper presented at the Value-Added Learning Conference, Empire College, State University of New York, 4–6 June.

Elsworth, G. (1994) 'Confronting the biases in connoisseur review and performance indicators in higher education: a structural modelling approach.' *Higher Education 27*, 163–190.

Elton, L. (1980) 'Evaluation of an institute for university teaching and learning.' In D. Billing (ed) *Indicators of Performance*. Guildford: The Society for Research into Higher Education.

Elton, L. (1984) 'Evaluating teaching and assessing teachers in universities.' *Assessment and Evaluation in Higher Education 9*, 2, Summer, 97–115.

Elton, L. (1987a) 'UGC resource allocation and the assessment of teaching quality.' *Higher Education Review 19*, 2, Spring, 9–17.

Elton, L. (1987b) 'Warning signs.' *Times Higher Education Supplement*, 11 September 1987.

Elton, L. (1988a) 'Book review.' *Studies in Higher Education 23*, 337–338.

Elton, L. (1988b) 'Appraisal and accountability in higher education: some current issues.' *Higher Education Quarterly 42*, 3, Summer, 207–229.

Evans, T. and Clift, R. (1987) Letter to *Times Higher Education Supplement*, 18 September 1987.

Evered, D. and Harnett, S. (eds) (1989) *The Evaluation of Scientific Research*. (A CIBA Foundation Conference). Chichester: John Wiley and Sons.

Ewell, P. (ed) (1985) *Assessing Educational Outcomes, New Directions for Institutional Research 47.*

Ewell, P. (1991) 'Assessment and public accountability: back to the future.' *Change 23*, 6, 12–17.

Ewell, P. (1994) 'Developing statewide performance indicators for higher education: policy themes and variations.' In S. Ruppert *Charting Higher Education Accountability: A Sourcebook on State-Level Performance Indicators*. Denver: Education Commission of the States.

Ewell, P. and Jones, D. (1994) 'Pointing the way: indicators as policy tools in higher education.' In S. Ruppert (1994) *Charting Higher Education Accountability: A Sourcebook on State-Level Performance Indicators*. Denver: Education Commission of the States.

Fairweather, J. (1988) 'Reputational quality of academic programs: the institutional halo.' *Research in Higher Education 28*, 4, 345–355.

Feldman, K. (1976) 'The superior college teacher from the student's view.' *Research in Higher Education 5*, 243–288.

Feldman, K. (1978) 'Course characteristics and college students' ratings of their teachers and courses: what we know and what we don't.' *Research in Higher Education 9*, 199–242.

Feldman, K. (1988) 'Effective college teaching from the students' and faculty's point of view: matched or mismatched priorities.' *Research in Higher Education 28*, 4, 291–344.

Feldman, K. (1989) 'Instructional effectiveness of college teachers as judged by teachers themselves, current and former students, colleagues, administrators, and external (neutral) observers.' *Research in Higher Education 30*, 2, 137–168.

Field, J. *et al.* (1992) 'Quality counts? citation analysis and performance measurement.' *Higher Education Review 24*, 37–42.

Fox, D. (1984) 'What counts as teaching.' *Assessment and Evaluation in Higher Education 9*, 2, Summer, 133–143.

Frackmann, E. (1987) 'Lessons to be learnt from a decade of discussions on performance indicators.' *International Journal of Institutional Management in Higher Education 11*, 2, 149–162.

Frame, J.D. (1983) 'Quantitative indicators for evaluation of basic research programs/projects.' *IEEE Transactions on Engineering Management EM-30*, 3, August, 106–112.

Frey, P. (1973) 'A two-dimensional analysis of student ratings of instruction.' *Research in Higher Education 9*, 69–91.

Frey, P., Leonard, D. and Beatty, W. (1975) 'Student ratings of instruction: validation research.' *American Educational Research Journal 12*, 327–336.

Fulton, O. (1986) 'Entry standards.' Paper presented to the Anglo-American Seminar on Quality Judgements in Higher Education at Templeton College.

Fulton, O. (1992) 'Higher education studies.' In B. Clark and G. Neave (eds) *The Encyclopedia of Higher Education*. Oxford: Pergamon Press.

Fulton, O. and Ellwood, S. (1989) *Admissions to Higher Education: Policy and Practice*. Sheffield: The Training Agency.

Further Education Unit (1986) *Research Project 304 – Towards an Educational Audit: Feasibility Study*. London: Further Education Unit and the Association of Colleges of Further and Higher Education.

Furumark, A. (1981) 'Institutional self-evaluation in Sweden.' *International Journal of Institutional Management in Higher Education 5*, 3, 207–216.

Gardner, D. (1985) 'Managing the American university.' *International Journal of Institutional Management in Higher Education 9*, 1, March, 5–12.

Garfield, E. (1970) 'Citation indexing for studying science.' *Nature* 227, 25 August 1970, 669–671.

Garfield, E. (1977) 'The 250 most-cited primary authors, 1961–1975. Part II. The correlation between citedness, Nobel prizes and academy memberships.' *Current Contents 50*, 12 December 1977, 5–16.

Garfield, E. (1979) *Citation Indexing: Its Theory and Application in Science, Technology and Humanities*. New York: John Wiley & Sons.

Gevers, J.K.M. (1985) 'Institutional evaluation and review processes.' *International Journal of Institutional Management in Higher Education 9*, 2, July, 145–148.

Gibbons, M. and Georghiou, L. (1987) *Evaluation of Research: A Selection of Current Practices*. Paris: OECD.

Gibbons, M. *et al.* (1994) *The New Production of Knowledge: The Dynamics of Science and Research in Contemporary Societies*. London: Sage Publications.

Gibbs, G. (1995) 'Quality in research and in teaching.' *Quality in Higher Education 1*, 2, 147–158.

Gilbert, G. and Woolgar, S. (1974) 'The quantitative study of science: an examination of the literature.' *Science Studies 4*, 279–294.

Gillett, R. (1986) *Serious Anomalies in the UGC Comparative Evaluation of the Performance of Psychology Departments*. Leicester: Paper from Department of Psychology, University of Leicester.

Gillett, R. (1989) 'Research performance indicators based on peer review: a critical analysis.' *Higher Education Quarterly 43*, 20–38.

Glenn, N. and Villemez, W. (1970) 'The productivity of sociologists at 45 American universities.' *American Sociologist 5*, 224–252.

Goedegebuure, L., Maasen, P. and Westerheijden, D. (eds) (1990) *Peer Review and Performance Indicators*. Utrecht: Uitgeverij Lemma.

Haas, P. (1992) 'Introduction: epistemic communities and international policy co-ordination.' *International Organisation 46*, 1–36.

Haladnya, T. and Hess, R. (1994) 'The detection and correction of bias in student ratings of instruction.' *Research in Higher Education 35*, 6, 669–687.

Hansen, H. and Jorgensen, B. (1995) *Science Policy and Research Management: Can Research Indicators be Used?* Copenhagen: Institute of Political Science, University of Copenhagen (mimeo).

Hare, P. and Wyatt, G. (1988) 'Modelling the determination of research output in British universities.' *Research Policy 17*, 315–329.

Harley, S. and Lee, F. (1995) *The Academic Labour Process and the Research Assessment Exercise*. Occasional Paper 24. Leicester: Leicester Business School, De Montfort University.

Harris, G. (1989) 'Research output in Australian university research centres in economics.' *Higher Education 18*, 397–409.

Harris, G. and Kaine, G. (1994) 'The determinants of research performance: a study of Australian university economists.' *Higher Education 27*, 191–201.

Harris, M. (1986) 'Judgements of quality in higher education: the role of the University Grants Committee.' Paper presented to the Anglo-American Seminar on Quality Judgements in Higher Education at Templeton College.

Harvey, L. (ed) (1992) *Quality Assessment in Higher Education: Collected Papers of the QHE Project*. Birmingham: University of Central England in Birmingham.

Harvey, L., Burrows, A. and Green, D. (1992) *Criteria of Quality*. Quality in Higher Education Project. Birmingham: University of Central England in Birmingham.

Harvey, L. (1995) 'Editorial'. *Quality in Higher Education 1*, 1, 5–12.

Hativa, N. and Raviv, A. (1993) 'Using a single score for summative teacher evaluation by students.' *Research in Higher Education 34*, 5, 625–646.

Henkel, M. (1991) *Government, Evaluation and Change*. London: Jessica Kingsley Publishers.

Henkel, M. (1994) 'PSSRU research on care management: Kent community project.' In M. Buxton *et al.* (1994) *Assessing Payback from Department of Health Research and Development, Vol. 2: 8 Case Studies*. Uxbridge: Health Economics Research Group, Brunel University.

Hicks, D. and Skea, J. (1989) 'Is big really better.' *Physics World*, December, 31–34.

Higher Education Council (1993) *Achieving Quality*. Canberra: Australia Government Publishing Service.

Higher Education Funding Council for England (1993a) *Assessment of the Quality of Higher Education*, Circular 3/93. Bristol: HEFCE.

Higher Education Funding Council for England (1993b) *Assessors'*
Handbook. Bristol: HEFCE

Higher Education Funding Council for England (1993c) *Research*
Funding Method, Circular 7/93. Bristol: HEFCE.

Higher Education Funding Council for England (1993d) *Research*
Assessment, Consultation Paper 6/93, (including UFC 1992 RAE
Report). Bristol: HEFCE.

Higher Education Funding Council for England (1994) *The Quality*
Assessment Method from April 1995, Circular 39/94. Bristol: HEFCE.

Higher Education Funding Council for England *et al.* (1994) *1996*
Research Assessment Exercise, Circular RAE96 1/94. Bristol: HEFCE .

Higher Education Funding Council for England (1995a) *Report on*
Quality Assessment 1992–1995. Bristol: HEFCE.

Higher Education Funding Council for England (1995b) *Developing*
Quality Assurance in Partnership with the Institutions of Higher
Education. Bristol: HEFCE.

Higher Education Funding Council for England (1995c) *Funding for*
the Development of Teaching and Learning, Circular 29/95. Bristol:
HEFCE.

Higher Education Funding Council for England *et al.* (1995) *Research*
Assessment Exercise: Criteria for Assessment and Working Methods of
Panels, Circular RAE96 3/95. Bristol: HEFCE.

Higher Education Management Statistics (HEMS) Group (1995)
Higher Education Management Statistics: Publication in 1996. London:
CVCP/SCOP/COSHEP.

Higher Education Quality Council (1993; 1995a) *Notes for the Guidance*
of Auditors. London: HEQC.

Higher Education Quality Council (1994) *Learning from Audit.*
London: HEQC.

Higher Education Quality Council (1995b, unpublished) *Report on the*
QAEN Consultative Seminars: 'Graduate Standards'.

Higher Education Quality Council (1995c) *Graduate Standards*
Programme: Interim Report. London: HEQC.

HMI (1989) 'In pursuit of quality: an HMI view.' In *Quality in Higher*
Education: a Report on an HMI Invitation Conference. London: HMI.

Hoare, A. (1995) 'Scale economies in academic excellence: an
exploratory analysis of the United Kingdom's 1992 research
selectivity exercise.' *Higher Education 29,* 241–260.

Hoggett, P. (1991) 'A new management in the public sector?' *Policy and Politics 19*, 4, 243–256.

Hölttä, S. (1988) 'Recent changes in the Finnish higher education system.' *European Journal of Education 23*, 1/2, 91–104.

Howard, G., Conway, C. and Maxwell, S. (1985) 'Construct validity of measures of college teaching effectiveness.' *Journal of Educational Psychology 77*, 187–196.

Hüfner, K. (1987a) 'The role of performance indicators in higher education: the case for Germany.' *International Journal of Institutional Management in Higher Education 11*, 2, 140–148.

Hüfner, K. (1987b) 'Differentiation and competition in higher education: recent trends in the federal republic of Germany.' *European Journal of Education 22*, 2, 134–144.

Hüfner. K. and Rau, E. (1987) 'Measuring performance in higher education – problems and perspectives.' *Higher Education in Europe 12*, 4, 5–13.

Ince, M. (1990) 'Costing the origin of the thesis.' *Times Higher Education Supplement*, 12 October, p.8.

In't Veld, R., Spee, A. and Tseng, H. (1987) *Performance Indicators in Higher Education in the Netherlands*. Paper presented at the OECD Conference on Education Indicators, Washington DC, 3–6 November.

Irvine, J. (1989) 'Evaluation of scientific institutions: lessons from a bibliometric study of UK technical universities.' In D. Evered and S. Harnett (eds) *The Evaluation of Scientific Research*. (CIBA Foundation Conference). Chichester: John Wiley & Sons.

Jackson, P. (ed) (1995) *Measures for Success in the Public Sector, A Public Finance Foundation Reader*. London: CIPFA.

Jappinen, A. (1987) 'Current situation regarding the development and use of performance indicators in Finland.' *International Journal of Institutional Management in Higher Education 11*, 2, 163–170.

Jarratt Report (1985) *Report of the Steering Committee for Efficiency Studies in Universities*. London: CVCP.

Jenkins, A. (1995) 'The research assessment exercise, funding and teaching quality.' *Quality Assurance in Higher Education 3.2*, 4–12.

Jesson, D. and Mayston, D. (1990) 'Information, accountability and educational performance indicators.' In C. Fitzgibbon (ed) *Performance Indicators*, British Educational Research Association Dialogues No. 2. Clevedon: Multilingual Matters.

Johnes, G. (1986a) *Determinants of Research Output in Economics Departments in British Universities* (discussion paper). Lancaster: University of Lancaster, Department of Economics.

Johnes, G. (1986b) *Research Performance Indicators in the University Sector*. Lancaster: University of Lancaster (mimeo).

Johnes, G. (1988) 'Research performance indicators in the university sector.' *Higher Education Quarterly* 42, 1, Winter, 54–71.

Johnes, G. (1990) 'Measures of research output: university departments of economics in the UK, 1984–1988.' *Economic Journal* 100, June, 556–560.

Johnes, G. (1995) 'Scale and technical efficiency in the production of economic research.' *Applied Economic Letters* 2, 7–11.

Johnes, G. and Johnes, J. (1990) *Measuring the Research Performance of UK Economics Departments: An Application of Data Envelopment Analysis* (Discussion paper EC/17/90). Lancaster: Lancaster University Management School.

Johnes, G. and Johnes, J. (1993) 'Measuring the research performance of UK economics departments.' *Oxford Economic Papers* 45, 332–347.

Johnes, J. (1990a) 'Determinants of student wastage in higher education.' *Studies in Higher Education* 15, 1, 87–99.

Johnes, J. (1990b) 'Unit costs: some explanations of the differences between UK universities.' *Applied Economics* 22, 853–862.

Johnes, J. and Taylor, J. (1987) 'Degree quality: an investigation into differences between UK universities.' *Higher Education* 16, 581–602.

Johnes, J. and Taylor, J. (1989a) 'Undergraduate non-completion rates: difference between UK universities.' *Higher Education* 15, 3, 209–225.

Johnes, J. and Taylor, J. (1989b) 'The first destination of new graduates: comparisons between universities.' *Applied Economics* 21, 357–373.

Johnes, J. and Taylor, J. (1990a) *Performance Indicators in Higher Education*. Buckingham: SRHE and Open University Press.

Johnes, J. and Taylor, J. (1990b) 'The research performance of UK universities: a statistical analysis of the results of the 1989 research selectivity exercise.' Discussion Paper.

Johnes, J. and Taylor, J. (1991) 'Non-completion of a degree course and its effects on the subsequent experience of non-completers in the labour market.' *Studies in Higher Education* 16, 1, 73–82.

Johnson, H. (1975) *Technology and Economic Interdependence*. London: Macmillan.

Johnston, R. (1989) 'Do you use the telephone too much? A review of performance indicators, evaluation and appraisal in British universities.' *Journal of Geography in Higher Education 13*, 1, 31–44.

Johnston, R., Jones, K. and Gould, M. (1995) 'Development size and reseach in English universities.' *Quality in Higher Education 1*, 1, 41–47.

Joint Performance Indicators Working Group (1994) *Management Statistics and Performance Indicators in Higher Education: Consultative Report*. Bristol: HEFCE.

Jones, L.V., Lindzey, G. and Coggeshall, P. (1982) *An Assessment of Research Doctorate Programs in the USA*. (five volumes). Washington DC: National Academy Press.

Jongbloed, B. and Westerheijden, D. (1994) 'Performance indicators and quality assessment in European higher education.' In V. Borden and T. Banta (eds) *Using Performance Indicators to Guide Strategic Decision Making. New Directions for Institutional Research 82*, 37–50.

Jordan, T. (1989) *Measurement and Evaluation in Higher Education*. London: The Falmer Press.

Joss, R. and Kogan, M. (1995) *Advancing Quality: Total Quality Management in the National Health Service*. Birmingham: Open University Press.

Kells, H. (1983) *Self Study Process*. New York: Macmillan.

Kells, H. (1986) 'The second irony: the system of institutional evaluation of higher education in the United States.' *International Journal of Institutional Management in Higher Education 10*, 2, July, 140–149.

Kells, H. (1989) *The Inadequacy of Performance Indicators for Higher Education: The Need for a More Comprehensive and Developmental Construct*. (mimeo).

Kells, H. (ed) (1990) *The Development of Performance Indicators for Higher Education: A Compendium for Eleven Countries*. Paris: Programme on Institutional Management in Higher Education, OECD.

Kells, H. (ed) (1993) *The Development of Performance Indicators for Higher Education: A Compendium for Twelve Countries*, (second edition). Paris: Programme on Institutional Management in Higher Education, OECD.

Kingman Report (1989) *Costing of Teaching in Universities*. London: CVCP.

Kishor, N. (1995) 'The effect of implicit theories on raters' inference in performance measurement: consequences for validity of student ratings of instruction.' *Research in Higher Education 36*, 2, 177–195.

Klein, R. and Carter, N. (1988) 'Performance measurement: a review of concepts and issues.' In D. Beeton (ed) *Performance Measurement: Getting the Concepts Right*. London: Public Finance Foundation.

Knudsen, D. and Vaughan, T. (1969) 'Quality in graduate education: a re-evaluation of the rankings of sociology departments in the Cartter report.' *American Sociologist 4*, 12–19.

Kogan, M. (1989) 'The evaluation of higher education: an introductory note.' In M. Kogan (ed) *Evaluating Higher Education*. London: Jessica Kingsley Publishers.

Kogan, M. (1994) 'Assessment and productive research.' *Higher Education Quarterly 48*, 56–67.

Kogan, M. and Henkel, M. (1983) *Government and Research: The Rothschild Experiment in a Government Department*. Oxford: Heinemann Educational Books.

Kogan, M. and Tuijnman, A. (1995) *Educational Research and Development: Trends, Issues and Challenges*. Paris: OECD.

Koon, J. and Murray, H. (1995) 'Using multiple outcomes to validate student ratings of overall teacher effectiveness.' *Journal of Higher Education 66*, 1, 61–81.

Kyvik, S. (1995) 'Are big university departments better than smaller ones?' *Higher Education 30*, 295–304.

Laband, D. (1985) 'An evaluation of 50 ranked economics departments – by quantity and quality of faculty publications and graduate school placement and research success.' *Southern Economic Journal 52*, 1, 216–240.

Laegreud, P. (1991) *Malstyring og virksomhetsplanlegging i offentlig sektor*. Bergen: Alma Mater.

Laurillard, D.M. (1980) 'Validity of indicators of performance.' In D. Billing (ed) *Indicators of Performance*. Guildford: The Society for Research into Higher Education.

Layard, R. and Glaister, S. (eds) (1994) *Cost-Benefit Analysis.* Cambridge: Cambridge University Press.

Le Grand, J. and Robinson, R. (1979) *The Economics of Social Problems.* London: Macmillan.

Liebowitz, S. and Palmer, J. (1984) 'Assessing the relative impacts of economics journals.' *Journal of Economic Literature* March, 77–88.

Lindop Report (1985) *Academic Validation in Public Sector Higher Education, Cmnd. 9501.* London: HMSO.

Lindsey, D. (1989) 'Using citation counts as a measure of quality in science: measuring what's measurable rather than what's valid.' *Scientometrics 15,* 3–4, 187–203.

Linke, R. (1990) 'Australia.' In H. Kells (ed) *The Development of Performance Indicators for Higher Education: A Compendium for Eleven Countries.* Paris: OECD.

Linke, R. (1991) *Report of the Research Group on Performance Indicators in Higher Education.* Canberra: Department of Employment, Education and Training.

Linke, R. (1993) 'Australia.' In H. Kells (ed) *The Development of Performance Indicators for Higher Education: A Compendium for Twelve Countries,* (Second Edition). Paris: Programme on Institutional Management in Higher Education, OECD.

Linke, R. (1995) 'Improving quality assurance in Australian higher education.' *Higher Education Management 7,* 49–62.

Maassen, R. (1987) 'Quality control in Dutch higher education: versus external evaluation.' *European Journal of Education 22,* 2, 161–171.

Maassen, R. and Van Vught, F. (1988) 'An intriguing Janus Head: the two faces of the new governmental strategy for higher education in the Netherlands.' *European Journal of Education 23,* 1/2, 65–76.

MacRoberts, M. and MacRoberts, B. (1986) 'Quantitative measures of communication in science: a study of the formal level.' *Social Studies of Science 16,* 151–172.

Mallier, T. and Rodgers, T. (1995) 'Measuring value added in higher education: a proposal.' *Education Economics 3,* 2, 119–132.

Marsh, H.W. (1984) 'Students' evaluations of university teaching: dimensionality, reliability, validity, potential biases and utility.' *Journal of Educational Psychology 76,* 707–754.

Marsh, H.W. (1987) 'Students' evaluations of university teaching: research findings, methodological issues, and directions for future research.' *International Journal of Educational Research 11*, 253–388.

Marsh, H.W. (1991a) 'Multidimensional students' evaluations of teaching effectiveness: a test of higher order structures.' *Journal of Educational Psychology 83*, 285–296.

Marsh, H.W. (1991b) 'A multidimensional perspective to students' evaluation of teaching effectiveness: a response to Abrami and d' Apollonia.' *Journal of Educational Psychology 83*, 416–421.

Marshall, N. (1995) 'Policy communities, issue networks and the formulation of Australian higher education policy.' *Higher Education 30*, 273–293.

Martin, B. and Irvine, J. (1983) 'Assessing basic research: some partial indicators of scientific progress in radio astronomy.' *Research Policy 12*, 61–90.

Martin, B., Irvine, J. and Crouch, D. (1985) *Science Indicators for Research Policy in Bibliometric Analysis of Ocean Currents and Protein Crystallography*. Brighton: Science Policy Research Unit, University of Sussex.

Mathias, H. and Rutherford, D. (1982) 'Lecturers as evaluators· the Birmingham experience.' *Studies in Higher Education 7*, 1, 47–56.

Matland, R. (1987) 'Kor flinke er universitetstilsette og korleis kan vi bli betre?' *Norsk statsvitenskapelig tidsskrift 2*, 65–86.

Mayston, D. (1985) 'Non-profit performance indicators in the public sector.' *Financial Accountability and Management 1*, 1, 51–74.

McClain, C., Krueger, D. and Taylor, T. (1986) 'Northeast missouri state university's value-added assessment program. A model for educational accountability.' *Journal of Institutional Management in Higher Education 10*, 3, 252–271.

McMillan, J. (1988) 'Beyond value-added education.' *Journal of Higher Education 59*, 564–579.

McVicar, M. (ed) (1990) *Performance Indicators and Quality Control in Higher Education*. Papers presented to an International Conference held at the Institute of Education (University of London) on 27 September 1989. Portsmouth: Portsmouth Polytechnic.

Mertens, F. and Bormans, R. (1990) 'Background to the development of a system of performance indicators in the Netherlands.' In F. Dochy, M. Segers and W. Wijnen (eds) (1990) *Management*

Information and Performance Indicators in Higher Education: An International Issue. Assen/Maastricht: Van Gorcum.

Mertens, P. (1979) 'Comparative indicators for German universities.' *International Journal of Institutional Management in Higher Education* 3, 1, 155–168.

Miller, R.I. (1986) 'A ten year perspective on faculty evaluation.' *International Journal of Institutional Management in Higher Education* 10, 2, July, 162–168.

Miller, R.I. (1987a) Correspondence with Prof. M. Kogan.

Miller, R.I. (1987b) *Evaluating Faculty for Promotion and Tenure.* San Fransisco, CA: Jossey-Bass.

Ministry of Education, Finland (1986) *Development Act.*

Ministry of Education, Finland (1994) *Higher Education Policy in Finland.* Helsinki: Ministry of Education.

Ministry of Education, The Netherlands (1985) *Higher Education, Autonomy and Quality.* Den Haag: Staatsuitgeverij.

Minsitry of Education, The Netherlands (1988) *Higher Education and Research Plan.* Den Haag: Staatsuitgeverij.

Minogue, K. (1986) 'Political science and the gross intellectual product.' *Government and Opposition 21,* 4, 185–194.

Mitchell, M. (1996) 'Activity based costing in UK universities.' *Public Money and Management 16,* January–March, 51–57.

Moed, H.F. *et al.* (1985) 'The use of bibliometric data as tools for university research policy.' *International Journal of Institutional Management in Higher Education 9,* 2, 185–194.

Moore, P. (1987) 'University financing 1979–1986.' *Higher Education Quarterly 41,* 1, January, 25–42.

Moravcsik, M. (1986) 'Assessing the methodology for finding a methodology for assessment.' *Social Studies of Science 26,* 534–39.

Morris Report (1990) *Performance Indicators: Report of a Committee of Enquiry Chaired by Mr Alfred Morris.* London: PCFC.

Morrison, H., Magennis, S. and Carey, L. (1995) 'Performance indicators and league tables: a call for standards.' *Higher Education Quarterly 49,* 2, 128–145.

Moses, I. (1985) 'High quality teaching in a university: identification and description.' *Studies in Higher Education 10,* 76–86.

Moses, I. (1986) 'Student evaluation of teaching in an Australian university – staff perceptions and reactions.' *Assessment and Evaluation in Higher Education 11*, 2, 117–129.

Moses, I. (1989) 'Role of problems of heads of departments in performance appraisal.' *Assessment and Evaluation in Higher Education 14*, 2, Summer, 95a9696.

Murray, H. (1984) 'The impact of formative and summative evaluation of teaching in north American universities.' *Assessment and Evaluation in Higher Education 9*, 2, Summer, 117–132.

Muth, J. (1961) 'Rational expectations and the theory of price movements.' *Econometrica 29*, 6.

NAB (1987) *Management for a Purpose: The Report of the Good Management Practice Group.* London: NAB.

Nandy, S., Brown, N. and Woollard, L. (1993) 'United Kingdom.' In H. Kells (ed) *The Development of Performance Indicators for Higher Education: A Compendium for Twelve Countries*, (second edition). Paris: Programme on Institutional Management in Higher Education, OECD.

Narin, F. (1987) 'Bibliometric techniques in the evaluation of research programs.' *Science and Public Policy 14*, 99–106.

National Academies Policy Advisory Group (1996) *Research Capability of the University System.* London: The British Academy, the Conference of Royal Medical Colleges, the Royal Academy of Engineering and the Royal Society.

Neave, G. (1985) 'Elite and mass higher education in Britain: a regressive model?' *Comparative Education Review 29*, 3, 347–361.

Neave, G. (1987) 'Editorial.' *European Journal of Education 22*, 2, 121–122.

Neave, G. (1988) 'On the cultivation of quality, efficiency and enterprise: an overview of recent trends in higher education in western Europe, 1986–1988.' *European Journal of Education 23*, 1/2, 7–23.

Nederhof, A. and Van Raan, A. (1989) 'A validation study of bibliometric indicators: the comparative performance of Cum Laude Doctorates in chemistry.' *Scientometrics 17*, 5–6, 427–435.

Nederhof, A. and Van Raan, A. (1993) 'A bibliometric analysis of six economics research groups: a comparison with peer review.' *Research Policy 22*, 353–368.

Nedwek, B. and Neal, J. (1994) 'Performance indicators and rational management tools: a comparative assessment of projects in north America and Europe.' *Research in Higher Education 35*, 1, 75–103.

Newby, H. (1990) 'New answers to searching questions.' *Times Higher Education Supplement*, 30 March 1990.

Niemi, A., Jr. (1975) 'Journal publication performance during 1970–1974: the relative output of southern economics departments.' *Southern Economics Journal 42*, 97–106.

Niiniluoto, I. (1990) 'Finland.' In H. Kells (ed) *The Development of Performance Indicators for Higher Education: A Compendium for Eleven Countries.* OECD.

Nimmer, J. and Stone, E. (1991) 'Effects of grading practices and time of rating on student ratings of faculty performance and student learning.' *Research in Higher Education 32*, 2.

O'Brien, P. (1994) 'Research selectivity exercises: a sceptical but positive note.' *Higher Education Review 26*, 7–17.

OECD (1995) *Higher Education Policy Review: Finland.* Paris: OECD.

Office of Science and Technology (1993) White Paper. *Realising our Potential – A Strategy for Science, Engineering and Technology,* Cm.2250. London: HMSO.

O'Leary, J. and Cannon, T. (1995) *The Times Good University Guide.* London: Times Books.

Ory, J. and Parker, S. (1989) 'Assessment activities at large research universities.' *Research in Higher Education 30*, 4, 375–385.

Osborne, M.J. (1989) 'On the marginal cost of a student in the public sector of higher education in the UK.' *Journal of Further and Higher Education 13*, 1, Spring, 55–65.

Oxburgh Report (1987) *Strengthening University Earth Sciences.* London: UGC.

Page, E. (1987) Letter to *Times Higher Education Supplement*, 25 September 1987.

Page, E. (1988) Letter to *The Times*, 8 October 1988.

Pettifor, J.C. *Print Out.* Nottingham: Nottingham Polytechnic.

Phillimore, A. (1989) 'University research performance indicators in practice: the university grants committee's evaluation of British universities 1985–6.' *Research Policy 18*, 255–71.

Phillips, D. (1989) 'Chairman's remarks.' In D. Evered and S. Harnett (eds) *The Evaluation of Scientific Research*. (CIBA Foundation Conference). Chichester: John Wiley and Sons.

Phillips, D. and Turney, J. (1988) 'Bibliometrics and UK science policy.' *Scientometrics 14*, 185–200.

Pike, G. (1991) 'The effects of background, coursework and involvement on students' grades and satisfaction.' *Research in Higher Education 32*, 1, 15–30.

Platt, J. (1987) 'Research dissemination: a case study.' *The Quarterly Journal of Social Affairs 3*, 181–198.

Pollitt, C. (1986) 'Beyond the managerial model: the case for broadening performance assessment in government and the public services.' *Financial Accountability and Management 2*, 3, 155–170.

Pollitt, C. (1987) 'The politics of performance assessment: lesson for higher education?' *Studies in Higher Education 12*, 1, 87–98.

Pollitt, C. (1988) 'Bringing consumers into performance measurement: concepts, consequences and constraints.' *Policy and Politics 16*, 2, 77–87.

Pollitt, C. (1989) 'Performance indicators in the longer term.' *Public Money and Management 9*, 3, Autumn, 51–55.

Pollitt, C. (1993) *Managerialism in the Public Services*, (Second edition). Oxford: Blackwell.

Pollitt, C. (1995) 'Justification by works or by faith? Evaluating the new public management.' *Evaluation: An International Journal of Theory, Research and Practice 1*, 1, 135–157.

Polytechnics and Colleges Funding Council (1989) *Recurrent Funding Methodology 1990/91. Guidance for Institutions*. London: PCFC.

Polytechnics and Colleges Funding Council (1990) *Recurrent Funding and Equipment Allocations for 1990/91*. London: PCFC.

Polytechnics and Colleges Funding Council (1992) *Macro Performance Indicators*. Bristol: PCFC.

Polytechnics and Colleges Funding Council and Council for National Academic Awards (1990) *The Measurement of Value Added in Higher Education*. London: PCFC/CNAA.

Porrer, R. (1984) *Higher Education and Employment*. London: Association of Graduate Careers Advisory Services.

Porter, A. (1977) 'Citation analysis: queries and caveats.' *Social Studies of Science 7*, 257–267.

Pratt, J. (1989) 'The context.' In *Report of a Conference on Performance Indicators in Teacher Education*. London: Centre for Institutional Studies, Polytechnic of East London.

Psacharopoulos, G. (1985) 'Returns to education: a further international update and implications.' *Journal of Human Resources* 4, 583–604.

Raiten, D. and Berman, S. (1993) *Can the Impact of Basic Biomedical Research be Measured?: A Case Study Approach*. Bethseda, MD: Life Sciences Research Office, Federation of American Societies for Experimental Biology.

Ramsden, P. (1991) 'A performance indicator of teaching quality in higher education: the course experience questionnaire.' *Studies in Higher Education 16*, 2, 129–150.

Ramsden, P. and Entwistle, N. (1981) 'Effects of academic departments on students' approaches to studying.' *British Journal of Educational Psychology 51*, 368–383.

Rasmussen, P. (1985) 'A case study on the evaluation of research at the technical university of Denmark.' *International Journal of Institutional Management in Higher Education 9*, 1, March, 58–66.

Reynolds Report (1986) *Academic Standards in Universities*. London: CVCP.

Rhodes, D.M. and Rumery, R.E. (1980) 'Student reports as indicators of instructor performance.' In D. Billing (ed) *Indicators of Performance*. Guilford: The Society for Research into Higher Education.

Rhodes, R. and Marsh, D. (1992) 'New directions in the study of policy networks.' *European Journal of Political Research 21*, 181–205.

Richardson, A., Jackson, C. and Sykes, W. (1990) *Taking Research Seriously*. London: Department of Health.

Richardson, J. (1994) 'A British evaluation of the course experience questionnaire.' *Studies in Higher Education 19*, 1, 59–68.

Richardson, R. (1994) 'Effectiveness in undergraduate education: an analysis of state education indicators.' In S. Ruppert (ed) *Charting Higher Education Accountability: A Sourcebook on State-Level Performance Indicators*. Denver: Education Commission of the States.

Rimson, J. (1991) *Activity Accounting: An Activity Based Costing Approach*. New York: John Wiley and Sons Inc.

Robey, J. (1979) 'Political science departments: reputations versus productivity.' *Political Science 12*, 202–209.

Roe, E. and McDonald, R. (1983) *Informed Professional Judgement*. St. Lucia: University of Queensland Press.

Rogers, A. and Scratcherd, T. (1986) Letter to *Times Higher Education Supplement*, 7 November 1986.

Rogers, B. and Gentemann, K. (1989) 'The value of institutional research in the assessment of institutional effectiveness.' *Research in Higher Education 30*, 3, 345–355.

Roith Report (1990) *Research in the PCFC Sector: Report of the Committee of Enquiry Appointed by the Council*. London: PCFC.

Roose, K. and Andersen, C. (1970) *A Rating of Graduate Programs*. Washington D.C.: American Council on Education.

Rossi, P. (1982) 'Some Dissenting Comments on Stake's Review.' In E.R. House (ed) *Evaluation Studies Review Annual 7*. London: Sage.

Royal Society of Chemistry (1995) *Chemistry in the UK – Will it Survive? Conclusions of the Royal Society of Chemistry Workshops*. London: Royal Society of Chemistry.

Ruppert, S. (ed) (1994) *Charting Higher Education Accountability: A Sourcebook on State-Level Performance Indicators*. Denver: Education Commission of the States.

Rutherford, D. (1987) 'Indicators of performance: reactions and issues.' *Assessment and Evaluation in Higher Education 12*, 2, Summer, 94–104.

Rutherford, D. (1988) 'Performance appraisal: a survey of academic staff opinion.' *Studies in Higher Education 13*, 1, 89–100.

Schmitz, C. (1993) 'Assessing the validity of higher education indicators.' *Journal of Higher Education 64*, 5, 503–521.

Science and Engineering Policy Studies Unit (1991) *Quantitive Assessment of Departmental Research: A Survey of Academics' Views*, Policy Study No. 5. London: SEPSU.

Scottish Education Department (1992) *Performance Indicators: Final Report of the Conference of Scottish Centrally Funded Colleges/Scottish Office Education Department Working Party*. Edinburgh: SED.

Scottish Higher Education Funding Council (1992) *Quality Assessment: The SHEFC Approach*. Edinburgh: SHFCE.

Segers, M., Wijnen, W. and Dochy, F. (1990) 'Performance indicators: a new management technology for higher education? The case of the United Kingdom, the Netherlands and Australia.' In F. Dochy, M. Segers and W. Wijnen. (eds) *Management Information and*

Performance Indicators in Higher Education: An International Issue.
Assen/Maastricht: Van Gorcum.

Selmes, C. (1989) 'Evaluation of teaching.' *Assessment and Evaluation in Higher Education 14*, 3, Autumn, 167–178.

Sheppard, R., Last, R. and Foulkes, P. (1986) *The UGC Research Evaluations: Some Observations on Their Methodology and Results with Particular Reference to Departments of German.* New Alyth: Lockee Press.

Sher, I. and Garfield, E. (1966) 'New tools for improving and evaluating the effectiveness of research.' In M.C. Yovits *et al.* (eds) *Research Program Effectiveness.* New York: Gordon and Breach.

Sizer, J. (1979) 'Assessing institutional performance: an overview.' *International Journal of Institutional Management in Higher Education 3*, 1, 49–77.

Sizer, J. (1981) 'Performance assessment in institutions of higher education under conditions of financial stringency, contraction and changing needs: a management accounting perspective.' *Accounting and Business Research 11*, 43, 227–242.

Sizer, J. (1982) 'Assessing institutional performance and progress.' In Leslie Wagner (ed) *Agenda for Institutional Change in Higher Education.* Guildford: Society for Research in Higher Education (Monograph 45).

Sizer, J. (1989) 'Performance Indicators and control quality in higher education.' Keynote Address to an International Conference, Institute of Education, London.

Sizer, J. (1990) 'Performance Indicators and the management of universities in the UK: a summary of developments with commentary.' In F. Dochy, M. Segers and W. Wijnen (eds) *Management Information and Performance Indicators in Higher Education: An International Issue.* Assen/Maastricht: Van Gorcum.

Sizer, J. (1992) 'Performance indicators in government institutional relationships: lessons from government' *Higher Education Management 4*, 156–163.

Sizer, J. and Frost, R. (1985) *Criteria for Self Evaluation of Department Research Profiles. Responsible and Responsive Universities Research Project* (Working Paper). Loughborough: Loughborough University of Technology (mimeo).

Sizer, J., Spee, A. and Bormans, R. (1992) 'The role of performance indicators in higher education.' *Higher Education 24*, 133–155.

260   *The Use of Performance Indicators in Higher Education*

Skolnick, M. (1989) 'How academic program review can foster intellectual conformity and stifle diversity of thought and method.' *Journal of Higher Education 60*, 619–643.

Skoyles, J. (1990) Letter to *Times Higher Education Supplement*, 23 February 1990.

Smith, R. and Fiedler, F. (1971) 'The measurement of scholarly work: a critical review of the literature.' *Educational Record 52*, Summer, 225–232.

Smith, T. (1987) 'The UGC's research ranking exercise.' *Higher Education Quarterly 41*, Autumn, 303–316.

Smyth, F. and Anderson, J. (1987) *University Performance Indicators*. Science Policy Support Group Seminar Aide-Memoire No. 1. London: SPSG.

Solmon, L. and Astin, A. (1981) 'Departments without distinguished graduate programs.' *Change 13*, September, 23–28.

Spaapen, J. and Sylvain, C. (1994) *Societal Quality of Research*. London: SPSG.

Spee, A. (ed) (1990) 'Development of performance indicators and quality assessment in higher education in The Netherlands.' Position Statement prepared for the meeting of the IMHE Project Group on the development of Performance Indicators in Higher Education, Danbury Park, UK, 23–26 January.

Spee, A. and Bormans, R. (1992) 'Performance indicators in government-institutional relations: the conceptual framework.' *Higher Education Management 4*, 2, 139–155.

STEAC Report (1985) *Report of the Scottish Tertiary Education Advisory Council. Future Strategy for Higher Education in Scotland*, Cmnd. 9676. London: HMSO.

Sub-Committee on Research Indicators (SCRI) (1989) *Issues in Quantitative Assessment of Departmental Research*. CVCP/UFC Performance Indicators Steering Committee (reported in CVCP N/89/147. London: CVCP).

Sutherland Report (1989) *The Teaching Function. Quality Assurance.* (VC/89/160a) London: CVCP.

Swinnerton-Dyer, P. (1986) Statement made at the Higher Education Works for Schools Conference, Royal Institution, 24 November 1986.

Talbot, R.W. and Bordage, G. (1986) 'A preliminary assessment of a new method of course evaluation based on directed small group discussions.' *International Journal of Institutional Management in Higher Education 10*, 2, July, 185–193.

Tan, D. (1992) 'A multivariate approach to the assessment of quality.' *Research in Higher Education 33*, 2, 205–226.

Taylor, J. (1985) *Comparing Universities: Some Observations on the First Destinations of New Graduates*. (Discussion Paper). 85/11. Lancaster: University of Lancaster.

Taylor, J. (1995) 'A statistical analysis of the 1992 research assessment exercise.' *Journal of Royal Statistical Society, A, 158*, 241–261.

Taylor, J. and Johnes, J. (1989) 'An evaluation of performance indicators based upon the first destination of university graduates.' *Studies in Higher Education 14*, 2, 201–217.

Taylor, M. (1989a) 'Recent changes in national higher education policies.' *Higher Education Management 1*, 3, 314–322.

Taylor, M. (1989b) 'The implications of new organisational patterns of research.' *Higher Education Management 1*, 1, March, 7–19.

Taylor, T. (1985) 'A value added student assessment model: northeast Missouri state university.' *Assessment and Evaluation in Higher Education 10*, 3, 190–202.

Teichler, U. (1988) *Changing Patterns of the Higher Education System: The Experience of Three Decades*. London: Jessica Kingsley Publishers.

Terenzeni, P. and Pascarella, E. (1994) 'Living with myths. Undergraduate education in America.' *Change* January/February, 28–32.

Thomas, P. (1985) *The Aims and Outcomes of Social Policy Research*. London: Croom Helm.

Times Higher Education Supplement (THES) (1987) 20th February.

Times Higher Education Supplement (1987) 5th June.

Times Higher Education Supplement (1987) 4th December.

Times Higher Education Supplement (1989) 8th September.

Times Higher Education Supplement (1989) 10th November.

Times Higher Education Supplement (1989) 1st December.

Times Higher Education Supplement (1990) 23rd February.

Times Higher Education Supplement (1990) 15th June.

Times Higher Education Supplement (1995) 29th February.

Tomkins, C. and Green, R. (1988) 'An experiment in the use of data envelopment analysis for evaluating the efficiency of UK university departments of accounting.' *Financial Accountability and Management 4*, 2, 147–164.

Torode, P. (1980) 'Course review at Newcastle upon Tyne polytechnic.' In D. Billing (ed) *Indicators of Performance*. Guildford: The Society for Research into Higher Education.

Treasury (1987) *The Government's Expenditure Plans, 1987–8 to 1989–90.* (Public Expenditure White Paper) Cm 56. London: HMSO.

Treasury (1990) *The Government's Expenditure Plans, 1990–91 to 1992–93.* (Public Expenditure White Paper) Cm 1021. London: HMSO.

Trow, M. (1986) 'Academic standards and mass higher education.' Paper prepared for the Conference on Quality Assurance in First Degree Courses, sponsored by Higher Education International, 1986.

Universities Funding Council (1989a) *Research Selectivity Exercise 1989: The Outcome*, Circular Letter 27/89. London: UFC.

Universities Funding Council (1989b) *Funding and Planning: 1991/92 to 1994/95*, Circular Letter 39/89. London: UFC.

Universities Funding Council (1989c) *Report on the 1989 Research Assessment Exercise*. London: UFC.

Universities Funding Council (1990) *Funding and Planning Exercise*, Circular Letter 29/90. London: UFC.

Universities Funding Council (1992) *Research Assessment Exercise 1992: The Outcome*, Circular 26/92. Bristol: UFC.

University Grants Committee (1984a) *Planning for the Late 1980s*, Circular Letter 17/84. London: UGC.

University Grants Committee (1984b) *A Strategy for Higher Education into the 1990s*. London: UGC.

University Grants Committee (1985a) *Planning for the Late 1980s*, Circular 12/85. London: UGC.

University Grants Committee (1985b) *Planning for the Late 1980s: The Resource Allocation Process*, Circular Letter 22/85. London: UGC.

University Grants Committee (1986) *Planning for the Late 1980s: Recurrent Grant for 1986/87*, Circular Letter 4/86. London: UGC.

University Grants Committee (1988a) *The Next Research Selectivity Exercise: Consultative Paper*, Circular Letter 15/88. London: UGC.

University Grants Committee (1988b) *Research Selectivity Exercise, 1989*, Circular Letter 45/88. London: UGC.

Valimaa, J. and Westerheijden, D. (1995) 'Two discourses: researchers and policy-making in higher education.' *Higher Education 29,* 385–403.

Van der Meulen, B. and Rip, A. (1995) *Indicatoren en Indicaties Voor de Beoordeling Von Maastschappelijke Kwaliteit Van Onderzoek.* Enschede: University of Twente.

Van Vught, F. (1988) 'A new autonomy in European higher education? An explanation and analysis of the strategy of self-regulation in higher education.' *International Journal of Institutional Management in Higher Education 12,* 16–26.

Warde, A. (1996) 'The effects of the 1992 research assessment exercise.' *Network 64,* 1–2.

Warnock Report (1990) *Teaching Quality. Report of the Committee of Enquiry Appointed by the Council.* London: PCFC.

Watkins, D. (1994) 'Student evaluations of university teaching: a cross-cultural perspective.' *Research in Higher Education 35, 2,* 251–266.

Weale, M. (1992) 'The benefits of higher education.' *Oxford Review of Economic Policy 8,* 35–47.

Webster, D. (1981) 'Advantages and disadvantages of methods of assessing quality.' *Change 13,* October, 20–24.

Weiss, C. (ed) (1977) *Using Social Research in Public Policy Making.* Lexington, Mass: Lexington/Heath.

Weiss, C. (1979) 'The many meanings of research utilisation.' *Public Administration Review 39,* 426–431.

Whiston, T. (1990) *The Evaluation of ESRC Research Centres.* (mimeo).

Whiston, T. and Geiger, R. (eds) (1992) *Research and Higher Education: the United Kingdom and the United States.* Buckingham: SRHE and Open University Press.

Williams, G. (1994) *Achieving Quality in Higher Education: a Student Centred Approach to Self-Evaluation: Proposal for a Student Progression Profiling Model.* Newport: Gwent College of Higher Education.

Winter Hebron, C. de (1984) 'An aid for evaluating teaching in "higher education".' *Assessment and Evaluation in Higher Education 9, 2,* Summer, 145–163.

Woolgar, S. (1991) 'Beyond the citation debate: towards a sociology of measurement technologies and their use in science policy.' *Science and Public Policy 18,* 319–326.

Wright, G. (1989) 'Draft report of the directorate resources network steering group on performance indicators, 1987.' In J. Pratt (ed) *Report of a Conference on Performance Indicators in Teacher Education*. London: Centre for Institutional Studies, Polytechnic of East London.

Wright, J. (1987) 'A big stick without a carrot.' *Times Higher Education Supplement*, 27 February 1987.

Yin, R. and Gwaltney, M. (1981) 'Knowledge utilisation at a networking process.' *Knowledge: Creation, Diffusion, Utilisation 2*, 555–580.

Yorke, M. (1991) *Performance Indicators: Observations on Their Use in the Assurance of Course Quality*. CNAA Project Report 30. London: CNAA.

Yorke, M. (1995) 'Siamese twins? Performance indicators in the service of accountability and enhancement.' *Quality in Higher Education 1*, 1, 13–30.

Zander, M. (1986) Letter to *The Times*, 11 July 1986.

Ziman, J. (1987) *Science in a Steady State: The Research System in Transition*. London: Science Policy Support Group.

Ziman, J. (1989) *Restructuring Academic Science: A New Framework for UK Policy*. London: Science Policy Support Group.

Ziman, J. (1994) 'Not the white paper.' *Higher Education Quarterly 48*, 12–23.

Index

A level scores, 51, 126, 127,130, 140
Aaronson, S. (1975) 182
Abrami, P. (1982) 150
Abrami, P. and d'Apollonia (1991) 150
Academic Standards Group 110
Academy of Finland 93–4, 95
activity based cost (ABC) 119–20
Adams, A., and Krislov, J. (1978) 72–3
Adelman, C. (1986) 73
Advisory Board for the Research Councils (ABRC) 11–12, 156, 186
age participation rate 10
Agricultural and Food Research Council (AFRC) 156, 200
Ahn, T., Charnes, A. and Cooper, W. W. (1988) 33
Aitken, D., (1991) 108
Alewell, K., and Göbbels–Dreyling, B. (1993) 90, 91, 92
Allen, D., Harley, M. and Makinson, G. (1987) 53

Allsop, P., and Findlay, P. (1990) 48, 216
American College Test (ACT) 72, 131–2
American Council on Education (ACE) 172
American Psychological Association 169
American Sociological Review 170
Anderson, J. (1989) 156, 157, 172, 190–191, 200
Ashworth, Professor 191
Assessment for Instructional Development (AID) 148
assessment of teaching performance 207
Association of Co-operating Universities, Netherlands 85
Association of Graduate Careers Advisory Services (AGCAS) 143, 144
Association of Graduate Recruiters (1995) 145
Astin, A. (1982) 73, 76–7, 126, 136
Audit Commission (1985) 6
(1986) 6
Australia 84, 87–90, 100, 101, 108, 147, 152, 176, 192, 194

Australian Committee of Directors and Principals (ACDP)(1988) 88
Australian Higher Education Performance Indicators Project 150
Australian Research Council 108
Australian Vice-Chancellors' Committee (AVCC) 88
Australian Vice-Chancellors' Committee/Australian Committee of Directors and Principals (AVCC/ACDP) (1988) 88, 100
average cost data 118–19
Ayers, R. (1994) 196

Baker, K. 4
(1986) 138
(1987) 138
(1988) 109
Baldwin, G. (1995) 89, 177
Banta, T., and Borden, V. (1994) 2, 39, 70, 145, 153, 213, 214, 215
Barnett, R.
(1988) 127
(1993) 114
(1994a) 19, 114, 116
(1994b) 104
Barrow, M. (1990) 26
Bath University 195

Higher Education Policy Series
Edited by Maurice Kogan

Higher education is now the subject of far reaching and rapid policy change. This series will be of value to those who have to manage that change, as well as to consumers and evaluators of higher education in the UK and elsewhere. It offers information and analysis of new developments in a concise and usable form. It also provides reflective accounts of the impacts of higher education policy. Higher education administrators, governors and policy makers will use it, as well as students and specialists in educational policy.

Maurice Kogan is Professor of Government and Social Administration at Brunel University and Director of the Centre for the Evaluation of Public Policy and Practice.

Graduates at Work
Degree Courses and the Labour Market
John Brennan
and Philip McGeevor
ISBN 1 85302 500 3
Higher Education Policy Series 1

Degrees of Success
Career Aspirations and Destinations of College, University and Polytechnic Graduates
Chris J Boys with John Kirkland
ISBN 1 85302 502 X
Higher Education Policy Series 2

Higher Education and the Preparation for Work
Chris J Boys, John Brennan, Mary Henkel, John Kirkland, Maurice Kogan and Penny Youll
ISBN 1 85302 505 4
Higher Education Policy Series 4

Changing Patterns of the Higher Education System
The Experience of Three Decades
Ulrich Teichler
ISBN 1 85302 507 0
Higher Education Policy Series 5

Evaluating Higher Education
Edited by Maurice Kogan
ISBN 1 85302 510 0
Higher Education Policy Series 6

Governmental Strategies and Innovation in Higher Education
Edited by Frans van Vught
ISBN 1 85302 513 5
Higher Education Policy Series 7

Jessica Kingsley *Publishers*
116 Pentonville Road, London N1 9JB

**Public Expenditure
on Higher Education**
A Comparative Study
in the Member States of the
European Community
*Frans Kaiser, Raymond J.G.M.
Florax, Jos. B.J. Koelman,
Frans A. van Vught*
ISBN 1 85302 532 1
Higher Education Policy Series 18

**Postgraduate Education
and Training in the Social
Sciences**
Processes and Products
Edited by Robert G Burgess
ISBN 1 85302 533 X
Higher Education Policy Series 19

Academic Community
Discourse or Discord?
Edited by Ronald Barnett
ISBN 1 85302 534 8
Higher Education Policy Series 20

Students, Courses and Jobs
The Relationship Between
Higher Education
and the Labour Market
*J L Brennan, E S Lyon,
P A McGeevor and K Murray*
ISBN 1 85302 538 0
Higher Education Policy Series 21

**Innovation and Adaptation
in Higher Education**
The Changing Conditions
of Advanced Teaching
and Learning in Europe
Edited by Claudius Gellert
ISBN 1 85302 535 6
Higher Education Policy Series 22

**Assessing Quality in Further
and Higher Education**
*Allan Ashworth
and Roger Harvey*
ISBN 85302 539 9
Higher Education Policy Series 24

Are Professors Professional?
The Organisation
of University Examinations
David Warren Piper
ISBN 1 85302 540 2
Higher Education Policy Series 25

Information Technology
Issues for Higher Education
Management
*Gordon M Bull, Carry
Dallinga-Hunter, Yves Epelboin,
Edgar Frackmann
and Dennis Jennings*
ISBN 1 85302 542 9
Higher Education Policy Series 26

Staffing Higher Education
Meeting New Challenges
*Maurice Kogan,
Elaine El-Khawas
and Ingrid Moses*
ISBN 1 85302 541 0
Higher Education Policy Series 27

Transition to Work
The Experiences of Former
ERASMUS Students
*Ulrich Teichler
and Friedhelm Maiworm*
ISBN 1 85302 543 7
Higher Education Policy Series 28

Jessica Kingsley *Publishers*
116 Pentonville Road, London N1 9JB

**Academic Mobilty
in a Changing World
Regional and Global Trends**
*Peggy Blumenthal, Craufurd
Goodwin, Alan Smith
and Ulrich Teichler*
ISBN 1 85302 545 3
Higher Education Policy Series 29

**Improvement and
Accountability
Navigating Between Scylla
and Charybdis**
A I Vroeijenstijn
ISBN 1 85302 546 1
Higher Education Policy Series 30

**Goals and Purposes
of Higher Education
in the 21st Century**
Edited by Arnold Burgen
ISBN 1 85302 547 X
Higher Education Policy Series 32

**Higher Education in Ireland
North and South**
Robert Osborne
ISBN 1 85302 379 5
Higher Education Policy Series 33

**The Use of Performance
Indicators in Higher
Education
A Critical Analysis of
Developing Practice 3rd edition**
*Martin Cave, Stephen Hanney,
Mary Henkel
and Maurice Kogan*
ISBN 1 85302 345 0
Higher Education Policy Series 34

**Study Abroad
and Early Career
Experiences of Former
ERASMUS Students**
*Freidhelm Maiworm
and Ulrich Teichler*
ISBN 1 85302 378 7
Higher Education Policy Series 35

**Crisis and Change
in Vocational Education
and Training**
Geoffrey Elliott
ISBN 1 85302 393 0
Higher Education Policy Series 36

**Standards and Quality
in Higher Education**
*Edited by John Brennan,
Peter de Vries and Ruth Williams*
ISBN 1 85302 423 6
Higher Education Policy Series 37

Jessica Kingsley *Publishers*
116 Pentonville Road, London N1 9JB